THE TRENDM

DRESS, BODY, CULTURE

Series Editor: **Joanne B. Eicher**, *Regents' Professor Emerita,*
University of Minnesota

Advisory Board:

Ruth Barnes, *Ashmolean Museum, University of Oxford*
Djurdja Bartlett, *London College of Fashion, University of the Arts*
Pamela Church-Gibson, *London College of Fashion, University of the Arts*
James Hall, *University of Illinois at Chicago*
Vicki Karaminas, *Massey University, Wellington*
Gwen O'Neal, *University of North Carolina at Greensboro*
Ted Polhemus, *Curator, "Street Style" Exhibition, Victoria and Albert Museum*
Valerie Steele, *The Museum at the Fashion Institute of Technology*
Lou Taylor, *University of Brighton*
Karen Tranberg Hansen, *Northwestern University*

Books in this provocative series seek to articulate the connections between
culture and dress which is defined here in its broadest possible sense as any
modification or supplement to the body. Interdisciplinary in approach, the series
highlights the dialogue between identity and dress, cosmetics, coiffure and body
alternations as manifested in practices as varied as plastic surgery, tattooing and
ritual scarification. The series aims, in particular, to analyze the meaning of dress
in relation to popular culture and gender issues and will include works grounded
in anthropology, sociology, history, art history, literature and folklore.

ISSN: 1360-466X

Previously published in the series

Helen Bradley Foster, *"New Raiments of Self": African American Clothing in the*
Antebellum South
Claudine Griggs, *S/he: Changing Sex and Changing Clothes*
Michaele Thurgood Haynes, *Dressing Up Debutantes: Pageantry and Glitz in Texas*
Anne Brydon and Sandra Niessen, *Consuming Fashion: Adorning the*
Transnational Body
Dani Cavallaro and Alexandra Warwick, *Fashioning the Frame: Boundaries,*
Dress and the Body
Judith Perani and Norma H. Wolff, *Cloth, Dress and Art Patronage in Africa*
Linda B. Arthur, *Religion, Dress and the Body*
Paul Jobling, *Fashion Spreads: Word and Image in Fashion Photography*

Fadwa El Guindi, *Veil: Modesty, Privacy and Resistance*

Thomas S. Abler, *Hinterland Warriors and Military Dress: European Empires and Exotic Uniforms*

Linda Welters, *Folk Dress in Europe and Anatolia: Beliefs about Protection and Fertility*

Kim K.P. Johnson and Sharron J. Lennon, *Appearance and Power*

Barbara Burman, *The Culture of Sewing: Gender, Consumption and Home Dressmaking*

Annette Lynch, *Dress, Gender and Cultural Change: Asian American and African American Rites of Passage*

Antonia Young, *Women Who Become Men: Albanian Sworn Virgins*

David Muggleton, *Inside Subculture: The Postmodern Meaning of Style*

Nicola White, *Reconstructing Italian Fashion: America and the Development of the Italian Fashion Industry*

Brian J. McVeigh, *Wearing Ideology: The Uniformity of Self-Presentation in Japan*

Shaun Cole, *Don We Now Our Gay Apparel: Gay Men's Dress in the Twentieth Century*

Kate Ince, *Orlan: Millennial Female*

Ali Guy, Eileen Green and Maura Banim, *Through the Wardrobe: Women's Relationships with their Clothes*

Linda B. Arthur, *Undressing Religion: Commitment and Conversion from a Cross-Cultural Perspective*

William J.F. Keenan, *Dressed to Impress: Looking the Part*

Joanne Entwistle and Elizabeth Wilson, *Body Dressing*

Leigh Summers, *Bound to Please: A History of the Victorian Corset*

Paul Hodkinson, *Goth: Identity, Style and Subculture*

Leslie W. Rabine, *The Global Circulation of African Fashion*

Michael Carter, *Fashion Classics from Carlyle to Barthes*

Sandra Niessen, Ann Marie Leshkowich and Carla Jones, *Re-Orienting Fashion: The Globalization of Asian Dress*

Kim K. P. Johnson, Susan J. Torntore and Joanne B. Eicher, *Fashion Foundations: Early Writings on Fashion and Dress*

Helen Bradley Foster and Donald Clay Johnson, *Wedding Dress Across Cultures*

Eugenia Paulicelli, *Fashion under Fascism: Beyond the Black Shirt*

Charlotte Suthrell, *Unzipping Gender: Sex, Cross-Dressing and Culture*

Irene Guenther, *Nazi Chic? Fashioning Women in the Third Reich*

Yuniya Kawamura, *The Japanese Revolution in Paris Fashion*

Patricia Calefato, *The Clothed Body*

Ruth Barcan, *Nudity: A Cultural Anatomy*

THE TRENDMAKERS

Behind the Scenes of the Global Fashion Industry

Jenny Lantz

Bloomsbury Academic
An imprint of Bloomsbury Publishing Plc

B L O O M S B U R Y
LONDON · OXFORD · NEW YORK · NEW DELHI · SYDNEY

Bloomsbury Academic

An imprint of Bloomsbury Publishing Plc

50 Bedford Square   1385 Broadway
London   New York
WC1B 3DP   NY 10018
UK   USA

www.bloomsbury.com

BLOOMSBURY and the Diana logo are trademarks of Bloomsbury Publishing Plc

First published 2016

© Jenny Lantz, 2016

British Library Cataloguing-in-Publication Data
A catalogue record for this book is available from the British Library.

ISBN: HB: 978-1-4742-5979-8
PB: 978-1-4742-5978-1
ePDF: 978-1-4742-5980-4
ePub: 978-1-4742-5982-8

Library of Congress Cataloging-in-Publication Data
Names: Lantz, Jenny, author.
Title: The trendmakers : behind the scenes of the global fashion industry / by Jenny Lantz. Description: London, UK ; New York : Bloomsbury Academic, an imprint of Bloomsbury Publishing, Plc, [2016] | Series: Dress, body, culture | Includes bibliographical references.
Identifiers: LCCN 2015037933| ISBN 9781474259781 (pbk.) | ISBN 9781474259798 (hardback) | ISBN 9781474259804 (ePDF) | ISBN 9781474259828 (ePub)
Subjects: LCSH: Fashion merchandising. | Fashion designers. | Fashion.
Classification: LCC HD9940.A2 L37 2016 | DDC 338.4/774692–dc23
LC record available at http://lccn.loc.gov/2015037933

Typeset by Integra Software Services Pvt. Ltd.
Printed and bound in India

CONTENTS

LIST OF IMAGES

Chapter 1

Photo by Michael Gottschalk/Photothek via Getty Images 2

Chapter 2

Photo by Franziska Krug/Getty Images 26

Chapter 3

Photo by John Downing/Getty Images 38
Photo by BOTTI/Gamma-Keystone via Getty Images 45

Chapter 4

Photo by Fernanda Calfat/WireImage via Getty Images 52

Chapter 5

Photo by Antonio de Moraes Barros Filho/WireImage 80
Photo by JP Yim/Getty Images 82
Photo by Vittorio Zunino Celotto/Getty Images 87

Chapter 6

Chapter 7

Chapter 8

Chapter 9

PREFACE

As a twenty-four-year-old, in 1970, my mother moved from the small town of Hedemora to Gothenburg, Sweden's second largest city, where she worked as a secretary to the CEO of Bröderna Edstrand, a steel and aluminum company located in a hideous blue-and-white building in one of the city's industrial areas. Bröderna Edstrand was an old-fashioned company. My mother, who had a great interest in fashion and sewed most of her wardrobe, and the two other secretaries devoted much thought to whether they dared wear trouser suits to work. Trouser suits as office attire were out of the question in Hedemora, but my mother had imagined things would be different in the relatively big city of Gothenburg. All three were well aware that the banks forbade women employees to wear trousers, but at Bröderna Edstrand there was no formal ban.

A trouser suit consisted of trousers and a long waistcoat that compensated for the absence of a skirt. One day my mother could no longer resist the lure of a trouser suit, and she bought an all-red one in thick cotton jersey with double white stitching around the neckline, armholes and hem, and sewn creases. A white polo-neck jumper and white pumps with chunky heels completed the ensemble. "Tomorrow I'm going to wear it," she told her office friends.

An excited suspense prevailed in the office the following morning. How would the revered Executive Director Mr. Haner react?

"Could Miss Johansson please come in?" My mother, whose room was next to the executive director's office, nervously took her stenography notebook. She had barely entered the room when Mr. Haner exclaimed, "Oh, how nicely dressed you are, Miss Johansson, really lovely. How nice with trousers." From that day on, wearing trouser suits had the green light at Bröderna Edstrand.

For women, the twentieth century started with corsets and gowns and ended with being able to wear trousers without embarrassment. It is usually thought that fashion reflects social, political, economic and cultural changes in society, while simultaneously reacting to fashion's own cyclical developments. The latter implies that changes in fashion sometimes precede societal changes and can empower people by increasing their agency, that is, ability to act on their will.

Fashion emancipation can also compensate for an absence of economic and social emancipation, as when women took up cigarette smoking.

Fashion has always been obsessed with gender, as the renowned fashion scholar Elizabeth Wilson has put it,[1] constantly creating and recreating gender boundaries. At the same time, fashion has long been gendered as feminine, and discussion of fashion has often concerned women's inherent vanity and frailty. Besides, fashion has moreover been considered superficial and ephemeral.

Over the forty years since this little episode at Bröderna Edstrand, fashion has altered its guise. Fashion's changes used to unfold at a drawn-out pace; for example, over a century elapsed from the time women wore trousers during the Utopian movement in the United States from the 1820s to 1840s, via the introduction of trousers into women's sports and leisure activities and the designs of Coco Chanel, to the social sanctioning of women's trousers in the offices of Bröderna Edstrand in the 1970s. In the mid-twentieth century, trends were often dictated from Paris and took a long time to appear in local media and be taken up by local fashion producers elsewhere in the West. Although the trends of the 1960s and 1970s were rarely transformational, they were clearly focused and packaged, for example, "the medieval trend" and "the Eskimo trend." Gone are the days when Yves Saint Laurent did the Russian peasant one season, Kenzo the Peruvian Indian the next and Vivienne Westwood responded with her pirates in the subsequent season.

Today some people even argue that trends are dead. "There are no more trends. Everything is in style," said David Wolfe, the famous trend analyst, at the beginning of the 2010s.[2] Many choose not to speak of trends at all. Perhaps today's fashion offering is more diverse than ever. Others argue that statements about the end of trends themselves constitute a trend.

The trend discourse is not so easily escaped. Fashion magazines, bloggers and retailers demonstrate that trends are alive and well, though they may have taken a new form.

*

I never felt comfortable with the word "trend." Before embarking on this study, I never used the word in everyday speech. This feeling probably stemmed from the herd behavior that the word conjures up, and from my desire not to be that predictable. Telling myself that I only bought fashion that I liked, I pretended to be unaffected by trends.

Still, there is something enticing about obviously significant phenomena that are at the same time experienced as problematic, which is why I previously conducted research into taste and quality. That started me contemplating the role of trends in the fashion industry. First, I was preoccupied with various French trend-forecasting agencies that I had heard of and with Swedish trend spotters who, on breakfast television, tell us what colors and key items the upcoming season will bring. How do these people gain their legitimacy? On what basis do they claim competence? What is their role in the fashion industry? My research gradually expanded as I realized the scope of the trend agencies' potential influence on the fashion industry and gained momentum when I received funding for it from the Swedish Research Council.

This book is based on ninety-five interviews with people in the fashion field on the topic of trends and their organizing function. The interviews were conducted during the 2008–2014 period, but most were conducted in 2011 and 2012. The informants range from representatives of fashion companies and trend-forecasting agencies, to magazine editors, journalists, bloggers, stylists, designers, department store buyers and financial analysts covering fashion businesses, mostly in London and also in Stockholm. London offers a cosmopolitan perspective on fashion and is home to representatives of all areas of global fashion. Relative to its small size, Sweden has a strong fashion industry that has produced one fashion giant (H&M) and numerous smaller fashion companies that have made their marks internationally, such as Acne, Filippa K and Hope. I also interviewed trend forecasters in New York, Paris and Tokyo. My position as the program director of an Executive MBA program specializing in globalization at the Stockholm School of Economics took me to the "BRIC" countries, that is, Brazil, Russia, India and China, so I also conducted interviews in these emerging economies. While these interviews were not conducted as systematically as the rest, they capture diverse discourses on trends and provide additional perspectives on a global industry.

Although primarily a book for scholars and students of fashion, the fashion industry and cultural industries, this book also addresses an audience beyond the purely academic. Unlike many anthropological or journalistic accounts that follow a small number of people in depth to give life to a larger phenomenon, this book includes a wide range of voices. As an organization scholar, I apply a sociological approach in which I try to discern patterns in people's behaviors and statements in order to understand the studied phenomenon, in this case, trends as an organizing principle in the fashion industry, and examine the conceptions and constructions of a particular "field."

ACKNOWLEDGMENTS

My greatest debt of gratitude is owed to all those who shared their time and experience with me and agreed to be interviewed for this study. I would also like to express a warm thank-you to those who read and commented on the manuscript in whole or part during various phases of the writing process: Ilinca Benson, Charlotte Holgersson, Ingalill Holmberg, Pia Höök, Kira Josefsson, Marianne Lantz, Frida Pemer, Linda Portnoff, Kristoffer Strandqvist, Lars Strannegård, Anna Wahl, Andreas Werr and Gunnar Westling. I would like to acknowledge the Stockholm School of Economics Institute for Research (SIR) for providing me with a research platform throughout the project, the Center for Advanced Studies in Leadership (CASL) at the Stockholm School of Economics, where I spent the last half year of the project, and the Center for Arts, Business and Culture (ABC) at the Stockholm School of Economics, my current research home. My Swedish publisher, Bokförlaget Atlas, and the editor of the Swedish edition, Tom Carlson, deserve my warmest gratitude for their patience and constructive comments. My sincere thanks to Hannah Crump and Ariadne Godwin at Bloomsbury Academic. I am indebted to Kira Josefsson who translated half of the text. Mayne Ellis and Stephen Sanborn are thanked for thoroughly editing the English edition of the book. My friend Annika Daal was a lifesaver by kindly offering me room and board in London when I started to run out of research money. Speaking of financial support, I would like to thank Handelsbanken's research foundation, whose Wallander stipend generously financed my pre-study of trend-forecasting agencies. Above all, I am deeply grateful to the Swedish Research Council for financially supporting the three-year research project "Organizing and trends in the fashion field," thus enabling this book. Finally, I want to thank my family for their unflagging support.

1 INTRODUCTION

"Impermanence is the theme for Autumn 2012/13." A French woman in matching skirt and blouse of black and green describes to an international audience of primarily fashion buyers and designers how trend information has been gathered and analyzed by the fashion team of Première Vision. She talks engagingly about "our nomadic lifestyle," "networking" and the desire to "piece together fashion from diverse sources." Before beginning the slide show, she emphasizes that there must be no photography or videotaping.

Her presentation treats three overarching themes—*uncompromising, having fun* and *redesigning rawness*—each illustrated by the principal new trends for womenswear and menswear. Being *uncompromising* is manifested in our desire to be more focused in terms of fashion. We have left *mix-and-match* behind us, she says as she highlights the new trend's coordinated dresses and coats, and the *determined elegance* in menswear in which new materials are mixed with old. The garments also express frivolity. Images of nature, details of buildings, close-ups of materials and color charts are shown, enlarging on the themes' links to design, architecture and manufacturing processes. The audience eagerly takes notes.

This seminar is part of the world's largest fabric fair, Première Vision, in Parc d'Expositions in Villepinte north of Paris. Twice a year, future trends are showcased at this venue, to the benefit of the agents, buyers, designers and fabric producers who attend. Lately, Première Vision has expanded into other countries and is now held in Beijing/Shanghai, Istanbul, New York and São Paulo. Attracting approximately 45,000 visitors, Première Vision Paris is still the largest and most important. The fair encompasses five halls replete with sample fabrics and garments. The manufacturers who exhibit—almost all European—are themselves divided by theme: *seduction* ("The fancy and fluid universe"), *distinction* ("The elegant, formal and tailored universe"), *relax* ("The casualwear, sportswear and jeanswear universe") and *pulsation* ("The sport, technical and performance universe"). Sometimes exhibitors display sample items, demonstrating how the fabrics can be used. An area at the fair's periphery, Maison d'Exceptions, is devoted to "the ultimate creativity" and is "against standardization," presenting an abundance of traditional and contemporary crafts and techniques.

The showcases in the seemingly endless corridors of shirt and denim fabric manufacturers differ from those in most other fairs. They are often constructed as individual rooms, accessible only by narrow entrances, like offices where business will be conducted. As the fashion industry's production and buying routines have changed and brands and retailers no longer buy just twice a year, Première Vision's role as a trade arena has changed. It has become a place where contacts are made and maintained, a networking arena. The participants' positions in the fashion industry are manifested in their showcase placements and sizes, their props and their visitors.[1]

More significantly, Première Vision is a venue where trends are created, packaged and communicated.

All the big trend-forecasting agencies are represented at the fair: Worth Global Style Network (WGSN), Stylesight, Promostyl, NellyRodi, Peclers Paris, Carlin, Trend Union and others. Having itself become an important trend player, the organization Première Vision offers a grand trend showcase, where fabric samples are displayed according to various themes, sketches, colors and patterns, all of which, according to the exhibitor, will be current trends in twelve to eighteen months. Everything is summarized on *trend boards*. Everywhere signs remind visitors that cameras, scissors and handling or taking fabric samples are all forbidden. Many visitors attempt to bypass these rules, covertly photographing or stealing pieces of fabric, but most offenders are soon warned

by the floor staff. Experienced—or possibly particularly anxious—visitors bring their own Pantone charts and take notes on the specific colors Première Vision has selected. Every day of the fair, Première Vision offers its own trend seminar.

Trends are negotiated not only at seminars and in trend showcases but also in small talk and introductions during the countless interactions, coffees and dinners involving fabric producers, agents, competitors and other visitors to the fair. Première Vision has traditionally shown sales figures for the fair on a large display in the main exhibition hall (and online for registered users), listing the most popular colors and materials traded for the new season. The significance of this information has diminished as the fair focuses much less on direct trading, but the information can be regarded as expressing the fair's trendmaker role.

*

This is a book about the trend machine of the global fashion industry, one in which supply and demand can never be taken for granted, as trends can affect either. The above description of Première Vision illustrates the role of trends as an organizing principle in the fashion field. I would even argue that fashion history shows that trends, existing at the intersection between production and consumption, play an organizing role. It is also my departure point for this book. Trends make it possible for manufacturers, designers, buyers and fashion magazine editors to agree on an approximate direction for fashion. Without trends, many fashion companies and consumers would be lost. They have a joint interest in identifying the "right new thing," even if they dismiss it. Few want to relate passively; everyone in the industry is keen to position themselves well in the fashion field. Certain actors and organizations, such as Première Vision and trend-forecasting companies, are capitalizing on this very need for trends.

Fashion is a social world, a *field*, where everyone is interdependent: fashion magazines need something to write about; designers need influences, buyers and consumers; stylists need assignments; buyers need new, interesting but also sellable brands; consumers need something to hanker after; financial analysts need promising companies to evaluate and investors need profitable homes for their money.

In the fashion field, inequality is the rule. There is an ongoing struggle for status, sometimes thinly disguised. A fashion show hints at the power struggles taking place: it matters who sits in the front row, what critics are present and how the show is received and by whom. In the fashion industry, some have greater influence than others. Individualism is often praised, but with the power game comes a widespread eagerness to copy, not only items and stores but even self-presentation among designers, stylists and fashion journalists. The black clothing worn by most fashion show guests is just one manifestation of this intense, high-stakes social game.

At the same time, fashion is utterly commercial. After all, all creators—whether local talents or worldwide conglomerates—want to sell their creations. Coordinating supply and demand becomes key, even if this process is far from being straightforward in the power struggles of the fashion industry. This means that many players have a common interest in trends such as *the return of the trousers, minimalism, seventies, outrageous shoes* or *colorful biker jackets.*

With the advent of the internet, many of the workings of the fashion industry have been turned upside down. In the era of globalization, the Web offers the possibility of participating in trends as collections are actually shown on the catwalk or when Suzy Menkes files a piece on the show or Style Bubble blogs about it. Anyone can comment on and disseminate fashion news via the internet. We can buy items from anywhere in the world and have them delivered in a few days. No one—producers, tastemakers or consumers—is unaffected. With the hunt for "the new" constantly being spurred by the internet, and investments (and thus risks) in the industry growing rapidly, creating, disseminating, adopting and translating trends have become ways to reduce uncertainty. The largest trend-forecasting agencies are taking advantage of this situation.

Other industries have also been inspired by the fashion industry's preoccupation with trends or ways of creating new "needs." Being on trend can be seen as a form of "insurance" for a fashion company. Consumer society likes to boast about "the democratization of fashion," about "trends for everyone." With the help of trends, companies hope not to be left without consumers, while consumers hope to be informed of the direction in which to look.

In 2011, the global fashion industry had a turnover of over USD 1.3 trillion.[2] The fashion industry experienced vast changes during the end of the last and the beginning of the current century. As globalization has increased, processes characterized as "lean"[3] have emerged, especially among mass-market fashion brands. The time needed for a garment to go from design to store rack has shortened considerably (e.g. the mass-market fashion chain Zara has a design-to-rack lead time of just two weeks[4]) thanks to modern production and distribution models and the exploitation of Third-World labor. Vast conglomerates with brand portfolios including everything from luxury to mail-order items have strengthened, with LVMH Moët Hennessy-Louis Vuitton and Kering (formerly Pinault-Printemps-Redoute, PPR) being prime examples. Ownership concentration has increased and barriers to entering the branded fashion market are now so high that it is absolutely necessary for a designer to obtain substantial financial backing at an early stage. Fashion is increasingly about the economy: Where the middle class grows at a remarkable speed, as in the BRIC countries,[5] expansive fashion companies try to stimulate demand.

The current transition toward "economization" and increased efficiency is not unequivocal, and the significance of fashion as cultural expression has also been accentuated. The early 2000s saw more artists and fashion designers join forces,[6] and museums vied with one another to present blockbuster fashion exhibitions. The boundaries between highbrow and lowbrow were blurred, and there were endless collaborations between ready-to-wear designers and mass-market brands. Reaching out to a wider audience became imperative even for the most renowned designers. Today, issues of corporate social responsibility (CSR) are at the top of the agenda for many fashion companies. To remain competitive, fashion companies must consider the needs and wishes of many different stakeholders, that is, consumers, competitors, owners, employees, environmental groups and the societies in which they operate. The fashion industry has been much criticized for exploiting cheap labor and for its industrial processes' negative effects on the environment, particularly through promoting over-consumption.[7]

Concurrently, there is strong movement in the opposite direction. People in the fashion industry time and again declare the end of trends. Who are trends for? Have trends escalated so quickly that they have played out their own role? Is the fashion industry imaginable without trends?

This book is a detailed examination of the significance of trends as an organizing principle[8] of the current fashion industry. It is interested in those forces that shape the role of trends in the fashion field. In it, I explore questions such as: How and why are trends created, translated and dispersed in the fashion field, how do organizations and individual actors in the fashion field relate to trends, how are consumers' relationships with trends constructed in organizations in the fashion field and how are these relationships gendered? The book focuses on womenswear, which constitutes the largest share of the fashion industry (i.e., 61 percent in the UK, 63 percent in the USA and 66 percent in Sweden),[9] but makes some comments and comparisons with menswear in passing. By extension, the book explores the development of the global fashion field in the early 2000s, through the lens of the trend concept.

In this book, the fashion field[10] refers to the relationships between the design, production, marketing and distribution of fashion to retailers, and how these are interconnected with fashion consumers. Financial intermediaries and owners are likewise influential. The field also includes all those institutions, organizations and individuals that participate in creating fashion—that classify garments as fashion (and not just clothes). Such "tastemakers"—cultural intermediaries that confer legitimacy—include critics, stylists, curators, some buyers and trend forecasters.

While the fashion field has been theorized in numerous studies, the same is not true of "trends." Its forward movement is usually said to set fashion apart, and trends are unquestionably part of that movement. I envision a trend as "a reduced form of change," a reified impending change that can be conveyed and communicated in the field and that must then be translated and interpreted, spread or dismissed. However, as I wanted to remain open and sensitive to various meanings of the term "trend," I refrained from imposing my own definition on the informants.[11] This approach is rooted in my social-constructionist view, in which our knowledge and perceptions of objects and phenomena are considered socially created. Together, we endow notions with meaning. This implies that the meaning of a concept varies over time and space; it is changeable although at times it may seem close to "natural." In other words, a basic tenet of this study is that notions such as "fashion," "trend," "quality," "fast fashion," "feminine," "masculine" and "Western" are constantly created and recreated in interactions between individuals.[12]

Labeling trends has become ever more important in the information age, as labels make trends searchable, summarizing and making them transmittable. This naming is powerful: The moment something is described as a trend, it is placed within a web of expectations, becoming something that can be spread.

Some may argue that a trend that makes a lasting impact on how we dress—for example, women's trousers—is no longer a trend but a *change*. While it is true that any fashion trend has the potential to make an enduring mark on our clothing style—we never know when kilts will be taken up by men beyond the catwalk or when the one-piece jumpsuit will become a staple—this book focuses on the *flow* of trends and their role in the industry. The people I interviewed cited many examples illustrating in detail their relationships with trends. Indisputably, "trend" is a concept frequently used in the fashion field, though in an unexamined manner. Throughout this study, informants took the concept for granted, as self-evident. Nobody ever asked me what I meant by "trend," with the interesting exception of the financial analysts who asked me whether I was referring to "fashion trend."

Today, the notion of trend is used far beyond the domains of fashion. By focusing on informants active in fashion, this book will touch on the influence of trends in this field on other parts of consumer society.

Reflections on methodology

I did not begin this study without preconceptions, as I have several years of experience in studying cultural production fields. Although the fashion field was unmapped research territory for me, I have long been interested in fashion. The research emanated from my interest in trend-forecasting agencies and in capitalization on trends. The research is permeated with my pre-knowledge of how cultural production fields work and with new analytical approaches added along the way as I read new literature concurrently with the empirical material from the interviews.

Broadly, I interviewed the informants in the following order: (1) trend-forecasting agency informants (twenty-five interviews), (2) other tastemakers (seventeen interviews), (3) informants from the BRIC countries (twenty-four interviews), (4) financial analysts (fifteen interviews) and (5) designer/brand informants (fourteen interviews). I did not interview all informants of the same type in the same round so that subsequent interviews with, for example, another trend forecaster would update me on developments in the area. The last interviews with tastemakers and trend forecasters, for example, were conducted in 2012 and 2014, respectively, just before putting together the English edition.

I was frequently reminded of how the fashion field is characterized by hierarchy. Trying to approach designers in London as an individual researcher based in Stockholm was difficult at times, as many fashion companies surround their designers with a nearly impregnable wall of PR people who fiercely control publicity. I contacted around thirty British designers and collection directors and in some cases corresponded assiduously with their associates before they eventually agreed to interviews. I found that the British informants had a greater understanding of what academic research entailed than did many others.

With the decision to conduct interviews in the BRIC countries I faced new problems: I lacked prior knowledge of the fashion fields in these countries and understood the difficulty of gaining a thorough overview in such a limited time. Other obstacles included my insufficient knowledge of languages together with often difficult-to-navigate Web sites where seemingly simple details such as names, titles and contact information were conspicuous by their absence.

Consequently, while the other interviews capture how people from diverse occupations relate to trends, depending on their position in the fashion field, the interviews in the BRIC countries are less systematic. Many positions and roles in the fashion field are ignored in this glance at the BRIC countries. Instead, these interviews capture, at a general level, trend discourses that can be juxtaposed with the dominant trend discourses in the West, offering a localized perspective on trends in the fashion field different from that presented earlier in the book.

Moreover, the interview situation in the BRIC countries differed from that elsewhere. It was not irrelevant that I came from Europe. One obvious limitation is that I needed informants fluent in English or French. At one point, in Japan, I used an interpreter, but it was seldom possible to arrange for interpreters when sending out interview requests (which were in English), so I was restricted to English-speaking informants. The informants viewed me as a Westerner, contrasting their situations with that in the West and pointing out the relevant differences. Because the fashion field has its roots and hub in the West, inequality, not only in economic terms, colored our discussions. Though these biases exist, I am still convinced that the interviews in the BRIC countries contribute to a more nuanced description of the role of trends in the global fashion field.

I also benefited from having been the program director of an MBA program on globalization offered by the Stockholm School of Economics, which provided study weeks at Fudan University (Shanghai) and Tsinghua University (Beijing), the Indian Institute of Management (Bangalore), the Fundação Getulio Vargas Business School (São Paulo) and the Stockholm School of Economics Russia (Saint Petersburg). This meant that I was reasonably up to date on developments in these countries and could test ideas for potential informants with local faculty and staff.

Before the interviews, I carefully outlined for informants the scope and direction of the project—both in writing and verbally in the interview itself—and informed them of the funding from the Swedish Research Council. I took care not to impose my own interpretive frame[13] onto the interviews, describing the project in general terms as about trends and organizing (my initial phrasing) and how various fashion actors related to trends. The interviews were semi-structured and usually lasted sixty to ninety minutes. All but two interviews were recorded and then transcribed; in those two cases, company policy forbade the recording of interviews, so I took notes instead.

As all cultural production fields are infused with both economic and cultural logics, the reasoning and behavior of the informants were closely connected to their particular positions in the studied field, which complicates anonymization. For a reader to judge the credibility of an interpretation in qualitative research, the position from which the informant is speaking must be made clear. This means, in the present context, that the person's specific occupation and endowment of fashion capital are necessary information. The situation is different when it comes to the financial analysts: they act within a purely economic logic and belong to the larger economic field. The financial analysts' positions among themselves are not based on fashion capital, and the economic field to which they belong is, to a greater extent than in cultural production fields, uniformly permeated by the idea that people are interchangeable and relate to each other as competitors ("*Gesellschaft* culture").[14] As a result, the specific financial institutions and the names and employment positions of these informants are less important, so in the book I generally refer to them as "financial analysts." Furthermore, anonymization was often a prerequisite for the participation of the financial analysts due to policy set by the institutions for which they worked.

Each named informant was allowed to read through the complete interview transcript; the rest of the informants, that is, the unnamed ones, were provided with the direct quotations of their own words. Slight revisions were made afterward; for example, an adjective might be changed or the name of a colleague or competitor might be anonymized. Sometimes, the benefits of having an interviewee speak openly under anonymity have been weighed against the revisions asked for by the interviewee in order to make statements under an identifiable name and affiliation, and if the latter hampers certain interpretations, anonymization has been favored. The publisher, Bloomsbury Academic, required each interviewee and their respective headquarters to sign an interview release form, a process that took several months to complete. Fourteen people asked to be anonymized after reading the interview material or did not respond to my contact attempts and were hence anonymized. In Chapters 2 and 3, I anonymized a few trend analysts, because certain informants were only quoted once or twice and I deemed it sometimes irrelevant exactly *who* in this occupational category said what. Some informants were not in the end quoted, sometimes because language problems yielded poor interview material and sometimes to avoid excessive repetition. If several informants expressed similar views or described similar experiences, I merely added comments such as "many others made similar observations" to indicate the range of the material. Since the time of the interview, several informants have changed jobs. I have not taken that into account, as only the position that the informant occupied when the interview took place is relevant to my interpretation. Interestingly, several tastemakers have moved between functions, for example, from being a fashion editor to being a fashion director at a department store, which verifies the importance of the social relationships in this field.

As a researcher, I always have the prerogative of interpretation, that is, the last word. Nevertheless, it has been essential that I respect the informants and give them more than just a few lines each in which to express themselves. I wanted to reveal their understandings of the fashion field while, as a researcher, going beyond their own interpretations.[15] I had no intention of challenging the informants' depiction of reality; for example, I did not question whether or not H&M engages in fast fashion, though I find an informant's denial of this interesting in itself. A few informants used business terms, such as "product life cycle," that I regard as part of the empirical material but not of my conceptual research framework.

*

The trend-forecasting agencies are introduced in Chapter 2. Informants from such agencies in New York, London, Paris and Tokyo spoke about their raison d'être. Why should anyone listen to them? Wherein lies their competence? How do these agencies legitimize themselves in relation to their customers? The chapter not only describes the rise of the trend-forecasting industry but also shows how trend forecasters organize the field with trends by capitalizing on the need to reduce uncertainty. Chapter 3 emphasizes that trend-forecasting agencies operate in a cultural production field, fashion, characterized by a set of conceptions of design, fashion and creativity. Together, Chapters 2 and 3 demonstrate the difficult balancing act of trend-forecasting agencies. On the one hand, these agencies point to the advantages of their trend-forecasting business model to gain clients' confidence. On the other hand, the trend forecasters have to take into account the position of the designers, and the conceptions of design, fashion and creativity that dominate the fashion field, and as a consequence, play down their own actorhood and seek legitimacy backstage. Chapter 4 canvasses other cultural intermediaries in the fashion field, tastemakers such as fashion journalists, stylists and buyers, and explores their relationships with trends. The social nature of the fashion field becomes very clear; many different actors cooperate in developing trends. The tastemakers challenge the role of the trend forecasters, as they see themselves as the ones who discover, recognize and define trends. In the information age, trends sometimes have the role of news hooks. The chapter also points at the increasingly low status associated with the word "trend," which is why some tastemakers prefer to talk about style rather than trends. The gendering of trends serves as the focal point for Chapter 5. The chapter asks how actors in the fashion field explain why womenswear trends tend to be shorter and more variable than menswear trends. The chapter then discusses the construction of femininity as more changeable and ephemeral and links it to the fashion industry, and this is followed by a section that connects interviewees' statements about women's desire to be "just right" to the modern construction of femininity and its emphasis on appearances. The chapter ends with a discussion about trends being perceived as not only restrictive but also empowering. Chapter 6 examines designers, brands and trends in three different segments: mass market, mid-market and designer/luxury. In this chapter, the fashion companies take center stage and, thus, the tension between *consistency* and *change* is stressed. Whereas fashion is said to have change as its very core, the ubiquitous practice of branding calls for consistency (according to dominating branding models). Many interviewees testify to seeing a more tolerant fashion scene, with more parallel trends, more knowledgeable consumers and more emphasis on individual styling than before. Several designers entirely dismiss the idea of using trend services, seeing themselves as the trendmakers or preferring to make niche products less subject to trends. Although the chapter illustrates how trends in general have become more demand-driven, the idea of an independent fashion *auteur* still thrives in the designer segment. Chapter 7, on financialization and trends, is based on interviews with financial analysts who must relate to trends in the fashion companies that they monitor and evaluate. As fashion companies want to expand, they go public to raise the necessary capital, and, thus, these companies submit to the logic of the financial markets. With the strong links between fashion and capitalism serving as a backdrop, the chapter highlights differences between those analysts who deal with luxury goods (the designer segment) and those analysts who deal with mass-market retail companies. The tendency among analysts to regard fashion trends as "fashion risks" is analyzed in light of Bourdieu's theory of cultural production; the fashion logic is seen as capricious and arbitrary by those who adhere to an economic logic. Under the influence of the financial markets, most fashion companies have adopted their range structures to fit the idea of trends as fashion risks, the "on trend" items representing only a small section of the total range. In the mass-market segment, however, analysts often address "the risk of not taking risks." Chapter 8 then takes the reader to the BRIC countries—India,

China, Russia and Brazil—to illustrate how tastemakers and designers relate to trends in these emergent markets. The interviews draw attention to the particular circumstances that stipulate the relation to trends in a high-growth fashion market with a rising middle class: *neomania*, the incessant strive for the new, is redirected toward trends rather than brands. The section on India casts light on the consequences of the restrictions in supply of fashion when interpreting the role of trends. The largest part of the chapter is devoted to China. The trend-forecasting agencies' presence, significance and growth in China is elaborated on from different perspectives. Likewise, the role of trends in Chinese culture as well as the social meaning of fashion in today's China is a popular topic among many interviewees. In a similar vein, the section on Russia emphasizes the construction of Russian fashion as *the other*, complementing the norm but never truly part of the fashion norm, the Western fashion scene. The piece on Brazil brings to the foreground one aspect of the globalization of the fashion field, namely how local tastemakers are losing ground to global tastemakers when it comes to trends. The book ends with a final discussion in Chapter 9, in which some of the overarching themes are summarized and expanded on, under the following headings: "Trends as organizing principle," "New ways of managing uncertainty," "Fashion capital strikes back," "The fashionization of consumer society," "Trend imperialism," "Trends have become low status," "The discourse of individuality," "The relationship between trends and fashion" and "Trendification." The theoretical and conceptual contributions of the book are found in the Appendix.

The one notable category absent from this text is that of manufacturers and the supply chain with all its subcontractors. This category has traditionally not created or influenced trends but has "followed orders," though the section on China identifies a nascent change.

2 TREND FORECASTERS— FASHION'S "INSURANCE COMPANIES"

We used to say that if you can find areas of *fear, uncertainty* and *doubt*, that's a sign that you should study them more closely. (Neil Bradford, CEO (2008–2009), WGSN)

Worth Global Style Network (WGSN), headquartered in London, is the world's largest fashion trend-forecasting agency. Its head office, in the impressive art deco building formerly housing the Carreras Cigarette Factory, has over 200 employees working on content. Neil Bradford, the company's CEO when I began the study, is impeccably dressed but does not present as a typical member of the fashion glitterati. After a few years with the management consultant firm McKinsey & Company, Bradford founded a company to help corporations navigate the decision process of buying large IT systems, providing "objective third-party opinion[s] ... We used to see it as an insurance policy." According to Bradford, Bloomberg and Reuters serve a similar function in the financial industries and IMS Health in the pharmaceutical industry.

Providing companies in the fashion industry with forecasting information helps WGSN's clients more easily avoid mistakes—"the insurance policy." Bradford points out that this does not mean that clients necessarily follow or copy the direction in which everyone else is moving; sometimes it is enough just to know where others are moving to choose a unique direction:

Even investing was an art a hundred years ago. But nowadays you have all these financial models and rocket scientists. In the same way, IT, when it emerged in the 1950s and 1960s, was considered an art. And today it is much better understood as a science ... What's fascinating with the fashion industry is that we are equally taking something that was very esoteric and hard to understand, and turning it into more of a science by giving people the tools they need to do their job better. (Neil Bradford, CEO, WGSN)

The big difference, according to Bradford, is what decisions are needed. In the IT industry, for example, decisions normally concern large corporations buying large IT systems. "Will I buy that new Microsoft Windows System for my company?" There is little use in asking Microsoft this question. Spending EUR 50,000 on a third-party opinion about a EUR 5 million investment is prudent, not wasteful. In the fashion industry, the clients are designers. Bradford sees WGSN's role not as helping clients make one big decision a year, but helping them make "fifty smarter decisions each day":

This is something I love about this industry, that people are using... the information literally on a daily basis. They'll come in, in the morning, for example, as a designer focusing on knitwear, they'll get their cup of coffee, fire up their email, and fire up their WGSN, and start exploring the latest colors, what their competitors are doing, what shapes we think are coming down. They go onto the site just to explore, to get some inspiration basically.

Bradford observes that the other big difference, compared with other industries where information always comes in the form of numbers and spreadsheets, is that WGSN's information consists largely of images.

Online trend forecasters: WGSN and Stylesight

WGSN was founded in September 1997 by the brothers Marc and Julian Worth. The Worth brothers previously ran the family business for twenty-five years, serving manufacturers in the fashion industry. A significant part of the company's services comprised badges, printing and T-shirts. The company had always offered clients a wide choice of design and graphic artwork from which customers could choose, leaving unused graphic resources. Inspired by Getty Images, the American stock photo agency, the Worths created an equivalent online resource, initially for their unused graphics and designs (WGSN still has a graphics library based on this).

The Worths' initial idea mushroomed to include trend forecasting, store windows, runway reports, travel directories and guides. After a year building their product, they launched WGSN in 1998. WGSN's yearly turnover was in the region of GBP 25 million in 2005, when the brothers sold WGSN for GBP 140 million to Emap, a media company specializing in business publications.

The Worths never regarded WGSN as an internet company but as an information business that used the internet to deliver content. The company initially used satellite broadcasting—despite the complicated technology of servers and dishes—to transmit information, because in 1998 the internet was simply too slow and WGSN did not want to compromise the quality of its images. As the internet improved by the end of the 1990s, WGSN became an online business. This was rather daring, since trend-forecasting information had previously only been published in books written by trend gurus who marketed, traveled and lectured.

The establishment of this online trend-forecasting agency coincided with an information revolution that would profoundly affect the fashion industry. Pivotal to changing fashion is sharing information. The more fashion information is shared, the more influence it will have on people and their behavior. Around the turn of the millennium, there was extensive talk of the "information society" and its potential to "democratize fashion." Suddenly, fashion information was available in all corners of the world: dissemination was instant and the images were of high quality.[1] Recognizing that images from the streets of Tokyo or São Paulo could make some designers' costly "inspiration trips" redundant, WGSN offered its users detailed material from cities around the world.

Bradford emphasizes that the speeding up of the fashion industry due to rapid information flow and "lean" production and distribution processes has made up-to-date business intelligence and trend-forecasting essential. Historically, there was a two-season system with long annual planning cycles. Now, although the fashion weeks' ready-to-wear shows still maintain the two-season system (i.e., autumn/winter and spring/summer), most fashion companies have continuous "drops" of new items. According to a WGSN survey, 59 percent of all fashion companies in the UK considered themselves to be designing "fast fashion" in 2008. WGSN offers a solution for companies that need timely fashion and trend information. The service's success rests on the collection of information from 140 fashion and trade shows and from various fashion-oriented cities. It sounds like a good deal. As a client, you pay GBP 16,500 and five users get access to the intelligence and research that WGSN spent GBP 6 million to compile. The rationale is economies of scale, as invoked by classic information intermediaries such as travel agencies and real estate brokers. Bradford stresses that it is up to individual users to employ the information, adapting it to their specific brands and intended consumer segments.

In 2011, WGSN was a trend-forecasting agency with 38,000 users in 3,000 companies in eighty-seven countries. Under the new leadership of Susanna Kempe, CEO from 2009 to 2011, WGSN still has about 200 employees.

In 2010, the company's annual turnover was close to GBP 40 million.[2] WGSN's clients include Armani, LVMH, Zara, Levi Strauss and C&A. Users of the site discover ongoing and upcoming trends, access analyses of trends and consumer insights, and can even use digital colors and patterns, runway images and street shots to create mood boards (i.e., collages of images, texts, colors and photos that illustrate what a designer wants to convey). WGSN provides users with patterns for key items representing a particular trend, including downloadable CAD pattern files that can be used in the industry-standard graphics software Illustrator and even sent directly to manufacturers. The archive contains 4.8 million searchable images.

WGSN's online fashion trend-forecasting services were almost unique until 2003, when Stylesight was established in New York. Launched as the low-cost alternative to WGSN, Stylesight has grown rapidly into a strong competitor. As of 2011, Stylesight offered basic subscriptions for USD 7,500 and had 25,000 users in 2,500 companies. Like WGSN, Stylesight's success lies in providing services that save its customers both time and money. Prada, Zara, Donna Karan, Polo Ralph Lauren, Club Monaco, Forever 21, Nordstrom, Bulgari and Abercrombie & Fitch are all Stylesight clients.

Both WGSN and Stylesight are eagerly expanding into new markets. Frank Bober, Stylesight's CEO, considers a customer base of ten to twenty thousand companies realistic when regions that were never before accessible to Western trend forecasting open up. Stylesight currently has thirty employees translating its Web site content into Spanish, Japanese, Chinese, Turkish and Korean.[3] WGSN provides daily updates in six languages and is planning a Chinese version of the Web site. The company has "creative labs" in New York, Los Angeles, Tokyo and Hong Kong and offices in fifteen other cities, including Seoul, Melbourne, Paris, Barcelona, Shanghai and São Paulo. Stylesight has large offices in New York, London, Shanghai and Hong Kong, and smaller locations in places such as Melbourne, São Paulo, Guangzhou, Bangalore, Tokyo and Istanbul.

In 2011, WGSN bought Denimhead, a Los Angeles-based trend-forecasting agency focusing on denim and casual sportswear. Kempe describes Denimhead as possessing a very high level of expertise in denim, an area where WGSN can offer more value to its international customers. Denim is extremely popular in India, for example, and acquiring Denimhead is seen as an investment in this rapidly growing market strongly dominated by menswear.

WGSN does not serve only the fashion industry. In WGSN's New York office, a head of content tells me enthusiastically about a colleague who just gave a presentation at Barilla's—apparently, womenswear silhouettes affect the shape of the pasta. Bradford describes the firm's entry into support for consumer goods as a result of being approached by car companies, mobile telephone producers and even shampoo brands. This took WGSN by surprise: "Why are you interested in this?" was their spontaneous reaction. However, the founders of WGSN realized the potential that followed in the footsteps of the aestheticization of society and chose the name Worth Global Style Network rather than Worth Global Fashion Network. Still, the content of WGSN's service is completely dominated by fashion. The aestheticization process means that Lufthansa, BMW, Microsoft, Procter & Gamble, IKEA, L'Oréal and others are now clients. Bradford explains:

> They're thinking of what is the next color that I should have in the interior of my plane, or what is the next color I should be using on my cars, or what is the next color or pattern I should be using on my computer to match the style of the day. I think there is one exciting megatrend here: everything is becoming stylish. If we were sitting in this office fifteen years ago, we would have boring chairs. But we now have quite nice chairs. Ten years ago phones were bricks and computers were beige. Now, what computer you have says a lot about you, what phone says even more about you. We all own six pairs of sunglasses for different looks. Style has exploded. I think it is also no longer the realm of the high-end products. Look at IKEA and Target in the States. Style is everywhere now. Today every consumer-focused company wants to have an edge style-wise.

In response to this expansion, WGSN's client list now consists of 60 percent fashion brands and retailers, 20 percent manufacturers and 20 percent companies in the consumer goods, automotive, technology and advertising industries. The fastest-growing client group is advertising, though Susanna Kempe explains it is from a small base and is a natural extension of advertiser's need to be close to their clients' inspiration source that the demand from this particular group is increasing. Kempe mentions that, after restructuring its Web site, WGSN now lists the client functions it serves, including marketing.

Kempe enthusiastically describes how WGSN's macro trend videos—the company releases three each season—are shown in the center foyer at Procter & Gamble, reaching almost every employee. Kempe believes that interest in WGSN's trend forecasting is increasing, in everything from design to packaging and branding.

WGSN also has a number of banks as clients. Their market analysts watch what is going on in the fashion industry and their specialists in mergers and acquisitions use WGSN to better evaluate companies before potential deals.

WGSN also offers a consultancy sideline representing about 5 percent of its annual turnover. Procter & Gamble, L'Oréal, Blackberry, some shoe manufacturers and even a few Russian department stores use this service. Stylesight, despite its fashion focus, also has several clients whose primary business area is something other than fashion—clients such as Mitsubishi, Mattel, Sephora, Amazon, eBay, Disney, Carrefour, Hard Rock Cafe and Bed Bath & Beyond.

In 2011, analysts estimated the trend-forecasting business to be worth GBP 36 billion[4] with two players, WGSN and Stylesight, being completely dominant. One question to keep in mind, as a first step in understanding trends as an organizing principle, is what the dominance of a few trend-forecasting companies means for the fashion field as a whole.

It all began in France

WGSN and Stylesight are not new or isolated phenomena. There is a long tradition of trend forecasting in the fashion industry. The first trend-forecasting agencies started in France: Fred Carlin founded Carlin International in the 1940s in Paris; Promostyl's founders Danièlle and Sébastien de Diesbach created the "trend book" concept, a book presenting the upcoming season's trends, in the 1960s; Dominique Peclers established Peclers Paris in 1970 and Nelly Rodi—also in Paris—established her eponymous agency in 1985.[5] These four French trend agencies are commonly referred to as "the first ones." Trend Union, the consultancy created by Li Edelkoort, is sometimes included in this group. Although Edelkoort herself is from the Netherlands, her trend agency is based in Paris. Many French trend-forecasting agencies, not exclusively Paris based, now have online presences but concentrate on publications such as trend books and on consultancy services.

Pierre-François Le Louët, explaining how his mother founded NellyRodi, describes a France that by the 1950s was lagging behind the United States in ready-to-wear. In 1947, Dior had supplied 5 percent of France's export revenues,[6] but in general France's fashion offerings at that time seemed not only muddled but dated. After a French trade delegation had traveled to the United States to learn how its fashion industry was structured, the French government formed a trend-coordinating agency, financed by the French textile industries, to reduce uncertainty in the industry. Le Louët observes:

If you give the same intelligence to those who sell the clothes, those who design them, those who buy the fabrics and those who supply them, there are enormous economic advantages for the fabric manufacturers, because they know what material will be in demand and where to concentrate their efforts. Similarly, if the retailers are all stocking violet that year, it inevitably creates a demand for violet, so they sell out their stock. The idea was to reduce the margin of error in the extremely risky field of fashion.[7]

Fashion, capitalism and modernity

Fashion, one of the most commercial fields of cultural production, is often said to have its origins in modernity and the rise of industrial capitalism. The latter contributed to increased trade and, with it, growing and developing cities, while feudal society and its hierarchies were broken down, creating the crucible for the development of fashion. Industrial capitalism created centers where new social roles emerged and a sharp division arose between street life and the private sphere. Appearance and self-presentation became increasingly important.[8] During the nineteenth century, gender became more explicitly marked in clothing.[9] The clear link between democratization and the establishment of fashion is clearer than ever in modern society: With increasingly blurred class distinctions, people tend to use fashion and other forms of cultural consumption both to set themselves apart and to demonstrate their group identity or allegiance.[10]

In addition to the obvious etymological correlation between *la mode* and *modernity*, the two concepts are related. One central feature of modernity is the ephemeral, the contemporary, and that is precisely what fashion expresses so well. Both fashion and modernity thrive on incessant change, self-fertilizing references to their own past and a constant adaptation to new factors that ensures continued existence. Ulrich Lehmann, author of *Tigersprung*, a book about fashion in modernity, argued that fashion must be studied at this very moment, while it is passing, rather than being historicized. Fashion is reborn every day, he wrote, in the form best suited and most relevant to the prevailing cultural and social milieu. Modernity will continue to exist as long as capitalism and the bourgeoisie exist, and fashion items express this.[11] In a globalized world whose various parts have adopted different capitalist systems and where the influence of modernity varies (in fact, one could speak of global modernities[12]), fashion can of course assume different meanings. The link between fashion and modernity also implies a historical link between fashion and the West.

Fashion's movements

Although the aim of this book is not to explain trends as such, the fashion field itself has spawned a plenitude of ideas about what causes changes in fashion. Sometimes informants refer to these as common knowledge about the spreading of trends. However, changes in fashion are not necessarily packaged and labeled as "trends." The numerous texts trying to explain fashion's movements suggest various theories from perspectives as different as psychology, semiotics, anthropology, art history, performance studies, sociology, economics and dress history. Despite fundamentally different approaches to and views of knowledge, these theories have points of convergence. In their book *Changing Fashion*, Annette Lynch and Mitchell Strauss identified four common threads that unite these theoretical perspectives and serve as the most prominent drivers of fashion change.[13]

Neomania: the never-ending search for novelty

References to an incessant striving for newness, called "neomania"[14] by Roland Barthes, appear in various forms. Psychoanalytic theories suggest that our subconscious sexual energy—part of the human condition—compels us to seek the visually and fashionably new. Usually, this neomanic instinct is taken for granted, for example, in cyclic economic models of fashion change. Fashion here consists of long cycles that repeat themselves consistently and predictably, independent of the environment, social changes, technological gains and individual designers. Other cyclical models have focused on various user groups, from innovators and early adopters to laggards and non-adopters. The existence of new, immediate fashion information through the internet and the growth of fast fashion have further sped up the hunt for the new.

Identity conflict

Another recurring topic in explaining fashion's shifts is identity conflict. When identities are in flux, for example, as social and cultural categories are being redefined, fashion is pushed in one direction or another. This generally occurs as prevalent constructions of gender, class, sexuality and ethnicity are put under external pressure and existing roles must be redefined. A classic example of a fashion change springing from this type of identity conflict is the emergence of punk style, a 1970s reaction to class and gender conventions in the UK, when the prospects for working-class youth were anything but bright. A theme throughout the literature is that fashion thrives in the tension between the strong wish to maintain one's individuality and the equally strong need to belong to a desirable group—the topic of a famous text on fashion by sociologist Georg Simmel.[15] In today's society, our identity is not set in stone but rather negotiable, to some degree, thanks to fashion.

Status

Status combat is another theme of theories that attempt to explain fashion changes. The idea is slightly time-worn and concerns how people of high status (typically economic and social) react disagreeably to supposed intrusions by "others." In the classic status combat, individuals in dominant positions develop new, alternative status symbols—new fashion—to distinguish themselves anew from those presumably "chasing" them. This is in line with Thorstein Veblen's description of conspicuous consumption in *The Theory of the Leisure Class*.[16] Globalization means that fashion consumers can be found in all corners of the world; at the same time, the gaps between them are enormous, both within and between countries, so status combat remains. In her book *Deluxe: How Luxury Lost Its Luster*, Dana Thomas described how some luxury brands' exposure in China, India and other Asian countries has made them less attractive as status symbols in Europe and the United States.[17] While much attention was previously paid to so-called trickle-down theories, that is, the idea that fashion starts in higher social classes and then spreads to other classes further down in the hierarchy, these ideas have given way to parallel theories in which inspiration is also seen to be gathered from vibrant "street" culture and elsewhere.

Mimetic behavior

People's mimetic behavior, their tendency to observe and copy what they see and like, is the last typical explanation of fashion change. Mimesis is a prerequisite for the mass adoption that now almost, but not entirely, defines fashion. The internet, globalization, urbanization and a stronger celebrity culture have all intensified mimetic behavior. Today, many people in the fashion industry reject this model, arguing that mimetic behavior is more complex and has taken new forms.

Trend-forecasting agencies as tastemakers

The above explanatory models describe fashion's movements from the consumer perspective. Certainly, society at large is sometimes taken into account, but the fact that fashion is also an industry and that changes in fashion may also result from the circumstances of production goes notably unremarked in the fashion literature. One way of capturing the flows between the consumption and production spheres is to scrutinize people whom sociologist Pierre Bourdieu calls "cultural intermediaries," that is, tastemakers.[18] In the fashion field, tastemakers can be seen as fashion promoters who move between production and consumption. Next to buyers, editors and journalists, stylists, bloggers and others, trend forecasters can also be seen as cultural intermediaries of the fashion field. By selecting and presenting trends in a certain manner, they shape people's interpretations of these trends in what sociologist Erving Goffman calls "framing."[19] Trend forecasters provide accounts of where and why trends have emerged and of what these trends are extending or reacting to, contributing to sensemaking concerning trends. Accordingly, these agencies have considerable power in relation to both producers and consumers.

Two kinds of trend-forecasting agencies

The competition between trend-forecasting agencies being fierce, they not uncommonly try to attract potential clients by describing reality in ways with which clients can easily identify. The agencies often use schematic diagrams of how their services meet the demands of different clients, in different stages of fashion production or in different segments of the industry. It is not unusual to cast competitors as providing limited services, their offerings being said to only cover a fraction of what the trend-forecasting agency in question promises.

In brief, one could say that online trend-forecasting agencies, primarily Stylesight and WGSN, present themselves as "the contemporary alternative." WGSN's constant updates of Web site content and rich information provided almost immediately keep customers informed about emergent trend developments. Broad coverage of fashion shows and fairs as well as street and travel reports from around the world mean the client can reduce expenditures of time and money.

The book-publishing French trend-forecasting agencies, on the other hand, stress their long historical legacies, their exclusive fashion knowledge and the anthropological interpretative frameworks they use to understand the long-term development of trends. Tactile information conveyed through fabric and material samples is emphasized. Claiming that their online competitors conduct mere "trend watching" and "reporting" rather than true trend analysis and forecasting, these traditional agencies only consider online services an option for big retailers with a fast-fashion profile.

It is hardly surprising that the online trend-forecasting agencies reject being characterized as mere "trend watchers," stressing their varied customer base and differentiated levels of trend information. The WGSN Web site cannot be briefly described, as it presents a vast amount of material (650,000 pages of content) from various angles. The heading *Inspiration* links users to themes such as *Celebrity, Street Shots, Vintage, Arts & Culture, Pop Culture* and *Photo Files*, each of which in turn leads to numerous other options for even more detailed material. All users in the client organization can be inspired by the same information. Under *Insight and Analysis*, for example, WGSN offers functions tailored to different phases in the product development cycle (i.e., *News, Think Tank, Creative Direction, Colour & Materials, Design & Product Development, Buying & Sourcing, Branding & Packaging, Marketing, Trade Shows, Catwalks, What's in Store, Retail & Visual Merchandising, Business & Strategy* and *City by City*). According to WGSN's CEO, Susanna Kempe, this can be seen as an adaptation to new user categories, such as buyers and marketers. The heading *Think Tank*, for example, encompasses macro trends several years ahead, while *What's in Store* offers reports from retailers around the world, close-to-season updates and a trend-tracker that identifies emerging trends and confirms others. *Buying & Sourcing* lists manufacturers and subcontractors around the world who subscribe to WGSN.

These two competing ways of describing reality will illuminate the material that follows, but I will focus on the trend phenomenon as an organizing principle. Some of my informants claim that their company was one of the earliest, if not the first, to conduct true trend forecasting. While it is not germane to my topic to know who was the very first, the fact that some informants stress their companies' histories is telling.

Offerings of trend-forecasting agencies: how do they claim their competence?

One step toward a deeper understanding of the role and expansion of trend-forecasting agencies in the fashion industry is to look more closely at how they legitimize their services in relation to their clients. How do they establish their competence? Why are their services necessary? On top of Bradford's "insurance policy" and the hope of saving time and money, they cite a number of other selling arguments.

Competence of the personnel

Common to all trend-forecasting agencies is that most of their employees have some sort of design background. Others may have studied art, social science or journalism, while business professionals and lawyers are exceptions. WGSN and many French trend-forecasting agencies take pride in having employees with vast fashion industry experience, people endowed with what sociologist Joanne Entwistle calls "aesthetic knowledge," a form of sensual, embodied knowledge obtained in the fashion field[20] in relation to objects. Since fashion largely concerns the relationship between the item and the body, people working in the industry develop what Entwistle calls a "sense and sensibility" that revolves around the body, often manifested in embodied metaphors describing their knowledge, such as "gut instinct" or "having an eye." This is generally referred to as tacit knowledge, as aesthetic knowledge is often difficult to articulate.[21] Typically, the employees have previously worked as designers or buyers, and trend-forecasting agencies increasingly profile their employees online and in marketing material to capitalize on their backgrounds. Besides industry knowledge and insights into the work processes, the significance of employees' networks within the industry cannot be underestimated. It is often said that WGSN's early success was explained by the Worth brothers' extensive network in the fashion industry. Such a network is particularly important at the outset as it strengthens credibility and provides an indication of the breadth of local competence in the company, helping it attract new clients. An account manager from an online trend service suggests that the French trend-forecasting agencies have the upper hand in Paris: "Most of the time [the clients] have a French trend-forecasting agency, Carlin, then Peclers, then NellyRodi, then Promostyl, and then, perhaps, they could imagine something new, but during recession times like these, they all have a tight budget."

As representatives of the trend-forecasting agencies describe what characterizes a good trend analyst, the prioritizing of the aesthetic knowledge becomes obvious. Those responsible for developing trend analyses are often said to have "a sixth sense," "an incredible eye" and the ability to "join the dots" and "see the big picture." One head of trends at a major trend-forecasting agency says:

> When I am looking to hire people, they have to have a creative background, they all need to have art school training. I think what makes a good trend forecaster is someone who is always looking around them, who sees things and gathers information in a particular way... Someone who is looking intellectually at what's happening in the greater sphere, whether it's economically, politically, or ecologically, in all the different spheres, and then linking it all back to fashion.

Many say that the job is less about stating that blue is the next big color than it is about being able to analyze how societal changes affect fashion trends.

Jane Kellock is the London-based trends consultant for WGSN responsible for coordinating long-term trends in the "trends," "colour," "graphics" and "material" categories. She manages a team representing analysts of fashion directions for womenswear, menswear, kidswear, footwear, interiors and materials, as well as a small research team. Every other Wednesday, the team holds a lunch meeting, discussing books, movies, exhibitions, places traveled to and other things that may have inspired them. Up to two years ahead of a season, WGSN organizes trend days with the company's trends teams from its largest offices, for example, in Los Angeles, New York and Hong Kong. Jane Kellock explains:

> We all get together for two days and we brainstorm our ideas, we do presentations for each other about what we think will influence the future. This time we did what we called "a box of ideas." Every single person in the trends team brought a box of ideas, a physical box with things in it which they thought would inspire the future. And it was fascinating, because there were things like people's knitting to... just anything. We don't get a brief, we say be as random as you possibly want to. So the sort of information we get comes from films, from art, from just what people are feeling, and then the trends team will get

together the day after and start putting it all together. Weirdly enough, every single time, key things come through. 'Cause you've got fifty creative people in a room, who are travelling all over the world, who are influenced constantly by all sorts of things, who are out there, the young ones are clubbing and so on. Weirdly enough, we get ten people who say things like "I'm really feeling like I want to do crafts" and "I want to bake cakes." So it creates… rough groups of information that we think are relevant.

The team members then pinpoint ideas, group them and give them names. The categories are later illustrated on trend boards with images of things people brought to the trend days. "Obviously, any thinking is based on what we did in previous seasons 'cause we've been doing this for ten years. We can call something a continuation of or an evolution of a specific trend" (Jane Kellock, Trends Consultant, WGSN).

The trends are given keywords and research references and are eventually published by the WGSN think tank. The trends teams then make these ideas relevant to their particular areas (e.g., womenswear, menswear and kidswear) and product type:

> Last season we had had *evolve, imagineer* and *outrageous*. Those were three main trends. The different areas will have different research references, different mood boards, but will be based along the same thinking. And that filters through all the way… From macro trends, which is think tank, down to "what's in store", trade show reports and eventually "what's in the shops right now?" (Jane Kellock, Trends Consultant, WGSN)

One such macro trend Kellock mentions is *being connected*, specifically, the relationship between online and off-line connection. Two relevant examples using social networks are the Web site Etsy, where people buy and sell handmade products, and the Occupy movement. Kellock recently identified the keywords that WGSN has been using since its inception and still finds them as relevant as ever: *sustainability, connections, mapping* and *emotional product*. Kellock laughs and says:

> The key thing is to evolve the overall trends, making them new, 'cause every season is like reinventing the wheel. We have to make sure that it looks new to our subscribers, because then it looks new to the customers. But at the same time we must make sure that we don't change it too much, because people don't like too much of a dramatic change. And also, it's not sustainable to make it completely different. So we do have a sense of morality, even if it doesn't come out in the shops at the end of it.

In the early days of the trend-forecasting business, the agencies usually each revolved around a person who was ascribed nearly supernatural insights and abilities. While most trend-forecasting agencies, often as their founders pass away, now downplay the significance of one individual's contribution, in one trend agency in Europe the cult of personality still thrives—Trend Union, owned by Lidewij Edelkoort.

The Trend Union headquarters, a narrow brick townhouse with floor-to-ceiling windows, is on the periphery of Paris' 14th arrondissement. The white interior is complemented by countless green plants: "For ten years now, Lidewij has published a magazine on plants, flowers and horticulture, *Bloom*, where she often talks about the meaning of plants for people," explains the office manager, Sophie Carlier. Edelkoort has developed a conglomerate of companies that complement one another. Besides Trend Union, there is a consulting company, a think tank and a free Web-based trend service focusing on interactivity. It is Edelkoort's role as a trend-forecasting agency director and chief analyst that is of most interest here. Twice a year, Trend Union's limited-edition *Trendbook* is released, forecasting trends two years in advance. In addition to this well-known publication, Trend Union also publishes books on trends in color, beauty, patterns, shapes and forms. These trend books cost EUR 1,700 to 2,400 each.

Many of those I interviewed describe Lidewij Edelkoort as in the avant-garde, as the last guru of the trend industry—a view her coworkers share. Carlier describes Edelkoort's special talent:

Already in school studying fine arts as well as at her first job, she realized that she had a special talent to foresee and forecast needs and tastes of consumers for the coming seasons and for the future. She has developed that ability further throughout her career, in different fields, and it forms the basis of her own vision of trend forecasting, which is very unique in the world of trend forecasting. Her competency is a balance between intuition, knowledge and expertise of the market and lifestyles.

Edelkoort's pre-eminence in the field is attested to by the many prizes and recognitions she has received, including an Honourary Doctorate of Art from Nottingham Trent University, Chevalier des Arts et des Lettres from the French Minister of Culture and appointment as the chair of the Design Academy in Eindhoven.

Carlier cites an example of how Edelkoort formulates a trend. The trend could be labeled "the importance of skin" and was closely connected to the importance of tactility, which, according to Carlier, originated in the early 1990s. At a flea market, Edelkoort discovered an intriguing vintage postcard of a tattooed woman. She then happened to view an exhibition of the artist Byron Kim whose paintings "sample" the skin of friends, creating mosaics of differing skin tones. Carlier mentions the book *Post-human*, published about that time, which described the body's importance and structure. Inspired by these disparate sources, Edelkoort translated her impressions into her 1992 trend book. One image Carlier shows me is of a bandage, suggesting the importance of skin color while underlining the feeling of elasticity and "softness to the touch." The following year, the trend book reiterated this trend and included more visual presentations of what the trend could mean to clients, such as latex samples that illustrated elasticity and "the new touch," and a leather corset created to highlight the shape of the body. In parallel, Edelkoort pushed for this trend in her magazine *View on Colour*. Carlier makes it clear that by 1994 this skin trend had reached materials and textiles, and skin colors were seen everywhere, as the trend inspired creative people in the fashion industry. Highlighting that the introduction of microfiber was critical to the trend's development, Carlier refers to "nude" lingerie from Marks & Spencer. In 1995, the trend arrived in catwalk shows, evident in both the variety of skin colors and the fluidity of fabrics. The following years, nude colors became popular in cosmetics such as lip gloss and nail polish. Thirteen years later, according to Carlier, Edelkoort stated that the trend was still relevant, citing the popularity of skeletons. This long-term perspective is continually emphasized by Trend Union and other French trend-forecasting agencies.

It is easy to discount the idea of guru status and assume that there is some arbitrariness in Edelkoort's storytelling. It is, however, crucial to keep in mind that Lidewij, like all trend forecasters, is operating in an aesthetic field. Edelkoort herself says that she has "trained her intuition" just as muscles can be trained. She has said, "Sometimes it is almost as if another person is sitting next to me, listening to the surroundings and observing interesting people, art, etc."[22] Aesthetic knowledge is difficult to verbalize and is often manifested in expressions such as "gut feeling," "intuition" or "eye" that allude to embodied knowledge directly attributable to the senses and their susceptibility—the be-all and end-all when operating in an aesthetic field. Such ability can only be acquired through practice *within* the fashion field. An individual such as Lidewij Edelkoort is often said to be irreplaceable in this respect. Carlier says, *"Elle est le moteur de son enterprise"*—she is the engine of her company.

*

Across the Atlantic, on 7th Avenue in midtown Manhattan, is David Wolfe, often called the trend guru of New York City. He is the creative director of The Doneger Group, a fashion trend-forecasting agency that combines trend intelligence with market information and expertise in retailing and merchandizing. If it were not for the clothing racks everywhere, the two carpeted floors of The Doneger Group offices could easily be mistaken for a software company. David Wolfe's account of his career clearly illustrates how the trend-forecasting business functioned before the information age and the advent of the internet, illuminating what was then considered cutting-edge aesthetic knowledge and skill.

In the mid-1960s, David Wolfe worked as an illustrator at a department store in Ohio, where he won some advertising awards. He and his British wife went to London for the first time to meet her family and to visit the city that was then the epicenter of all things fashionable. His wife encouraged Wolfe to bring samples of his work and make appointments with people in the London fashion industry.

I called the finest store in London at the time, which was Fortnum & Mason. I got an appointment with the Fashion Director. I was so intimidated when I walked into that room and directly I could tell she was wearing Yves Saint Laurent couture, and she was sitting by that desk with a hat on. I thought I was so far out of my league, it was terrible! But I went through my portfolio and I explained what was then a very unusual concept. I don't know if I invented it, but I certainly maximized it. What I had sold to this little chain of stores in Ohio was something that I called *image advertising*. That meant that they should use their advertising space to present a fashion level that they didn't expect to sell. Today, that sounds like Advertising 101, but back then, it was a brand new idea. So I finished off my presentation, closed my portfolio, and she didn't say anything! I thought, "God, I've made such a mistake!" And then, she asked me a question that changed my life: "Can you go to Paris for me this afternoon?" It turned out that she had done three things that morning. She had signed a contract with Condé Nast to buy the opening page of *British Vogue* for the next twelve issues, for her stores' advertising. She had fired her advertising agency, and she had sent a contract to Emanuel Ungaro to represent exclusively his ready-to-wear line. Now she wanted to fly me to Paris, meet Emanuel and go with him to *the Salon*. "He will have models and clothes. You will sketch whatever you want. It will be my ad in *British Vogue*." So I never went back to Ohio. From that moment on I had a career as an illustrator. I was the number one or two illustrator in Europe for about ten years. I was doing all the prime jobs—I was the illustrator for the *London Sunday Times* and I was working for the *Women's Wear Daily* in Europe.

Then I got bored. I thought I really understood how fashion works. The editor of *Women's Wear Daily* left and she said she had a great idea for a consultancy company. By this time, the American rag trade had wakened up to the fact that they could no longer copy what came down on the Paris haute couture runways, which is what they had been doing forever. Fashion in the 60s was really coming from young people, from the streets, from little boutiques in London and Paris, and places nobody knew about. Certainly, I was there, and I think about six companies sprang up at the same time. All were to feed this underground information to the American rag trade.

But because the ragtrade is so competitive, the companies soon started to say "All my competitors are getting the same information, can't you tell me what's going to happen next?" They did not just want to know what was happening at the time. I discovered that I have a real eye for discovering what is going to happen next and understanding why. Because I was an illustrator I could visualize what didn't exist yet. So in November 1969 I did the first fashion forecast that was ever published. It was so successful, I can't begin to tell you. In those days, trend forecasting was very much about creative ideas, not so business-oriented. I remember saying, for example, that the next big thing is going to be Medieval. Therefore, this would be the shape, these would be the colors, we would have Medieval-inspired jewellery and cross motifs. I would wing it from that point, and just let it grow. Even if we still use the word trend today, those are not trends as they were then. Back then, trends became very dramatic and neatly packaged like the "pirate trend" or the "Eskimo trend".

The beauty of it is that the fashion consumers at that time were the baby boomers,[23] and they were addicted to change … so they were used to absorbing an idea and digesting it, and then being hungry for a totally new idea. That's not different from what fashion had ever been, but the ideas used to come more slowly, at a seasonal pulse, but now it simply sped up. The entire fashion industry caught on to this idea of trends, and it stayed that way for a while. (David Wolfe, Creative Director, The Doneger Group)

The older generation of trend analysts has their *good eye* to thank for their career advancement, and the fact that the profession of trend forecaster was in the making can hardly have been to their disadvantage. Those talented few were attributed great powers and given guru status. Now, in the early twenty-first century, the guru era is essentially over (with the exceptions of Edelkoort and Wolfe), despite fashion's sustained popularity and the strong focus on celebrities and individuals in pop culture in general. This development perhaps has to do with the enormous amounts of information that must be processed in short times, so that trend-forecasting agencies, like so many other knowledge-intensive companies, have established ways of managing knowledge that depend less on particular individuals.

To the extent that they can explain why trends emerge, informants sometimes resort to the explanatory models presented earlier (i.e., neomania, identity conflict, status combat and mimetic behavior) but frequently simply refer to a "feeling." Again, it is common to hear competence described as a sixth sense, as aesthetic knowledge that does not have to be legitimized in any other way: it is simply *recognized* within the field.

Today, the trend-forecasting giants devote much time and effort to profiling their personnel, without foregrounding any one person. Successful careers in fashion as well as breadth of knowledge are highlighted. To attract credible names, companies need to invest large sums in starting up, a factor posing a significant obstacle for small companies. Marc Worth, WGSN founder, invested GBP 10 million in his "trend-tracking" company Stylus, founded five years after he sold WGSN to Emap:

> My view on trend forecasting is actually that nobody can really predict or forecast trends, and that's why we try not to use the term. Stylus is more about inspiration and tracking trends. We give our clients inspirational content. The people who create the trends are the ones using our product.

Worth describes Stylus' business as "online information, to inspire creatives." He claims not to know about trends, but that his forty-five full-time content staff and the eighty freelance contributors around the globe do. They all have backgrounds in fashion, interiors, product design and art and have worked in the industry for many years.

Attracting highly qualified personnel has been a key success factor for WGSN, according to CEO Susanna Kempe. Kempe repeatedly distinguishes between WGSN and those trend forecasters that, in her view, are "cheap and cheerful":

> It's about that authority that comes from objective expertise. If you are a business that just hires teens and interns who copy what comes from the catwalks you can only keep the information on that same level. It's a perfectly good business model—I'm not saying that [it's not]. If you want to be a cheap and cheerful trend forecaster, and charge people 5000 pounds, that's the way you have to produce the information. It's fine, but it's not our model.

Stylus, meanwhile, is riding on the wave of aestheticization. Marc Worth's first idea was to create a version of WGSN for the interiors and home furnishing industry, but conversations with clients and contributors made it obvious that the notion of a service for a single vertical design area is obsolete: "Everything is influenced by one industry and that is *design*," says Worth. Describing Stylus as a much bigger project than originally conceived, with both deeper and broader content, Worth claims that potential customers range from Target and Marks & Spencer to BMW, Tiffany & Co., Marriott Hotels, Mattel, Saatchi as well as various fashion companies.

Proof points

If economies of time and money and the competence of an agency's personnel are not sufficient selling arguments, the trend forecasters use proof points to support their forecasts. Although the forecasters do not invest in advertising, they put considerable effort into demonstrating their ability to predict trends long before they materialize. One marketing and PR assistant from an online trend bureau explains: "It's very easy. You just ask someone to choose a trend, maybe a color or maybe a trend such as *ink*. And you will find it on the Web site. So [we] knew that it would be an upcoming trend." Being early is essential. It is not uncommon to hear trend analysts say, "My only problem is the timing, I'm always too early."

A WGSN head of content points to the company's vast archive as an excellent source of proofs showing, for example, that WGSN identified *sustainability* as a trend as early as 2000. In a 2004 report, *Sustain*, WGSN gave clients directives on how to make their businesses more sustainable and environmentally friendly, effectively predicting the sustainability trend. CEO Susanna Kempe, for example, points to the increasing weight given to confirmations and proof points as among the biggest changes in the fashion industry in recent years. Trend forecasters' heightened awareness of the role of proof points is well illustrated by Trends Consultant Jane Kellock's description of how her team tries to "frame" the season's trends as developments of previous ones. If the trend-forecasting agencies succeed in being convincing storytellers, not only do the trends they identify seem more likely, but the storytelling itself becomes a part of the proof, encouraging a particular interpretation of the past that favors the agency's trend selection. In this way, the agency tries to take charge of the sensemaking process.[24]

Customer relations

The trend-forecasting agencies assiduously cultivate their customer relations. One account manager at WGSN notes that job descriptions in the fashion industry often include a requirement that the successful applicant must be proficient at using WGSN. CEO Neil Bradford goes even further:

> Having WGSN access is seen as a mark of prestige, because normally a company can't afford to give everybody access. So they choose their top five or ten designers. The mentality is "I've been chosen, this is great, the company is investing in me, I'm learning all this stuff, I'm improving, isn't this fantastic?"

WGSN also uses online seminars—webinars—where customers from around the world virtually attend trend presentations. The customers can then interact with one another, resulting in further trend coordination.

A recurring problem for online trend forecasters is that some customers do not use the Web site to its fullest potential because they lack time to learn how to navigate it. One account manager from an online trend service says that clients often think that they can easily master the Web site "just because it's Internet" and describes how the company sometimes has to train its clients. The perceived inaccessibility of the site also depends on the information seeker. One head of trends at an online trend forecaster categorizes users as of two types:

> The broad user is a natural in the fashion business. She—most of our clients are female—will log on in the morning, she will get a rundown of what is happening in the industry and the top topics, information that she will use throughout the day. So she'll look at lots of different things on the site. Then we have the other user, who will drill down to one specific area directly. Let's say she is a knitwear designer. Then she will find everything about knitwear. "This is the cardigan of the week that I need to look at."

That customers use the site in very different ways poses problems for marketing communication. There are ongoing discussions about expanding the site to include non-fashion information to accommodate the growing customer base beyond the domain of fashion. Still, most users are looking for fashion information.

Most trend-forecasting agencies collaborate with design schools such as Parsons The New School for Design and the Fashion Institute of Technology (FIT), both in New York. By offering students subscriptions for free or at a significant discount, the trend-forecasting companies hope to establish relationships with future customers at an early stage. By the time these students graduate and start working they may recommend the service to clients and employers.

The need to adapt and translate

Sometimes customers want the same information as their competitors have, to make sure that they are headed in the right direction. Customers often want something extra, of value only to themselves: tailored information. The trend-forecasting agencies are equipped to provide customers with individualized consultancy to help them interpret the information and determine what is relevant to their brand and market.

Global trends are indeed a fact. The fashion shows in Paris, Milan, London and New York directly affect how people dress in the streets of Tokyo. These trends must be translated, however, especially in a market such as Japan's that is in itself highly differentiated. The sales director of Peclers Paris in Japan explains:

> Japan is a massive country. Tokyo is arguably the largest city in the world. There are nearly forty million people in the Tokyo metropolitan area, which is more people than in most European countries. This means that each city in Japan has its own individual trends. What's hot in Tokyo is not hot in Osaka or Nagoya. Therefore you have to update the information you receive through the trend books with the very last-minute trends and with trends that are happening in the specific local market that you are going to sell to. So, for example, leggings might be hot in Tokyo this month, but no one wants to wear leggings in Osaka. Certain hats may be very popular in Nagoya but people in Tokyo say that they hate them.

Local trends in Japan are reinforced by the fact that Japanese fashion brands are typically vertically integrated, that is, large parts of the production and distribution chain are owned by the same company. It is not unusual for a retailer to sell clothes that the company itself has designed and manufactured, sometimes to the level of fibers and fabrics. This gives the fashion companies great production flexibility. They can adapt to specific markets and to prerequisites for fashion with an extremely short "product life cycle"[25]—in other words, fast fashion.

All trend-forecasting agencies with book publishing at their operational core also offer consultancy services to their customers. On behalf of a client, they can undertake a brand identity project or design a footwear line or a particular collection. The consultancy side of the business allows them to be a great deal more directive. Suggesting a clear direction—in French, *parti pris*—to a company considering various alternatives is central to their offering and competence, according to these trend-forecasting agencies.

A man responsible for sports and leisure trends at a Parisian trend-forecasting agency says that if he wants to push for the trend "urban mobility," he points out signs that this trend is already underway: "Mobility in town, cycling, is [a] huge market for tomorrow. It's about well-being, but also about mechanical and ecological sports, which are very important in our time." To convince the client, he identifies successful cases of trend forecasting, stressing that it is not an exact science: "Nobody reads the future—we're not magicians." The big companies, he says, buy many different trend books and attempt to synthesize them.

Online trend-forecasting agencies have a slightly different approach. Their service is profitable because it is scalable, that is, the cost of adding new subscribers is extremely low. In light of the high costs associated with human resources, it is not difficult to see that these agencies prefer to use their personnel in ways that benefit all users, that is, for Web publishing rather than for consultancy jobs that create value for only a few. Still, Stylus, WGSN and Stylesight offer limited consultancy. Trend analysts from agencies with a modest presence on the internet like to tell discouraging stories about how WGSN and Stylesight reports create more work for their customers. A trend forecaster from a book publishing trend bureau notes that, since the early 2000s, a fast-moving consumer goods company has had a staffer whose sole task is to sort all the WGSN information, forwarding only pertinent material to the appropriate people.

Susanna Kempe, WGSN CEO, is familiar with the problems associated with too much information: "When you are travelling, you always know what to wear because you only have five items with you, but at home you have closets full and you never know what to wear." It is WGSN's ambition to ensure that their information is not overwhelming from the outset but is organized to allow users to delve into specific areas at their own pace.

*

In the autumn of 2013, WGSN acquired Stylesight, forming a trend-forecasting company with 60,000 users and 4,000 clients. The managing director of WGSN at the time, Steve Newbold, explains the rationale, "We felt that if we could create a high quality, single website that offered enhanced value to all of our customers, then it would be a significant step forward."

According to him, the global content team is now a combination of the best of Stylesight and WGSN delivered on a dynamic and reliable digital platform. Newbold stresses that the overlap of customers between the two companies was quite limited. The trend-forecasting industry is still thriving on the impact of fast fashion. Cycles of two, three or four weeks are now commonplace to the industry. "That means that the designers, merchandisers and buyers need to get detailed trend analysis to enhance and enable fast and commercially reliable decision making," says Steve Newbold.

*

The notion of "insurance" has been key to the rise of trend-forecasting agencies: customers expect to save time and money by using their services and, in so doing, reduce risk. Trend-forecasting agencies make themselves indispensable by acquiring personnel who are deeply knowledgeable about the fashion industry and trend analysis, capitalizing on their self-claimed identification of previous trends, building strong customer relationships, translating trends to the specific brand of the customer or adapting trends to a certain market. The next chapter will examine in greater detail the legitimacy of trend-forecasting agencies in the fashion field.

3 TREND-FORECASTING AGENCIES—BACKSTAGE LEGITIMACY

> We think we have over 50 per cent market share. We are what Google is to search ... We are the giant of the group. The Worth brothers were there at the right time and they flipped it from being a publication model coming two times a year to being an online model, which has really mirrored and enabled the fast fashion movement, so WGSN has been the key driving force in fashion the last ten years. (Neil Bradford, CEO, WGSN)

Neil Bradford's observations establish the primacy of WGSN. This raises a few questions: Why does WGSN not boast about how outstanding and influential it is in the fashion field in all its communications? If the entire endeavor is about reducing risk, why not stress the benefits of having one dominant industry actor?

Fashion is not like other industries as it exists within the larger field of cultural production. Many individuals and organizations in the fashion field are not driven solely by the prospect of making money; rather, they want to produce "interesting fashion," "nice clothing," "cool fashion" or "empowering fashion" and possibly win recognition for this. In other words, there are alternative but simultaneously operative ways of legitimizing fashion production, in addition to earning money, that is, a cultural logic or, more specifically, a fashion logic. The French sociologist Pierre Bourdieu, who has studied several cultural production fields, explored the fashion field in his 1975 book *Le Couturier et sa Griffe*.[1] The fashion field has since undergone colossal changes, and the Parisian fashion scene described by Bourdieu does not resemble the global fashion field on which the present study is based. I interpret the fashion field along the lines of Agnès Rocamora, who has criticized and built on Pierre Bourdieu's original ideas.[2] The fashion field can be said to be constituted by numerous individuals (e.g., designers, models, journalists, editors, stylists, bloggers, celebrities, fashion students and buyers) and institutions or organizations (e.g., museums, design schools, fashion shows, trade fairs, magazines and fashion companies) that follow certain rules of the game and that compete for the same things (e.g., honor and recognition). In other words, the fashion field comprises a system of relationships in which certain key designers, stylists, magazines, journalists, retailers and department stores dominate others.

Martin Margiela, for example, is more prestigious than French Connection. In the fashion field, these brands occupy different "objective positions," arguably playing in different leagues—the former in cosmopolitan designer fashion and the latter in global high-street fashion. In designer collaborations, mass-market fashion chains take advantage of the luster of designer and high-status brands. It is not rare for brands or designers to seek international positioning and acknowledgment as well. In the UK, several designers have obtained prominent positions in French fashion houses, as Phoebe Philo did at Chloé and Céline. For designers from smaller countries, it can provide important recognition for their products to be sold through the luxury e-commerce site Net-A-Porter.

The positions are not always clear. Some designers strike a balance between prestige and breadth, so it is not a simple hierarchy. Magazines such as *Vogue*, *Harper's Bazaar*, *W*, *Elle* and *Grazia* all occupy significant power positions in the fashion field, but so do smaller prestige magazines such as *Love*, *Pop*, *A Magazine*, *Around the World*, *Gentlewoman*, *AnOther Magazine* and *Lula*. Department stores with strong positions in the fashion field include long-established institutions such as Liberty, Harvey Nichols and Selfridges in the UK; Barneys, Bergdorf Goodman and Saks in the United States; and shops such as Browns and Dover Street Market, which focus on the designer fashion segment. These department stores have a legitimizing function: if they endorse a certain designer they also open doors for the brand. They can endow others with prestige.

From a position of power in the fashion field, it is possible to use one's prestige, one's symbolic capital[3]—which in this field can be translated into fashion capital—to legitimize others. The legitimizing individuals or organizations determine whether something is to be recognized as interesting or "fashion forward."

In the traditional fashion field outlined by Bourdieu, the fashion designer occupied an elevated position similar to that of an artist in the field of fine arts. In Bourdieu's system of relationships, the success of a fashion designer did not just result from performance, but from the significance ascribed to her or him by other individuals and organizations rich in fashion capital, such as journalists, buyers and designers. The fashion field is now permeated by enormous economic interests, representing the "economization" of the field. Actions, behaviors and claims legitimized with reference to an economic logic could be said to be justified outside the fashion field in the surrounding corporate world, that is, the economic field. Practices in the fashion field are often far from unambiguous. For example, the launch of a brand, collaboration or magazine can be legitimized by an economic logic, a cultural logic or, often, a combination of both. To raise the required financial capital to realize their fashion vision, many companies must relate to financial analysts and the financial press to demonstrate their financial credibility. This external legitimacy is necessary to participate in fashion shows, to produce enough to be relevant to notable department stores and to engage renowned fashion photographers and models. Today, economic capital is closely linked to pure fashion capital.

Given the structure of the fashion field, it is insufficient for trend-forecasting agencies to insist that customers can save money by using their services. It may be difficult for clients to admit to needing creative assistance, that is, that they lack sufficient fashion capital. The trend-forecasting agencies need to relate to dominant ideas about fashion, fashion design and creativity.

Inspirational or directive

Many trend-forecasting agencies present themselves as "inspirational." Anticipating criticism for "destroying creativity" and "encouraging copying," they try hard not to be too "directive." The late 2000s saw lengthy online discussion of WGSN as a killer of creativity. (WGSN staff suggest that this debate was initiated by certain people behind Stylesight.) WGSN's employees constantly point to travel tips, suggestions about new designers and market research as inspirational trend information, in contrast to the "close-to-season" updates that are indeed more directive. The online trend-forecasting agencies are quick to stress the amount of information they provide, and that it is impossible to be directive when offering clients so many images and possible paths. In line with this idea, Sophie Carlier, Lidewij Edelkoort's office manager, remarks that Edelkoort is famous for the creativity she brings to the industry and for never being overly directive: Edelkoort gives inspiration to create and respects the creativity of the designers she addresses. The handful of trend forecasters who pride themselves on being "directive" are usually those who offer tailored consultancy.

More often than not, trend-forecasting agencies speak of providing their clients with inspirational trend intelligence, whether through books or online. The trend-forecasting agencies' consideration of the client's designer(s) or design team, and their unwillingness to challenge the client's fashion capital, reflect the relationships within the fashion field. The behavior of the trend forecasters mirrors the rules of the game and the established positions. Ascribing creativity and fashion knowledge to legitimate actors is fundamental to the existence of the fashion field.

Still, the largest online trend-forecasting agencies, Stylesight and WGSN, offer vast numbers of detailed patterns under the heading "close-to-season" that can easily be downloaded to Illustrator. Again, it is worth remembering that these two companies completely dominate the trend-forecasting business. The habit of responding to accusations of destroying creativity is evident among many trend forecasters. A head of content at an online trend bureau defends the trend-forecasting industry, arguing that it only reflects how the fashion industry has always worked: "People are not going to copy because of us":

> Before we existed, people were buying other brands' lines or photographing them in stores. That aspect has always been there. If you want to be successful, you need to have the right trends. And then you are going to look like your neighbor on the high street to some extent.

The online trend service may offer silhouettes in the form of downloadable patterns, but the client does not need to use them exactly as presented, she points out. CEO Susanna Kempe repeatedly stresses that WGSN's service is not about limiting creativity but about giving people tools to be on trend in a way that is completely appropriate for their brand and market—as fashion creators who choose to stay away from trends risk losing considerable money.

Fashion capital

One way that the fashion forecasting agencies can improve their position in the field is to recruit people from companies with a lot of fashion capital in the hope that it "rubs off," so to speak. Another way to gain legitimacy is to collaborate with credible institutions such as design schools and museums. Some trend forecasters teach at Parsons The New School of Design, the Fashion Institute of Technology (FIT) and Central Saint Martins and, as mentioned, some trend-forecasting agencies offer their services to students at heavily reduced prices. Lidewij Edelkoort sometimes works as a museum curator and is art director at the Design Academy in Eindhoven. Contributing to field legitimacy, a non-profit organization that works to preserve handicraft techniques is included in Edelkoort's Trend Union group. With Pierre Bergé, she has initiated an annual exhibit called *Talent*, where she presents work by talented and innovative fashion and design students from all over Europe. It is imperative that fashion leaders manifest concern for the growth of creative power and help foster values that are not entirely commercial.

The fashion field is also characterized by international positioning. Representing a British trend-forecasting company in France when France, especially among the French, is considered the leading fashion country is sometimes a problem, says a French marketing assistant at WGSN in Paris. History is crucial. WGSN puts considerable effort into safeguarding its legitimacy on the contemporary fashion scene. In recent years, the company has become a sponsor of New York Fashion Week, initiated a fashion industry competition, WGSN Global Fashion Awards, and, together with *Vogue*, launched the digital archive and the vintage resource *Vogue Archive*, which contains every issue of the fashion magazine since 1892.

Fashion capital can also be expressed as a penchant for "good taste." As in all cultural fields, there are various views of taste in the fashion field. Most of the fashion people I met are very well aware of the prevailing commercial rules and embrace them in one way or another. Rita Nakouzi, director of Promostyl Americas, for example, previously worked at an art gallery but found it exceedingly difficult to sell art to which she had become emotionally attached. She finds fashion to be more about commerce and hence less difficult to sell. She thinks that taste still matters a great deal. When asked why a client should turn to Promostyl rather than to another trend forecaster, she mentions the company's long experience and also stresses its "taste level": "In my humble opinion, I think we have one of the best colorists ever, and I think no one compares to her level of taste. She to me epitomizes good taste." Nakouzi knows that customers choose Promostyl to gain a new avenue of growth and develop their businesses, but she thinks that the choice of forecaster is often made on the basis of taste. She herself knows that Promostyl is good, the oldest agency, and has exquisite taste—"Either you see that, or not," she laughs, adding that maybe she is not the "best salesperson" in that sense.

Confidentiality

Many US informants maintain that European fashion companies are less inclined to admit to using trend-forecasting services. A US content manager suggests that Europeans want to see themselves as trailblazers. Neil Bradford, WGSN CEO 2008–2009, confirms this. He finds it fascinating that every sector of the industry—even those in high fashion—buys WGSN's product. Some clients do not allow WGSN to publish their names, and WGSN has signed confidentiality agreements with fashion companies in Europe that "do not want people to know." Susanna Kempe, WGSN CEO 2009–2011, sees such confidentiality agreements as understandable:

> I think that's completely fine. Years ago they called us "Fashion's Secret Weapon" in the *Wall Street Journal*. I think that's fine. I want to enable our clients to be successful. If there is a creative director who prefers that his or her board does not know that they use somebody's support and assistance, that's completely fine.

Since boards of directors are interested in minimizing uncertainty, one wonders whether there might be an upside to revealing the use of WGSN. Kempe observes:

> I really believe that we minimize the risk. But I think that in a creative industry where people consider their value as based on those ideas they come up with, I suppose admitting that you use any kind of source of inspiration might make somebody nervous. So whatever works best for each individual client is fine.

The trend-forecasting agencies' concern about treading on anyone's toes clearly reflects the fashion field and its positions. Since the legitimacy of fashion companies depends on the designers and their ability to create, the position of trend-forecasting companies is not such that they can openly boast of their clients' success. At the same time, the trend-forecasting companies advertise both their raison d'être and abilities by referring to both economic considerations (e.g., uncertainty reduction, comprehensive information offering and customer relations) and the fashion capital they possess in the expertise of their personnel (i.e., first-hand fashion information). The trend-forecasting agencies have an organizing function in the field, but they gain their legitimacy *backstage*, out of the public eye. On top of that, the spread of confidentiality agreements implies a problem for me as an interviewer. Sometimes I doubted particular interviewees who professed not to be familiar with either Stylesight or WGSN.

WGSN CEO Neil Bradford discusses the need for confidentiality agreements, while being clear about his caveats with respect to the assumed character traits of countries. He maintains that there is a huge culture of self-improvement books in both the UK and the United States. In line with this, sellers in London can insist that WGSN is a great tool to help clients do their jobs and that access to WGSN means status. In continental Europe and to some extent in Japan, he says, clients view themselves more as "the experts" thinking, for example: "I'm a menswear designer. I've worked in this industry for twenty years. I was hired because I know something about menswear. So I don't need any service to tell me about menswear."

In fact, an expert might consider it a "slight insult" to be accused of relying on a trend-forecasting service, Bradford claims, but such a client may nevertheless be interested in employing a trend consultant for a specific task. Despite thorough knowledge of menswear suits, for example, a design team may have insufficient knowledge of jackets, and a trend consultant may be hired to assist. Italian or French fashion companies may use WGSN's expertise in the US and UK markets to gain insight into trends in the American market. Even if continental European fashion companies do not see themselves as needing assistance with tailoring or high fashion, they might be interested in information on street style, retail coverage, prices and sales.

Merely communicating or creating and influencing trends

When the trend-forecasting agencies describe themselves as *inspirational* rather than *directive*, they are concerned with how they present themselves to their customers, and the distinction may give customers an idea of how to use the trend information provided. A closely related but separate distinction is whether the trend-forecasting agencies merely *communicate* already active trends or whether they *create and influence* trends. This distinction captures how the trend agencies want to present themselves in the fashion field at large and, occasionally, how they truly see themselves.

It is common practice for trend-forecasting agencies to stress that they do not influence trends but that trends are disseminated through them. A fashion director at an American trend forecaster explains:

> We observe the consumers, we observe the retail scene—we are observing retail at the highest level so we see things bubble up. Eventually it's going to impact the end consumer. Sometimes you just see one thing and you know that's going to change everything. Like Tory Burch. You knew that she captured something in her design aesthetic—it wasn't young, it was kind of missy, but it had this kind of *1960 country club* sensibility. She's been the biggest influence in the marketplace. She's influenced J. Crew and she's influenced many other designers. Or a TV show like *Mad Men*.

WGSN CEO Neil Bradford notes that the closer to the start of the season, the more precise WGSN's confirmation reporting becomes, as the company identifies which of the previously identified trends are the most popular: "We're just making more efficient what would have happened anyway. It's not a new force." If WGSN had arbitrarily decided to push green as the new trend color at a time when most designers, retailers and brand representatives were insisting blue is in, Bradford says such an effort "wouldn't last very long," regardless of how much WGSN published to the contrary. "At WGSN, we are a representative of everything we see out there … we are going to shows, catwalks, tradeshows, visiting cities, designers. We are an amalgam of all that information."

Many trend forecasters mention clients who claim to use trend forecasts as "confirmations," suggesting that the forecasted trends are already in the making and customers want to verify that they have interpreted them correctly. One woman at WGSN who formerly worked at Zara commented that when she and her colleagues spotted a trend on WGSN, whether about an item, color or fabric, they would tell their buyers "It's on WGSN." Such was the buyers' confidence in WGSN's expertise that only then were orders (often thousands of pieces) placed.

In New York offices that exude an atmosphere of the low-cost alternative, which is exactly how Stylesight has positioned itself in relation to WGSN, I meet with CEO Frank Bober and a number of his co-workers. The desks are crammed together and the walls and shared spaces seem slightly neglected. Stylesight has grown at a furious pace since its launch in 2003.

One of Stylesight's senior trend analysts insists that trend forecasters are only communicating trends already in motion, albeit at an *extremely early* stage. She cannot overemphasize the small size of the trend-forecasting industry. In New York

City, where she lives, she knows everyone in the business: they are friends outside the workplace although they work for different companies. People involved in qualitative fashion trend forecasting are "birds of a feather," she says. At Stylesight, analysts look for trends that evolve, and nothing is considered a trend unless it can be followed not just through seasons but for years. She likens her job to that of an investment banker: while she cannot predict what is going to happen in the market, she can give a "pretty darn accurate opinion of it."

Anyone can call himself or herself a trend forecaster or trend hunter. Self-proclaimed trend forecasters seem to proliferate by the day, especially online. How easily can someone gain the necessary credibility and legitimacy? In an industry that stresses the need to reduce uncertainty, there is a corresponding need to use well-established and well-regarded trend-forecasting agencies with known impact in the fashion and design industry. The large online trend-forecasting agencies such as WGSN and Stylesight, which are relatively young, took a new approach to trend forecasting with their continual updates and wide scope. Marc Worth,

founder of both WGSN and Stylus, emphasizes the financial capital required to attract the right people. Along with the legitimacy that comes from the ability to manage business intelligence, the company's history and the backgrounds of its employees—the trend forecasters—are also critical. Cultural capital[4] in the form of knowledge of the fashion history, fine arts and the humanities is highly valued. Established trend forecasters frequently decry fashion bloggers' lack of perspective and lack of the cultural capital the trend forecasters themselves possess and share. This is why the bloggers, according to the trend forecasters, have more difficulty understanding trend changes in the fashion industry, and some even suggest that it can be "dangerous for us as a society [i.e., the fashion sphere] to lose the respect of people who have spent time studying and, you know, the intellectual power that is put into their knowledge." Many trend forecasters must maintain a delicate balance: they claim not to be creating or influencing trends but rather to be recognizing trends already in the making; on the other hand, they describe themselves as far ahead of the bloggers, whom they say can only confirm existing trends.

WGSN's CEO Susanna Kempe observes that bloggers, the fashion press and the trend agencies she refers to as "cheap and cheerful," which produce lists of hot trends in season, are mainly concerned with reporting what already exists. WGSN, she says, does not say "in two years, it will only be blue." The company can, however, tell its clients in March that cobalt blue will be the color that resonates with consumers in the coming summer.

The phenomenon of self-fulfilling prophecies

Whether the trend-forecasting agencies merely channel trends already in motion or whether they actually create trends, and irrespective of whether they choose to present their service as "inspirational" or "directive," they do turn the attention of the industry in one or a few directions, which suggests the production of self-fulfilling prophecies.

The self-fulfilling prophecy phenomenon is repeatedly mentioned by informants and is of course related to the trend forecasters' role as risk-minimizing tastemakers. The position of trend-forecasting agencies in the fashion field means that they should keep a low profile and downplay their own actorhood, lest it threaten their existence. Still, several trend analysts confirm the existence of the self-fulfilling prophecy, as one of them observes:

> The old joke about "I'm never wrong" is often true because it's like a self-fulfilling prophecy. If I say *sky blue pink* for next year everyone will do *sky blue pink*. The real test comes as to whether I have second-guessed that the consumer will buy

sky blue pink. But very often if it's the thing, everyone is talking about it, the color is promoted, and the consumer is sort of sheep-like.

A senior trend analyst from an online trend bureau explains that certain clients do not want to follow the agency's advice, believing that everybody else will be jumping on the trend. She believes that their forecasts often become self-fulfilling prophecies and cites some examples:

> [There] is a television advert for a big retail chain. And we do these trends videos where we take our trends, present them in video format and add music to it. This particular advert looks exactly like one of our trends videos. We were all sending it around the office going "is this because of us or ...", you know. We have no way of tracking how people are using our trends. Which in some ways is really frustrating. Sometimes, when you go into a shop, you can see that they've got our whole color palette. You ask yourself, was it because they just did ours straight off or is it a coincidence?

The accusations of self-fulfilling prophecies have always been around. A trend forecaster recounts how Calvin Klein was thinking at the peak of his career:

> I said "here you are, a leader, no matter what you do it's like a license to print money—why do you want to buy forecasting information from me?" And he said: "I want to buy it so that I know what everyone else is doing. Then I make sure that I don't do that."

With this, the trend forecaster wants to illustrate that there are many different ways to use the information to benefit your own interests. Although these allegations have been around for ages, it cannot be denied that with the launch of the online trend-forecasting services, a more tangible form of trend information (e.g., patterns for tops) is spreading widely, something that increases the possibility of self-fulfilling prophecies at a time when there is so much *more* information than before. Marc Worth, the founder of both WGSN and Stylus, says:

> WGSN has become a self-fulfilling prophecy. When so many people are looking at the same content, everything will look the same. Many new clients have come from manufacturing countries like China, India, Marocco and Turkey, areas where all they want to do is to see what's on the catwalks and get similar designs into the shops. So with that, in my opinion, the WGSN concept has really removed the creative aspect.

Worth takes the existence of self-fulfilling prophecies as a sign that the industry is ripe for change. According to him, the market is now turning against the WGSN concept and the uniformity that it implies, and many actors are now looking to do something different. However, one should probably bear in mind that Marc had just launched Stylus.

Some trend analysts blame their customers for having failed to translate the trend information to their own brands. What some perceive as uniformity in fashion has less to do with the trend information itself than with the clients' inability to adapt the information to specific brands.

Any adaptation of trend information inevitably affects the production process. Fashion companies typically use certain manufacturers and distribution systems, and all actors want to contain costs in their particular segments. Such constraints can be difficult for designers, as a trends research consultant elaborates:

> Having watched the design process as a designer in the industry, seeing where you say it should be in the very beginning and then seeing where it ends up, can be so destroying. All these factors come in—price, fabric, where it's manufactured, what the buyer thinks, what the customer might demand—and at the end you start to think "Why did I bother? By the time it gets into the shop it looks hideous. And it doesn't sell." Sometimes I hear: "You told me to do so." But I never told you to do it quite like that. Here at [the online trend bureau] we get to do the best part: "Here's what we think it should look like, now go away and do it. You can either do it really well or you can ruin it." We don't really know what happens to the product at the end. It's a quite nice part of the job.

The role of trend-forecasting agencies in the fashion field is a difficult juggling act in which the agencies must not only win the trust and confidence of customers and convince them of the superiority of their model, but also take into consideration the designers' conceptions of fashion, design and creativity while downplaying their own actorhood. In seeking this delicate balance, and when speaking of *other* trend-forecasting agencies, the agencies often expose the hidden contradictions in their own approaches.

4 TASTEMAKERS—HUNT FOR THE INCIPIENT TASTE

The discussion about trends has been sinking to a lower, very public level. Sofi Fahrman's[1] fashion magazine writes about trends. I would never humiliate myself and write about stuff like trends. Fashion intellectuals don't do trends. I only work with trends when I have advertising clients.

Thus speaks a stylist who divides his time between editorial jobs and assignments for various brands. He believes that trends have become a way of packaging and selling clothes, though he distinguishes between different types of selling. When a fashion brand sells a jacket for GBP 1,500 it is not about a trend, he says, but about a "lifestyle or an ideology or something else."

A fashion editor clarifies the significance of trends for the British fashion magazine she works for:

Trends are our fashion news. Fashion is a constantly evolving industry. It used to anchor twice a year. But Britain has made high-street retailing with a fashion edge our specialty. And we're a weekly magazine, where trends and the quickness at which they change are really our bread and butter.

Another fashion editor comments that she is not the intended reader of the magazine she works for. A copy of the magazine has never been brought into her home.

These remarks illustrate the difficulty of capturing the tastemakers' relationships with trends. Believing that only those who use the word "trend" are the true trendsetters is like trusting a shop called, for example, "Top Fashion" to provide the most fashionable items. The concept of "trend" suffers from many preconceptions.

Tastemakers

Unlike the trend forecasters, the tastemakers covered in this chapter—that is, magazine editors, fashion photographers, stylists, buyers at fashion-oriented department stores and boutiques, and even certain bloggers—are open about their legitimizing positions. Many of them are engaged as experts in various fashion events and organizations. They have the power to make a mark on fashion. As intermediaries between the production and consumption sides, their distance from the end consumer varies and they face various kinds of risk. Acting on the basis of specific conceptions of the customer, consumer and reader, tastemakers must also consider various economic and fashion-related risks. On one hand, they need to secure advertisers, readers and sales; on the other, they constantly need to reinforce their artistic authority, their legitimacy, by continuing to publish spectacular magazines, offering exciting selections of brands and collections in their department stores, making credible trend forecasts and writing engaging fashion stories. How, then, do they relate to trends?

The tastemakers represent only a few cogs in the global trend machinery, which is why I focus on their *relationships* in the fashion field. Sometimes, as with the fashion editor quoted above, the tastemakers categorize and package trends. At other times, the tastemakers help legitimize something already existing in the fashion field, classifying it as good and interesting, even though the word "trend" is not uttered. This does not prevent others in the fashion field from taking the recognition of a phenomenon as licence to consider it a trend. Trends do not emerge out of a vacuum: their packaging, communication, diffusion and interpretation are dependent on many in the fashion field.

In the 1960s, sociologist Herbert Blumer studied buyers at a fashion house in Paris. He noticed that the buyers' independent aesthetic choices converged remarkably, despite their competitiveness and secrecy with one another. When asked to explain their purchasing choices, they referred to their personal taste, saying that they found certain items "stunning." Blumer was fascinated that these tastemakers seemed to arrive at very similar feelings concurrently. He argued that the buyers acted in anticipation of the *incipient taste* of the consumers and that their buying decisions manifested a collective social experience driven by the attempt to capture the proximate future and to portray "the direction of modernity," the *zeitgeist*. Blumer did not agree with Georg Simmel's or Thorstein Veblen's ideas about taste spreading as the lower classes imitated the upper classes. Blumer claimed, instead, that the elite is caught up in the need to respond to rather than set the direction of fashion. Blumer used the concept of "fashion trend" to describe the predictable forward movement of fashion, which he said arose from people's desire to be different in the right direction.[2]

Another sociologist who has illustrated how seemingly individual choices are in fact socially conditioned is Stanley Lieberson, who studied how parents name their children, a phenomenon free of commercial interests. He found that parents are guided by how other parents name their children, which results in an internal taste mechanism in the choice of names. In other words, shifts in the popularity of names do not just reflect societal changes.[3]

In the fashion field, many decisions revolve around judging collections, individual items, photos, models and brands—assessments with no correct answers. Yet some form of consensus regularly emerges regarding what collections and items are the most interesting. This consensus building is a collective process in which some people and organizations, however, have more legitimacy than others do. In the fashion field, people often read the same magazines, such as *Women's Wear Daily*, browse *style.com* and visit the same fairs and shows. Often, the tastemakers attended similar schools. This process of socialization gives rise to a certain range of taken-for-granted knowledge, that is, the aesthetic knowledge discussed in Chapter 2, or *doxa*, to use Pierre Bourdieu's term.[4] "The eye" for fashion trends is not innate in tastemakers but an acquired skill.

Tastemakers at a British fashion magazine

Amanda Palmer is the fashion director of *Lauren*[5] and has many years of experience with this magazine and European fashion houses. Through her mix of editors, chosen for various assignments, the editor-in-chief covers certain taste profiles. The readership is varied, ranging from students and "women who lunch" to loyal subscribers outside of London and women in the City who "don't always have a great interest in fashion—they just want to know that they are looking okay for their job."

Palmer is clearly proud of working on the magazine's fashion stories. She thinks their images all have a fantasy or dream element to them, taking fashion out of its context, making it theatrical, dramatic, exciting or eccentric so that the readers can dream. The house photographers with whom she frequently works have high status in the fashion field.

By associating with high-status people, individuals can confirm their position as "in the game," giving them more symbolic capital and status with which to drive and forge collaboration. It is as if high-status people offer some kind of "magic" that raises the status of their collaborators and, in turn, carries the prestige further: "She works with someone who collaborates with Steven Meisel."[6] While someone with low status can "contaminate" others, individuals with especially high reputations can effortlessly transcend boundaries. The status hierarchy within a cultural production field is relational, status always being dependent on others' recognizing it. One both confers and accepts status.

Assignments in *Lauren* usually revolve around a trend or "story," Palmer explains. Palmer is painfully aware that the fashion magazine's position in the fashion field means that it affects how fashion history is written. The editorial team wants the fashion magazine to be as supportive as possible of the British fashion industry, but there are several considerations. Today, everyone is an international shopper, so the content must reflect more than what is happening in the UK. During a recession, there is always pressure from big advertisers to be included in fashion stories. "If a brand has to close store after store, and never receives any support from the magazine, that brand might get slightly irritated. It's always a very fine line to tread," Palmer observes. She sees the system as self-perpetuating: the more the large brands spend on advertising, the surer the readers will be that they must be remarkable designers.

In fact, on occasion those designers who have actually initiated a trend may be left out of a shoot, simply because they are not advertisers. Palmer professes to experience endless internal conflict around these issues. She finds it sad to see someone, a designer, who is not an advertiser and lacks money, but who started the trend, excluded from the shoot. On other occasions, Palmer says the editor-in-chief insists on including those designers.

As fashion director, Palmer sometimes has conversations with British designers whose work she finds "one note, too singular," because she believes the magazine has a responsibility to explain to designers why their collections are not covered or are not as promising as previous ones, because "If we are not going to do that print story, then maybe … [the] collection will not receive that much coverage."

However, Palmer cannot praise British fashion enough. She thinks that what designers like Christopher Kane, Sarah Burton, Erdem and Jonathan Saunders all have in common is that they are both talented and business-oriented. Palmer would like to feature British designers even more but *Lauren* is still dependent on the bigger brands for its survival.

When Carine Roitfeld left her position as editor-in-chief of *Vogue Paris*, there was much talk about her having used her position to promote certain brands in which she had a vested interest. (Palmer also consults on the side for some brands.) Those consultancy jobs are contentious within the larger media group. The directors understand that fashion editors could earn large sums consulting for fashion companies. Palmer stresses the importance of keeping the two jobs separate. According to Palmer, she almost never suggests covering "her" brand in the fashion pages because she is committed to the magazine's integrity.

This two-pronged approach of working for a prestigious magazine while consulting for designers recalls what sociologist Ashley Mears in *Pricing Beauty* called the two circuits of modeling, the commercial and the editorial. A fashion model in New York receives extremely low compensation for jobs in *Vogue*, but appearing in the magazine garners prestige which in turn can generate additional, but again poorly paid, modeling jobs for designer brands' fashion shows. The model's jackpot comes when a sizeable prestige brand hires her or him for an advertising campaign.

In all cultural production fields, actors have a complicated relationship with profit. Pierre Bourdieu called the cultural production field "the economic world reversed." If one seeks to achieve status in the field, one must understand that too frequent commercial assignments sooner or later take a toll on symbolic capital: status is whittled away and the chances of an eventual pay-off diminish. Consequently, actors in the cultural production fields have an incentive to dismiss economic enticements: they have an interest in being economically disinterested—"the losers win," according to Bourdieu. However, by continually building symbolic capital, actors can, in certain fields, eventually reap outsized gains. The fashion capital resources that follow from being a fashion editor at a prominent magazine open up rare opportunities, such as work at prestigious fashion houses. For fashion editors, directors, critics and academics, who, like Palmer, are endowed with vast amounts of fashion capital, integrity in the face of commercial pressure is essential. The importance of this integrity varies with the actor's position in the fashion field, depending on the magazine, school or brand with which she or he is associated.

At the same time, the cultural and economic spheres of the fashion field are not sealed and separate compartments. Some individuals with significant fashion capital must act against their own professional logic in certain situations and roles. This is manifested in the jokes they tell about some of their dealings, downplaying the importance of their jobs and distancing themselves from both their assignments and the attendant economic capital. When the editor in the beginning of the chapter states that her magazine, with its broad appeal, does not belong in her house, or the stylist quoted above claims that he concerns himself with trends only when he works with advertising clients, their words can be interpreted as attempts to keep symbolic distance from the more market-oriented sides of their jobs.

Palmer thinks that trends have changed immensely since the turn of the century. For one, pre-collections, which bridge the gap between a fashion house's main autumn and spring collections, did not exist until recently. Today pre-collections often constitute around 70 percent of a designer brand's sales. Palmer believes that pre-collections attract early adopting consumers who want something "new" all the time and whose attention span is limited. Pre-collections began when American brands such as Ralph Lauren, Donna Karan, Calvin Klein and Michael Kors launched cruise collections for those traveling to warm climates during the winter months. Not as idea driven as the main collections, pre-collections are never shown on a catwalk but are geared to being worn and to selling well over a longer period in shops than are the main collections. However, it is the fashion shows that still garner the fashion companies the most publicity, with their eccentric and photogenic items. Palmer suggests that, taken together, these two elements—the pre-collections and main collections—constitute a winner: the main collections provide much-needed fashion capital, while the pre-collections "capitalize" on this and earn most of the money, the financial capital.

The fact that high-street shops always offer new things has affected designer fashion, Palmer says, forcing designers constantly to come up with new little ideas to engage consumers and the press. These ideas could be a new scarf collection, a plastic collection or an artist collaboration—"People don't want to see the same Prada bag that they saw two weeks ago." There is always room for another news story, another blog post. Palmer is concerned that if designers succumb to mounting pressure to come up with ever more new things, consumers may eventually simply tune out the increased product flow. Magazines have a harder time remaining relevant, since they photograph four months in advance and the information is no longer new when the magazine hits the stands.

Palmer claims never to have met a fashion trend forecaster, suggesting that WGSN is probably more relevant to bigger chains with many customers, chains such as Topshop. "They say things like polka-dots are going to be in, right?" Palmer comments. Yet she is familiar enough with the service to know that it provides downloadable patterns. It may be that Palmer distances herself from trend forecasters because of their low status in the fashion field. She suggests that trend forecasters may be slightly redundant, since a fast fashion company can copy a Prada item and have it in stores before Prada can offer the original item in its shops. She also notes that all designers respond to fashion cyclically, as when designers use or reject ideas and themes from previous seasons, citing explanations of fashion changes relating to neomania and cyclicality (see p. 20), constant self-referencing and the internal fashion mechanism studied by Stanley Lieberson (see p. 51).

Tastemakers at department stores

Several department stores in London have a legitimizing position in the fashion field. Being included in the assortments of Harvey Nichols, Liberty, Selfridges, Browns or Dover Street Market will attract attention throughout the fashion world. On Brompton Road, near its department store, are the Harvey Nichols headquarters. As with the other department stores I visited, the headquarters' decor seems strikingly *backstage* in relation to the store. April Glassborow, buying manager at Harvey Nichols, describes their department store as more like a big boutique. Harvey Nichols does not sell any basics "apart from a few white shirts, possibly" and not much daywear: "It's almost as if the customer is always dressed to go to a cocktail party." Unlike Harrods and Selfridges, Harvey Nichols can be more selective and focus on presenting an *interesting* assortment. Around 60 percent of the assortment is own-bought while around 40 percent is sold by concession.[7] However, the general rule is that, when times are tough, there is a desire to increase the concession portion of sales, as they make a guaranteed minimum contribution to the business: in other words, concessions entail less risk.

April Glassborow and the Harvey Nichols buyers are unmistakably tastemakers. The buying process begins with a meeting where the buying and merchandizing teams review the sales results line by line. They examine space versus sales performance and gather input from the shop floor staff. They consider where the market is going, discuss what they think of upcoming designers and brands and what they think of the new collections of designers already represented at Harvey Nichols. They then conduct a preliminary *range review* with the fashion director followed by a financial presentation for the CEO. Glassborow says that the buying teams have extensive autonomy, however, and that their vision influences what they buy; she merely indicates the general direction.

Glassborow's sense of what will suit the Harvey Nichols customer arises from her long experience in buying: "You can look at something, and say 'that is not very Harvey Nichols', but what does that mean?" This tacit but socially created knowledge is typical of the fashion field. The "eye" or "gut feeling" is a relational skill, acquired over years of experience. Bourdieu observes that the "eye" does not see fashion but various positions in a field in which one competes for prestige. Glassborow appears aware of this, relating the story of a buyer from a high-street chain who came to Harvey Nichols and needed a few seasons of experience before she assimilated the Harvey Nichols way of thinking: fashion that is sexy, quite dressy, with a strong fashion message. Sellers from the various designers and brands have learnt and internalized the tacit knowledge of what Harvey Nichols is: "Harrods would buy this," they say, "I know you wouldn't," and they are right most of the time, Glassborow says.

As the representative of a legitimizing actor in the fashion field, April Glassborow is bombarded with questions from aspiring designers who would like to gain a toehold in Harvey Nichols. She can almost always tell whether a designer's work is right after just a few questions on the telephone, about things such as distribution and price points, complemented with photos. Harvey Nichols can introduce only a few new designers each year, and a new designer should be given at least three seasons to understand Harvey Nichols' fit, pricing and customers. The new designers are introduced in the Knightsbridge store[8] and selected brands are supported by providing business advice regarding pricing and collection structure, by including their items in installations and public relations activities and by ensuring that new collections are exposed in areas easily accessible to customers.

To illustrate how Harvey Nichols has affected the fashion scene, Glassborow describes being the only store in the UK to buy Alber Elbaz' first collection for Lanvin. This investment in the brand at an early stage has ensured that the department store and Lanvin still have a very good relationship. Harvey Nichols was also among the first to buy Alexander McQueen.

> It's interesting that the fashion crowd knows this and recognizes it as important. To develop both those businesses to the level that they are now takes an awfully long time. We really struggled at the beginning, but the press picked up on the fact that we were among the first. So it creates Harvey Nichols' image, even if you are not making money on that one particular designer at the start. (April Glassborow, Buying Manager, Harvey Nichols)

If one belongs to the fashion field, one must acknowledge that there are meaningful differences between collections and designers, that good taste exists and that it is imperative to promote high-quality fashion. As Bourdieu might say, there exists a belief in *fashion for the sake of fashion*. People forget that the rules of the fashion field were socially created and that they adhere to social conventions. Everyone in the field behaves as if this game of fashion, this hunt for prestige, good taste and fashion for the sake of fashion, exists independently of their belief in it. The buyers act under this *illusio*, a belief in the autonomous pursuit of new fashion stars. This race reaches extremes during the fashion weeks, when fashion journalists participate in identifying the new rising stars and assessing which ones will keep on shining. Amid prevailing uncertainty, magic is created around the designer eventually identified as the most interesting. Together, the fashion buyers and journalists spot the "incipient taste."

As Georg Simmel pointed out, creating new fashion is a difficult balancing act between fitting into the existing fashion landscape and standing out. Identifying the "incipient taste" is no easy process but a struggle between fashion authorities to be the one who chooses. By playing and therefore affecting this game's outcome, Harvey Nichols gains further authority. Bourdieu says, "[T]aste classifies and it classifies the classifier."[9] Status in the fashion field, and in the cultural production field in general, cannot be translated to economic status but comes from one's authority as a tastemaker: to be recognized as someone with good taste.

The importance of the social aspects of fashion weeks—both catwalks and showrooms—cannot be overemphasized.[10] Gossip, status-seeking imitation and herd behavior give rise to what Robert Merton called the "Matthew effect," whereby small differences are exaggerated, success increases exponentially and "the rich become richer." If a designer is perceived as good, it improves the chances of further exposure and therefore of being seen as significantly better, maybe even as a genius. Together, people in the fashion field widen the gaps between those who have and those who have not.[11] Even actors in the fashion field may not understand why a certain designer or collection is embraced, making it highly rational for them to keep with the herd. As long as other tastemakers find the designer or the collection sufficiently legitimate as "the new," it will come to represent "the new." To follow a particular social order because one believes that other people find this order legitimate, and hence follow it, is a classic condition of legitimacy, according to the sociologist Max Weber.[12] Exactly who finds a designer or an item truly legitimate and who is just following the crowd is ultimately irrelevant. Legitimation requires consensus to exist at the collective level but not necessarily at the individual level.[13]

Harvey Nichols subscribes to WGSN, but April Glassborow is not fond of the service, which she thinks caters to too many markets at once. Another buyer agrees, noting that Harvey Nichols' buyers attend exactly the same fashion shows as do WGSN analysts and have the same opportunities to form their own opinions of what may fit the Harvey Nichols sensibility. Glassborow prefers the seasonal round-ups that David Wolfe and Chris Gilbert compile for The Doneger Group, which she compares with the buying decisions. These presentations are not essential, however, as Glassborow and her team pride themselves on editing a collection that will be relevant to the store. They see themselves as fashion authorities.

Glassborow considers trends important but not the driving force for Harvey Nichols' customers:

> I don't think our customers are saying that "this season, I must buy this dress or a red skirt". Maybe they say that "I must buy a camel coat this autumn"... but I don't know, I don't shop like that. Our customers have their own style, we can't dictate too much what the trends are for them. We don't lay out our stores by

trends. I think, if you are Topshop you can do that because it's all own label. Whereas we try to buy into the trend of the designer, and what the designer is presenting. What Balenciaga is presenting can differ immensely from what Givenchy is doing, rather than saying you must all be wearing miniskirts this season.

Harvey Nichols' trend packaging is aimed mostly at the sellers to give them a feel for the season. Like all fashion authorities, the buyers at Harvey Nichols speak with great certainty about taste-related phenomena that, by their very nature, are ambiguous. All cultural producers must make definite decisions about things that are inherently ephemeral and vague. To admit doubt is to question the entire field, and the actors need to believe in the game. The trend services may disturb the *illusio* of the independent game, of fashion for the sake of fashion, making their presence frequently problematic for those working in the fashion field. High-status actors such as Harvey Nichols and *Lauren* accordingly associate the trend services with mass-market fashion and purely economic capital.

Since the credit crunch, Glassborow has observed a rejection of trends: people are confident enough to dress in a way that suits them rather than as fashion dictates. Even though today's customers want today's fast turnover, it does not mean that they constantly change their wardrobes; rather, the new is mixed with the old. Even so, Glassborow firmly believes that trends as such are here to stay. She thinks that the trend-denying trend is an invitation to find one's own style. The fashion shows still convey the familiar feeling of everyone having attended the same party: suddenly all the colors are in the same palette or there is a common thread running through the fabrics. The fabric industry still has a significant impact on the offerings. What is shown at Première Vision (see Chapter 1) strongly influences the fashion season. Everyone, from raw material producers and manufacturers to trend and color forecasters, is mutually dependent, according to Glassborow: "It's not necessarily the designer that says this season I'll mainly be doing bright blue."

Selfridges' "designers" and "bridge"[14] womenswear buying manager, Shannon Adams,[15] describes the famous department store as inclusive, selling everything from Chanel to Topshop. She says that risk management is a natural part of her job. Although there is always risk in buying something new, she now has greater confidence in her choices. For example, she once bought an exclusive collection for Selfridges by a relative unknown, Jay Ahr, and within two days of roll-out, 70 percent of the order had been sold. The year before that, Sacai made its first appearance at Selfridges', with similar success. The buyers work closely with personal shoppers and sales clerks to ensure that the collections are presented in an exciting way.

Selfridges uses WGSN. She does, however, reject the use of statistics in buying decisions, except for sizing. "Buying designer fashion is so much about emotion, something you must not forget," she says, recalling the skills she and other actors have acquired in the field.

Adams is always traveling, spending most of her time in Paris, Milan and London. During the buying season, she explores what the season is going to be like. There is no time to decide on themes for the season. Instead, she and other buyers make their decisions based on feeling and intuition, identifying themes in hindsight. They focus on the pre-collections, choosing what is "most Selfridges" and ensuring that all the brands contribute to the overall impression. Adams compares the brands, calculates price points and ensures a degree of exclusivity. If there is a rumor that everyone is going to want a burgundy sweater for the season, it is not automatically a good thing to buy *every* burgundy sweater on offer. Adams' buyers always give the brands feedback on what they like in the collections and what Selfridges' customers like.

With the windows and creative teams, the Selfridges buyers then give a trends presentation to Selfridges staff and the press, identifying themes that tie the season together. Like the buyers at Harvey Nichols, Shannon Adams believes that trends will continue to appear: "If they disappeared completely, why would you then go shopping?" Adams distinguishes between "trends" and "trendy": very expensive does not necessarily mean "trendy," which she feels is "more of a cheaper thing." Trends are manifested differently in the more expensive markets. Céline exemplifies a brand that changed the whole market mood with its clean, chic style, replacing Balmain's rock aesthetic. Adams describes this transformation as a slow trend, in which people invest for emotional reasons. It is not a matter of a fashion consumer whose desire for a pair of blue trousers with a zipper on the front is replaced by a totally different desire the next week. Consumers who buy Céline want to be modern, chic, and understated. It is a desire driven by a variety of influences. Adams believes that a brand's attraction is based on what the brand signals and whether this is currently relevant. Adams relates to trends by handling Selfridges' portfolio of brands and collections in the "designers" and "bridge" categories, making sure that key items are included, and she remains vigilant as to how brands develop over time. What collections are embraced and seen as relevant in a specific season comes down to that "magic"—as Bourdieu would call it—created in the fashion field as everyone seeks to pin down the incipient taste.

At Harvey Nichols and Selfridges, trends are not spelled out; the windows and displays speak for themselves. In social media, however, these stores use images to emphasize trends, as in "the metal shoe trend" and "the neoprene trend." Even though Harvey Nichols and Selfridges do not explicitly use the actual word "trend" in their stores, it is evident that they have worked through the buying process in a trend-analytical way and that their personnel are trained accordingly and are well aware of their trend-initiating or trend-confirming role.

The accounts of all three women—Amanda Palmer, April Glassborow and Shannon Adams—contain clear examples of how they as tastemakers work with designers, providing feedback on collections, advising on how to proceed and managing the collections' structure and pricing. All of them stress the importance of financial backing. The notion of the solitary designer, whose aptitude is decisive, is explicitly challenged: the tastemakers take part in "creating the designer." All of them speak of the many aspiring designers who approach them, either wanting to be covered by the fashion magazine or be represented by the department stores. Designers whose breakthroughs are yet to come are well aware of the tastemakers' role in "creating the designer."

Tastemakers at newspapers

Hilary Alexander, long-time fashion director and journalist of the British newspaper *The Daily Telegraph*, has scaled back on writing for the paper. With more than 236,000 followers on Twitter, she is, among other things, the chair of Graduate Fashion Week in London where the final-year students of London's fashion schools show their collections. Alexander maintains that the internet accounts for the most noteworthy change in the significance of trends in the fashion industry. Fashion shows are now live-streamed and all designers have a presence on Web sites, Facebook, Twitter and Instagram. Fashion, says Alexander in July 2012, is made instantly accessible around the world, in a way beyond anything imaginable even five years ago. In her job as fashion critic, Hilary Alexander has not had to take responsibility for generating sales. She does not concede that the fashion field is socially created and believes in the independent quest for fashion stars. The "magic" still exists for her. Her approach is based on a cultural logic:

> It's the same principle as before: you have to be good. That is the ultimate test. These days there are more opportunities to get your work out to the world either through your own website, Facebook, Tumblr or any of the other social media platforms, and there is probably more competition ... But the decisive thing, if you are going to be successful, is to be good at what you do and to have people buy your clothes and like them.

The internet has not affected the work of fashion journalists "except they now have to be multi-tasking." The public has, in her view, been more affected and inspired: "If you lived in Iceland or Kazakhstan you could never hope to see a Burberry or a Alexander McQueen show, because they would only happen in London, Paris, Milan, and New York, and only for fashion press and buyers."

Today's fashion is not more tolerant, there is just a lot *more* of it, Alexander says. The basic inspirations have not changed. The spring and summer collections always have some navy and white nautical references. In the autumn and winter collections, military references are standard. Bohemian and ethnic inspiration recurs, perhaps in the forms of a hippie trend, an African trend or an Inuit trend. She sees the most significant changes as occurring in the development of fabrics and yarn, the surface textures of fabric and the boom in digital printing. Trend services are not that useful to Alexander, since she does not have to look far into the future, but she thinks that they are tremendously important to the industry.

Bloggers as tastemakers

In Stockholm, I meet with Johanna and Karin (not their real names, as they wished to remain anonymous), two women in their thirties who have been blogging since the dawn of blogs. They both have backgrounds in fashion media, which gives their blogs legitimacy and positions their comments differently in the fashion field from those of any random fashion blogger, for example, Colleen in Springfield, even if . she attracts several hundred thousand visitors. While it is easy for anyone to claim to be an expert on fashion or trends, it is less easy to be seen as authoritative, as this requires well-established relationships in the fashion field.

Both women think that trends are unquestionably important. Johanna likes to divide trends into various levels: local trends, trends among certain groups of people, global trends and larger trends or tendencies. She says that things happen faster today: trends come faster, peak faster and disappear faster. Johanna thinks there are always at least five parallel trends but, she says, perhaps we cannot see the overarching trends of this decade, since we are in the midst of them. Johanna characterizes the first decade of the 2000s as the boho trend, followed by the "edgier" Acne trend.

A fashion trend can be communicated in various ways, says Johanna, being identified either when a blogger captures its expression and illustrates it with an ensemble or, more analytically, when bloggers or journalists ask why this trend has emerged at this time, where it has come from, what it means and what influences are visible.

Karin, on the other hand, mentions the trend of dismissing trends. It has become untrendy, she says, to talk about trends. Few people want to talk about the trends of autumn and winter in terms of colors, coats, skirt lengths and so on. Fashion editors, celebrities and stylists are only interested in *personal* style— the idea that "you can dress however you want." Karin suspects that this trend-dismissing trend will last, seeing it as a result of anxiety. It is something that some of the fashion crowd embrace when they consider themselves too cool and competent to tell the masses what hem length a skirt should have. But the people who promote the "unique" style all look the same, Karin observes. These people are only unwilling to *talk* about trends. To her it feels disingenuous: it is clear to anyone who sees their advertising campaigns or collections that certain things are most definitely on trend. Bloggers have not been as afraid to identify and discuss trends, she says.

Both Johanna and Karin describe the Swedish fashion industry as a small group where everyone knows one another. Johanna observes that the most difficult thing is to remember that there is a world outside the fashion world, especially when a particular trend seems very strong—"right now everyone is talking about…"—when she has seen it on four blogs simultaneously or because it is dominant among the fashion people she knows. Even though the trend is not yet firmly established on a wide scale, it may still be worth writing about. The Swedish fashion industry is emotional, Karin believes, making it easy to hurt people's feelings.

In noting this, both women capture the social nature of the fashion field. In the face of social ambiguity, the rumors, gossip, stories and ideas that arise in the small group constituting the fashion field become vital. It is also because of this ambiguity that trends can seem urgent and that some people may feel that "everyone is talking about trends."

Tastemakers at Swedish fashion magazines

Madelaine Levy is editor-in-chief of the Swedish fashion magazine *Bon*, which is published four times per year. Levy describes the magazine as motivated by an interest in phenomena rather than taste, and its writers can explore something without necessarily considering it an example of good taste. *Bon* has legitimacy in the Swedish fashion field: being featured there is a way for fashion companies to make a name for themselves, to rebrand themselves as hotter or to reposition themselves.

Levy regards trends as incredibly important. Ideas travel the world at approximately the same speed everywhere, so people "are ready" for something new in several places at the same time. Levy believes that many who say they do not follow trends fail to realize to what extent they are governed by them. It is practically impossible to find a pair of jeans one has "dreamed up" or a piece of clothing with a collar one has imagined. It is difficult even to find one's own color to wear, since production is largely determined by what color companies such as Pantone have chosen for the season. Levy states that fashion journalism that tells people what to wear—"this fall, wear a yellow skirt"—has given trends a bad reputation because people are not keen on being lectured. She is more interested in analyzing trends as a phenomenon, identifying the tendencies and seeing what paths they take. *Bon* publishes trend reports from the shows, and Levy reads the trend agencies' complimentary reports, but for budgetary reasons *Bon* does not subscribe to a trend service. In her job as editor-in-chief, Levy comes across "a million different phenomena, names, ideas," and the task of sorting and grouping her impressions requires her to work a bit like a trend analyst.

Li Svärd Edwall, the fashion editor for *VeckoRevyn*, a younger and more commercial Swedish fashion magazine, thinks that trends have lost some of their relevance: "Since things happen so fast with fashion blogs, cruise collections, pre-fall, winter, pre-winter, spring collections—early spring comes during Christmas sales—there are no real releases, they overlap and there is a lot of repetition." Nothing is *totally* out of style. While she personally takes pleasure in the current permissive atmosphere of the fashion world, she thinks that the lack of clarity is difficult for producers to navigate: "You can see that many latch onto blogs to somehow gain some certainty. You know that this girl has a ton of readers. She's within our age interval and her *look* is right." Svärd Edwall's comments illustrate the organizing aspect of trends. When trends are undefined, or when there are too many of them, this creates uncertainty for producers. Instead, they turn to actors who might be popular but who sometimes lack fashion capital.

Tastemakers at *Grazia UK*

In a windowless conference room within a stone's throw of Covent Garden, I meet with Style Director Paula Reed and Editor-in-Chief Jane Bruton to learn how the fashion magazine *Grazia UK*, which sells 205,500 copies per week, relates to trends. The fact that *Grazia UK* can take in trends much more quickly than the traditional fashion magazines was, Bruton saw, the big advantage from its launch in the UK:

> If we go to Milan, Paris, New York or stay here in London, that's in the magazine the following Tuesday. And gone are the days when it was only the catwalks that determined the trends. Trends now come from the street, celebrities and the red carpet. We might notice that tuxedo trousers or flat monk shoes are hot all of a sudden. And that's not from sitting on the front row but from our reporters being out there spotting things.

On Monday mornings, the heads of the editorial department meet; Paula Reed presents the ideas of the fashion team. The department heads go through the photos that have arrived from PR agencies, brands and photographic agencies, often depicting celebrities, and discuss trends identified by the fashion reporters and chosen at the end of the week for the "Ten Hot Stories" pages. Bruton emphasizes that *Grazia UK* is not concerned solely with fashion but also covers news, politics, features and sometimes the economy: "Our readers are as interested in what's going on in Syria as they are in sandals."

Grazia UK uses trend labels as a news hook. Reed thinks that many fashion magazine covers make fashion seem a bit lofty and remote. *Grazia UK* instead presents fashion as something people can gossip about, be excited about; as Bruton says:

> We're not saying to everybody that we're fashionable and we've decided that this is what the trend is, and you need to go away and do it. Rather, we're saying: "this is interesting, we're excited about this, are you?"

Bruton explains that *Grazia UK*'s editors always alert retailers when the magazine intends to feature an item, well aware that the retailers will be inundated by inquiries:

> *Grazia* has the power to drive people into their stores. The readers know that they can go into the store the same Tuesday when the magazine comes out and buy that item. The retailers appreciate it if we can give them a bit of advance warning.

Bruton and Reed believe that trends are extremely important to the readers of *Grazia*. "They want to be one step ahead of the trend," Bruton says:

> They're *early adopters*, they're leaders in their group. Even if they're not going to rush out and buy a certain trend, they want to know about it. But they don't slavishly follow trends. They've got minds of their own. And we're not prescriptive; features of the type "your figure is an apple-shape, then you can buy this" are rare.

Reed finds the fashion landscape to be much more tolerant than before. With fewer fashion rules, she believes that many people are now uncomfortable and seek advice. For example, Reed loves it when her hairdresser makes suggestions that work but is unnerved when a hairdresser asks her what she wants. People are always looking for advice, Reed says, and *Grazia UK* tries to give them the confidence to cherry-pick the trends that are right for them.

The fashion magazine *InStyle*, where Reed used to work, focused on celebrities who started trends, such as Kate Moss. Bruton says, "The whole skinny jean thing probably started with her. And the tuxedo." Reed adds, "And that kind of lazy vintage dress that is massively influential." They mention Jennifer Aniston's girl-next-door Californian style, Chloé Sevigny and Alexa Chung. These senior *Grazia UK* women think that interest in how celebrities dress is waning and that people will eventually be interested in pictures of people who have put together a style without the help of a stylist.

Reed has access to Stylus and WGSN but seeks inspiration elsewhere:

These sites used to be good for some bits and pieces of stories, but it's like they service a different part of the industry, the retailers. So it's probably the buyers of Topshop who would be looking at the sites.

The trend-forecasting services, Reed observes, are "cotton and wool."

"They'll say things like the next big thing is *gentleness*. And then they'll cover that with anything from pastel colors and chiffon to unstructured tailoring and sportswear. There has to be something in there that you are going to hit right on the nail. It's ridiculous. We have to zoom in on the useful things, we can't say to our readers, it's all about *gentleness*."

Though she calls Lidewij Edelkoort a "goddess," her presentations and books are even more remote from the world of *Grazia UK*, of more interest to designers and fabric developers. Then she pauses: "Somebody like [Dior designer] Raf Simons would never use a trend forecaster. He is a kind of oracle of the next big thing."

Both women agree that, as designers are expected to come up with creations that turn the forecasters on their heads, there can be drawbacks to using trend services. As Reed points out:

These designers are buying fabrics from people who have been listening to trend forecasters. They are fishing in the same pool. Designers and magazine editors, everybody is looking for a singular point of view. A clear voice. A fresh way of saying things. They are not all trying to figure out if Nicolas Ghesquière is doing a mini-skirt, because then they better be doing one too.

Grazia UK's ambition to be inclusive can be interpreted based on the magazine's position in the fashion field. It has a broader appeal than many fashion magazines, and its eagerness to be on the same level as readers—manifested in features such as "What do you think?" and "Fashion jury" (where readers constitute the jury) in the magazine and the online *Graziadaily*—can be interpreted as reflecting the boom in blogs, whose recipe for success has been interaction with readers.

Nevertheless, despite their caveats about not being fashionistas behind dark glasses, *Grazia UK*, like the trend forecasters, directs everyone's attention in its trend reporting. The magazine chooses what it wants to convey. It is crucial to have concrete, identifiable and commercially valuable trends that can be disseminated, and the magazine's influence in this is evidenced by the fact that Bruton and Reed inform relevant retailers of trend choices before publication.

Stylists as tastemakers

In recent years, stylists have acquired high status in the fashion world. Daniel Linderoth,[16] an internationally successful Swedish stylist, describes a change of roles in which the photographer must now dance to the stylist's tune. Stylists are used by celebrities, magazines and fashion brands. *Grazia UK*'s Jane Bruton says of this trend, "Celebrities want to get it right so that they don't get headlines like 'Oh my God, what on earth was Eva Longoria thinking?'" Magazine stylists bring "a look," and stylists who work closely with designers become a sounding board in that exceptionally intimate design process. *Grazia UK*'s Paula Reed explains:

> Katie Grand, who has a massive personality, works closely with Marc Jacobs. It's almost as if she's part of that little creative family. They're part of the massive LVMH, the scary corporate business, in this big shiny building in Paris where it's all about bottom line and profit and loss. They don't speak that language naturally. So they do hunker down and come up with fabulous ideas and create amazing things that can then be marketed and makes Louis Vuitton one of the most successful companies in the world.

Other designer–stylist duos such as Karl Lagerfeld and Amanda Harlech, Alexander McQueen and Camilla Nickerson, and Yves Saint Laurent and Loulou de la Falaise have, Reed says, professionalized the muse. Reed sheds light on this mutual dependence, challenging the image of the headstrong and self-sufficient designer:

> Somebody like Katie is out there working with photographers and designers in the big wide world and with her magazine *Love*. She is out and about every day and lives in a very urban part of London. She lives in a real world. Marc Jacobs lives in a limiting world. Most of the designers do. When John Galliano left Dior he said "My God, I haven't walked down the street and bought myself a pack of cigarettes for ten years." So they've got no connection with the real world. The stylists become their eyes and ears. They're touch points to what's going on out there.

In Daniel Linderoth's view, the big fashion houses are so driven by money that magazines can be far more progressive and innovative. He started a fashion magazine claiming that "from the perspective of doing a contemporary analysis, it's much more fun than doing a collection." On trend services, Linderoth observes:

> WGSN is like a self-playing piano. What they say becomes the truth. They have a good position. When all designers pay to look at those trends they automatically become trends. I mean, I have tremendous problems as a stylist

when I step into different meetings with fashion companies, and they all show me inspiration boards and I can tell exactly what trend site they subscribe to. They all have the same inspiration. They even use the same words as those that WGSN pushes. It scares the daylight out of me.

While Linderoth has no support from trend services, he consults for some designers early in collection development, often in the trend analysis phase, but also during production. He concentrates on the totality and the colorings. Of a presentation by Lidewij Edelkoort, which by his own admission he attended because he got in free of charge, he said it was "damp lemons and one-year-old magazine clippings that I myself had grown tired of." The big clothing companies who have no wish to be at the cutting edge he sees as the most likely candidates for this type of inspiration. "Not everyone wants to be as ground-breaking as H&M."

It is in tastemakers' nature to engage in the game of who can identify the incipient taste first. The fact that some niche fashion magazines are considered more intellectually challenging than the collections of the fashion houses reflects the distribution of symbolic capital.

Online fashion retailer as tastemaker

There are more trends than ever before. And customers are used to searching for trends, in the same ways that magazines are featuring them. So they apply the same terms from when they read magazines when they search Google, and when they search websites.

Katie Rogers is the founder of the online retailer Lemon and Berries,[17] which sells "accessible luxury" designer fashion from APC to Preen. Rogers immediately rejects the suggestion that trends have lost their role because there are so many concurrent trends: "It's not applicable to luxury, to designer fashion, where collections are based on *one* trend." The customers of Lemon and Berries understand what trends are and want them to fit into their everyday lives and styles: "It's not about a 16-year-old who one week dresses head-to-toe in animal print and then next week in neon."

The search function is the biggest difference. In an online store, a customer can filter by size, color, trend, designer and event (in Lemon and Berries' case, for example, "Ascot," "Wimbledon" and "Wedding") and get an overview of the available offerings. Rogers identifies trends as very popular among her online customers, since they can find the five or six trends for the season on the site. Lemon and Berries' buying team has access to WGSN but also looks for recurring themes directly in the collections. Rogers finds WGSN useful for delving into a variety of specific markets. Though trends are global, she is in no doubt that some trends will be more relevant to one territory than to another, saying that "minimalism is a trend that will never work in the Middle East, where it's all about color." In contrast to Net-A-Porter, its competitor in the luxury segment, Lemon and Berries does not aspire to be a fashion magazine.[18] The firm collaborates with fashion magazines that compile, for example, "editor's style-picks" with products from the site, underlining the centrality of relationships in the fashion field.

*

In online stores, trends have names such as "Cavalry Calling," "Shoe Shine," "Velvet Goldmine," "Collar Cool," "Shimmer and Shine," "Trophy Knit," "MonoTones" and "Leather." Interestingly, online fashion stores use such trend labels while bricks-and-mortar department stores and fashion shops in the same segment prefer to organize items not by trend but by designer. As online customers search using trend labels that they have seen in magazines and online, consistency between these labels and the headings of the online store becomes critical. The magazine *Grazia UK* also pays special attention to trend labeling, calling it a "news hook." The frequent use of trend labels in social media could be seen as indicating their growing significance, as online search functions reinforce the importance of categorization.

Despite many reservations about the word "trend," the role of trends as an organizing principle was confirmed repeatedly over the course of my conversations. Nobody seems to seriously believe that the era of trends is over. Emblematic of fashion as a cultural production field is that everyone wants to be the one who recognizes and discovers—no one wants to be a follower. The tastemakers' competence to identify and communicate trends is challenged by the trend forecasters, so it is unsurprising that the tastemakers downplay or are even offended by the trend services' mere existence, let alone expansion. The position of a fashion editor in the field rests on his or her independence, fashion capital and taste. The tastemakers' claim that they consider themselves to be trend analysts can be seen as manifesting the struggle for authority in the field. The designer fashion segment, where the word "trend" is used only rarely, is, as Katie Rogers points out, permeated by the fact that one collection revolves around a single trend so that the mix of collections and designers or brands becomes vital to retailers.

There are several interpretations of why the trend concept has lost status. The first is based on overarching conceptions of the primacy of the designer and of fashion as an art form. Here, the tastemakers' authority comes from their ability to "follow the field," participating in forming the dominant views through their assessments of collections, designers, new talents and brands. Tastemakers are ascribed knowledge and are sensitive to movements in the field. As Bourdieu points out, the creators self-consciously create themselves, but then forget what they have created, that they have *created*.[19] Their strenuous work becomes invisible even to themselves, and instead they experience every new discovery as if it were *magic*. It follows that the idea of articulated trends dispels that magic.

Second, the low status of the trend concept can be interpreted in light of the rise of mass-market fashion that in recent decades has pushed trend-thinking and neomania, while the internet has enabled many actors beyond the fashion establishment, such as bloggers, to enter the field and offer services that benefit fast fashion. Trends have become associated with mass-market fashion, economic capital and a patronizing tone about what is right and wrong for the moment. Several informants related trends to shopping.

I have already acknowledged that the social aspect of the fashion field is immensely important when it comes to developing trends, interpreting collections, forming opinions and creating an aura of "magic" around certain creators, collections and brands. Those who cherish membership in and the security of easy identification of the fashion elite will eagerly act as gatekeepers to the fashion field's legitimate scene. The reluctance of the inner circle to share trend information in our information-saturated world can be understood from a power perspective, as Karin the Swedish blogger points out. Claims about trends being over and dismissals of trends as signifying dependent behavior in a time that celebrates individual free choice could also be seen as excuses or, alternatively, as support for the opposing force of trend dissemination.

5 GENDER AND TRENDS—ON VARIABILITY

Men always look a bit silly in a trend, don't they?

So says Paula Reed of *Grazia UK*. Jane Bruton, editor-in-chief of the same magazine, adds: "Men aren't so interested in getting it *right*; they are just more concerned with not getting it *wrong*, so they are much more conservative." Reed agrees: "Yes, they would hate to think that they were flashy. But actually, we're a country where men have a peacock gene."

Fashion magazines, blogs, shops and e-commerce sites are perpetually filled with trend news about womenswear. If neomania can be said to be the engine of fashion, trends serve as a form of guidance, ensuring the fashion industry of a constant demand for the "right" new. Why, then, are trends in womenswear infinitely more volatile—shorter and more diverse—than those in menswear? Even the word *style* has different connotations in menswear and womenswear: in menswear it is connected to continuity, while in womenswear it implies newness and change, being invoked primarily in fashion stories inviting readers to "steal the style" from celebrities or designers, or when actresses, who all look strikingly similar and who are dressed by stylists, are referred to as "style icons." We are relentlessly hurled back into variable women's fashion.

In a market economy, it ought to be in the interest of many fashion companies to incite change so that more items or styles are deemed out of fashion. With the shorter lifespan of current trends, it could be assumed that men also would wish to purchase new items more frequently, which would radically increase the demand for menswear fashion. I was curious as to why trend forecasters, fashion designers, fashion journalists, bloggers, buyers and stylists do not make more effort to make menswear trends more varied, or men's fashion more fluctuating, especially since the fashion field is highly reliant on change. Other consumer products, such as mobile phones, furniture and food, have proven receptive to a heightened emphasis on trends. Still, my question is neutral. I do not necessarily wish for quicker trends; rather, I am interested in why the phenomenon of trends is more variable in womenswear than in menswear.[1] Some of the interviewees below have already been featured in the book; others will be paid more attention in upcoming chapters.

Most informants appeared to regard male consumers as resistant to change via trends, uttering statements such as "men just don't think like that" or "men have a different approach to fashion." "Women have a different relationship with their bodies," said one French trend analyst. Many seemed almost unable to answer, claiming that so many societal and cultural factors were involved that they did not know where to begin. They usually referred to differences between men and women, between the feminine and masculine sensibilities. British designer Erdem Moralioğlu (see p. 117) describes women as more adventurous than men in terms of fashion. Another British designer, Inacio Ribeiro (see p. 120) from the brand Clements Ribeiro, says that for a while he felt slightly guilty for contributing to what he perceived as a cultural imposition on women, that is, being trophies. He has come to realize, however, that it is intrinsic to women's nature to dress up and that fashion expresses femininity in a way that does not apply to men and masculinity. Masculinity, Ribeiro says, is expressed through sports, cars and other pursuits; fashion is less important to men, so their fashion develops more slowly and less dramatically. Men are often portrayed as more conservative than women, and some designers noted men's penchant for types, for example, brats, mods and rockers, and their tendency to stick to styles that once captivated them.

Cecilia Björk (see p. 109), a Swedish designer, speaks of women being in more contexts, often in different roles—as professionals, mothers, friends and sometimes participants in social events. Compared with men, women change clothes in a different way and for different reasons, creating more and clearer trends in womenswear. Talking about menswear as less changeable and less "spaced out," Cecilia adds that despite the common belief, color and variation do not inevitably make the designer's work more *fun*.

These conceptions of masculine and feminine and of "demand" are interwoven with images of what a designer can offer, what a fashion editor or trend analyst can propose, where the boundaries of fashion lie and what is considered right and interesting from a fashion standpoint. The supply of fashion is often taken for granted but, instead of trying to interpret *why* menswear trends are shorter and less varied, the informants frequently described *how* men's and women's fashion differ. The constructions of womenswear and menswear are distinct to the degree that they are perceived as unalterable and self-evident.

A key account manager at a trend bureau says that women have more choice and can therefore experiment from day to day, building on the idea that the industry offers women a selection with which to "experiment." The same woman believes that men do not dare to experiment as much and that they are afraid of appearing gay if they are "overdressed." According to her, fashion companies are putting effort into making men more open-minded about fashion, but that "educational work" targeting men costs too much in the current cost-constrained environment—after all, it took years before men had the nerve to use face cream, she notes.

"The appetite for menswear is different," says Kate Phelan (see p. 96), the creative director of Topshop:

> Men are not the peacocks that I think women are. Women love their clothes, and buying fashion is a way of exhibiting yourself. Women have always showcased fashion more than men. I think there are more conventions around men, more conventional dressing—you know, the typical—they don't wear skirts and dresses. But within womenswear you have so much to choose from—you could dress like a guy, you could dress like a princess. But as a guy you're basically stuck with a pair of trousers or a pair of shorts, a shirt or a t-shirt, a coat or a jacket ... . I think men are especially affected by their peer group, that they tend to not want to stand out.

Informants reiterate the notion that menswear fashion is substantially more enduring. Roland Hjort, a designer for Whyred, suggests that the big fluctuations in womenswear are because more money is spent on clothes for women than for men, so the offering for womenswear must be wider ranging. That brings us back to the core of my question: Could it be that men spend less on clothes because the variations in them, the trends, are so small? Hjort notes that one constantly hears about changes in menswear, but that in reality these changes are minute:

> A woman can wear both a pair of truly wide trousers and a pair of really skinny trousers. That you can never do for a guy. There is just one pair of trousers for guys, so in that way it is rather limited.

Hjort observes that men act in more tradition-bound ways and keep returning to items that they have liked previously: men are more loyal as customers, some always buying the same type of product, for example, a parka.

When one of the online trend bureaus started a close-to-season department, the trends team discussed whether the same setup should be used for menswear and decided against it. A head of trends observed:

> Menswear doesn't move as quickly as womenswear. The turnaround of womenswear is much faster, and trends also come from celebrities. Men might look at celebrities but they don't want to wear exactly what those celebrities are wearing, they think differently.

Some informants are aware that their own preconceptions of how men should dress influence their buying decisions. Sarah Jordan, collection director at Imogen Brown (see p. 125), sees change in menswear but notes that it is slower than in womenswear, because fashion does not seem to interest men as much. She often shops for her husband at New York stores such as J. Crew and Brooks Brothers, developing different looks and trends each year:

> Men can still always wear a t-shirt or a shirt and a pair of trousers … You don't want that [i.e., the Prada AW12 collection items] to happen to your husband. It's like Dracula! It looks all right on the runway, and yes, I understand where Prada is coming from. But if I met a guy like that on the street, I would be so scared. So I agree, there should be more variation in menswear, but at the same time I'm also stuck with this image of how things should be.

Men are considered to think in terms of categories: Do I need a new shirt? A new suit? Women, to a much greater extent, are expected to ask themselves: Do I need something new? Nina Bogstedt, range manager at Filippa K (see p. 106), elaborates:

> Men go out and are more driven by their needs, they approach their shopping in a rational way. I have heard horror stories about people who make an Excel spreadsheet before they go out shopping, and that's something I believe few women would do. I think a lot of men approach fashion in that manner: here are the shirts, here are the suits, here are the t-shirts …. There are quite a few who make very directional menswear fashion, but maybe it isn't particularly wearable to the great many. If you don't want to go down that road, there is very little to play with. It's more of a classic cut. There's never much drama in terms of color or print. I think it all goes back to women's different behavior and their openness to change when it comes to clothes and to be inspired while shopping. And they engage in spontaneous shopping a lot more.

Claiming that there is less to "work on" in menswear, Bogstedt notes that, while in womenswear everything from skirt lengths and widths to necklines can change, a men's shirt is a men's shirt. It can be monochrome or print, the wings of the collar or the width of the cuffs can be changed, but a shirt still has two sleeves. Substantially more basics are sold in menswear, Bogstedt claims.

Jane Shepherdson, CEO of the British brand Whistles (see p. 102), regards the smaller variations in menswear as evidence that men are not as excited by fashion as are women. Some men just want whatever the mannequin is wearing, because clothes are a necessity purchase, though Shepherdson finds the success of luxury brands' menswear collections interesting.

By contrast, Geoffrey Finch, the creative director of Antipodium (see p. 111), regards the menswear consumer as more particular about details, such as the thickness of a button or the cut of an item. Men have the same eye for detail when it comes to shoes such as trainers: "To some people, these sneakers all look the same, but to others, the limited edition and the special finish mean everything." Finch thinks there are more subtleties in menswear than in womenswear, and even men who are not particularly fashion-conscious are interested in the details.

Several informants think that more trends have prevailed in men's fashion in recent years, that men's fashion has become *better* and that "lots of things are happening in menswear." The woman who initially described men as lacking fashion courage (see p. 73) is taken aback by the changes in the intervening three years: "It took time, but men are finally daring. There has been a significant shift in men's attitudes towards fashion consumption, especially among youth, for whom the feminine and masculine codes have blurred."

Rita Nakouzi from the trend forecaster Promostyl finds menswear exceedingly interesting because men are now spending more money on fashion; there is growing appeal in "having a wardrobe" and "wanting to accessorize." Menswear trends are normally manifested in fabrication: the lapel, two or three vents on the jacket and a slightly longer or shorter coat. Thom Browne changed the whole trends discourse in menswear by shrinking the male silhouette. Like many interviewees, Nakouzi points out that there has recently been more experimentation in menswear. She is not convinced that any industry effort to shorten trends would lead to increased sales because men shop *differently* from how women shop. Men are more fascinated by performance—by ripstop, antibacterial and wrinkle-free fabrics and by protective functions—than by the cut of a piece of clothing. If a certain cut works for a man, he will stay with it. A man will not wear skinny jeans if he is bulky. "I don't know how long it took to get men to wear skinny jeans," notes Nakouzi, adding that women may wear leggings, for example, even when they should not, just to be trendy. The reality is that changes are incremental in menswear, and any attempt to change this setup drastically will backfire on the industry.

April Glassborow (see p. 55), buying manager at Harvey Nichols, has also noticed considerable changes in menswear. She sees that a certain segment of the male population now wants to be fashionable and buys into trends, renewing wardrobes and shopping, unlike in the past, when most men just wanted to "get it over with." Harvey Nichols' menswear department attracts men who are interested in fashion, Glassborow says, while "the customers going to Harrods are very different." Unlike women, who are not that loyal to particular stores—to them it makes no difference whether an item is from Primark or Prada, from a shop or from Net-A-Porter—men tend to have favorites. At a certain fashion level, men buy proportionally more designer-level items than do women, not being as keen about *mix-and-match*, Glassborow claims.

Many informants use circular reasoning in reflecting on the quickness and variety of womenswear trends. Women want short and varied trends because they are *like that*. How do we know that they are like that? Well, they behave in that way. Men are not *like that*. How do we know that they are not like that? They do not behave in that way. Such explanations could go on and on. These presuppositions reproduce constructions not only of women's and men's fashion, but also of gender more generally. The fashion companies' ideas about their customers and offerings remain unexamined and unaltered.

While tastemakers and, as we will see, designers compete in exercising influence when it comes to the specific expressions of trends, they have downplayed their own roles in affecting the changeability of trends in men's and women's fashion.

History may offer some insight into existing gender constructions. Although many of the underlying reasons for these constructions are irrelevant to today's society, the constructions linger and, in the fashion industry specifically, as shown above, they are reproduced through persistent conceptions of how men and women relate to trends. Here, the invisible hand of the market economy takes the gender order into consideration and in fact reinforces it, even though this counteracts the ultimate aim of the capitalist market economy to generate profit.

The informants' answers can also be seen as another sign of the economic irrationality of the patriarchy.[2] The many faces of the gender order are frequently justified with reference to their being economically rational. Owing to gender stereotyping and the biased evaluations that they produce, one might, for example, hear that "the most competent" candidate, a man, was appointed director because he seems achievement-oriented and "profitability has to come first."[3] In other words, arguments frequently cite economic rationality although they are not necessarily economically rational. The burden of proof, that is, whether the choice of director really was the most economically justified, is on someone other than the one making the decision. The prevailing order is *assumed* to be economically rational.[4] In all power structures, those in dominant positions strive to make the dominated perceive the power structure as legitimate, for example, by making it seem as if those in power are the most suitable for the job, that is, the most "boss-like," most economically literate, most conventionally appropriate and most charismatic.[5] We create images of how managers should be, based on how they have been, while economic rationality in reality is secondary. As for men's relationships with trends, economic rationality is similarly subordinated to ideas about how men are, though in this case the issue is not position in society or organizations. Perhaps that is why people have more difficulties trying to justify this feature of the fashion field. Essentially all informants have difficulties explaining why trends are—and particularly have been—long-lasting and less varied in menswear. My impression is that most have not contemplated the differences between trends in women's and men's fashion in economic terms.

Femininity as volatile and capricious

Since the birth of fashion, which is said to coincide with the birth of modernity, fashion, the body, sexuality and sin have been more closely associated with the construction of femininity than of masculinity. In other words, fashion has been gendered as feminine. According to fashion historians, this equating of fashion and women, and the exclusion of men from the concept, comes from nineteenth-century Victorian ideas of the relationship between the sexes, social mores and sexuality.[6] By the same token, the fashion industry and its consumers are mostly women (see the statistics presented on p. 5), though when it comes to ownership and management in the fashion industry, power is less often in the hands of women.[7]

The essence of femininity has been characterized as superficiality, artifice and masquerade and constant changeability. Femininity and fashion, which has changeability at its heart, thus mesh well and this relationship affects trends. According to historian Jennifer Jones, women have been associated with capriciousness and change for centuries.[8] Valerie Steele and many other scholars have identified the First World War as the dividing line between nineteenth-century fashion and the modern era, when women were soon able to wear trousers without causing surprise. The evolution of women's fashion should not be viewed as merely reflecting economic and social change—for example, that short skirts followed women's emancipation; this evolution was as much a result of internal fashion mechanisms, including the inherent neomania of fashion. After the First World War, women tried to gain acceptance in lines of work dominated by men, appropriating certain symbols coded as masculine, such as the business suit and the tie. These symbols were often translated, as with the tie blouse for businesswomen.[9]

That women's fashion has been more fickle can also be understood by looking at the subordinate position of women as a group compared with men, which has meant that women gained from crossing gender lines and associating themselves with symbols coded as masculine. Parents, for example, consider it less problematic for girls to wear colors and clothing associated with boys, than the reverse.[10] Correspondingly, men have had less to gain, from the perspective of power, from adopting clothing viewed as feminine. Comme des Garçons, Yohji Yamamoto, Jean-Paul Gaultier, Rick Owens and Carin Wester have all launched skirts for men, while J.W. Anderson has made dresses but with a limited impact. The gender order clearly contributes to making variation greater in women's fashion than in men's.

Cultural theorist Jennifer Craik writes in *The Face of Fashion* that, while womenswear has been concerned with creating a *look*, an image to admire, men's appearance is about enhancing men's active roles, particularly as concerns their professional and social status. Craik says that the dominant menswear discourse is *fashionless*, its rhetoric characterized by denials: there is no fashion for men, men dress for fit and comfort, not style, women dress and buy clothes for men, men who dress up are peculiar, men do not notice clothes and men have not been duped into joining the endless pursuit of trendiness.

In European culture, the cycles of men's fashion have been longer and less dramatic since the eighteenth century. In the 1960s, however, men's fashion gained in popularity and a new relationship with the male body was discernable.[11] Men's fashion at this time became a part of the field of fashion, the heart of which is, of course, change, making relationships with tastemakers more important. As the seasonal logic became the norm for collections, the cycles of men's fashion became somewhat shorter and there is currently greater variation in cut, color and materials. Nevertheless, when some informants say that "quite a lot is happening" in menswear, this should be understood in relation to the past.

New forms of masculinity are accompanied by new attitudes to fashion. One example is the idea of the "metrosexual man,"[12] in turn followed by the notion of the "retrosexual man."[13] The fashion industry is global, and even though we see new forms of masculinity emerging locally,[14] it is far from certain that they will affect global fashion. Still, in the context of fashion trends, the dominant construction of masculinity is linked to stability rather than fickleness.

That femininity is associated with more variability is evident in sociologist Stanley Lieberson's study of the popularity of names in Europe and the United States. He demonstrates that naming became a matter of fashion and taste only in the twentieth century, finding a clear difference between girls' and boys' names. Fashion in girls' names accelerated earlier than in boys' names, and there is a higher "fashion turnover" in girls' than boys' names in most regions. Lieberson takes this to mean that boys' names have long-signaled continuity with the past and have less of a "decorative" function. As previously noted, parents are increasingly influenced by how others name their children, which activates internal mechanisms that drive fashion forward.[15]

Others have interpreted the "fickleness" of womenswear as arising from the evolution of production systems. Rather than viewing the industry structure as a response to the fashion scene, political economists Ben Fine and Ellen Leopold note an interdependence between the production system and the expression of fashion. Fine and Leopold interpret fashion's rapid changes as a way that the industry compensated for its failure to create mass production of the kind that was common in other industries, such as the auto industry. In the 1920s, the fashion industry's manufacturing and distribution structures were primitive. In menswear, where clothes were "staples," one could speak of widespread mass production. In womenswear, say Fine and Leopold, much was produced at home, partly because women's work rarely required specialized clothing and also because women generally had good sewing skills, augmented by the sewing machine, which facilitated production in both industry and the home. This meant that the clothing industry did not develop the same mass-production systems as were seen in industries such as the automotive industry. Fine and Leopold argue that the quickening fluctuations of fashion—that is, trends—compensated for the industry's long-standing lack of technological innovation.[16]

The importance of being right

Amanda Palmer, the fashion director of *Lauren*, is convinced that most women want to be told what is "right." They know what is in but do not have the time, "eye" or confidence to make their own fashion choices:

> A lot of women who have money work, and they don't want to look stupid or foolish, eccentric or stupid; they want to look right for the role they have in life. Even if you're the woman who lunches with her best girlfriend who maybe has got more money than you ... I think there are so many women for whom fashion isn't a pleasure.

Palmer is not one of those women: she loves jewelry, color and decoration. Palmer has even offered her fashion skills in charity auctions, doing wardrobe updates. At first, she disliked meddling with how people dressed but has become fascinated with those women who are successful in their professions and do not know how to present themselves. Despite being self-assured in many aspects of their lives, these women lack confidence when it comes to what looks good on them:

> It really is a wonderful thing to go to someone's house and say, "If you just went to Monsoon or Accessorize and bought a scarf. And don't do the scarf like that, take it from the corners and roll it up, because it will make it thinner." What pleasure it gives them is amazing—it's really lovely. And I think a lot of women just are not interested enough to spend time experimenting, so they never get better either. And most women, and men too, for that matter, are expected not to be fashion illiterate.

*

The idea of looking "right" as a woman characterizes much of the history of fashion and is linked to the Western tradition of thought in which a woman's appearance is crucial to her self-esteem and identity.[17] "Being right" is about having good instincts and finding the right balance. Of course, women's dress has been determined by class as well, and in this respect "being right" has been crucial. In the seventeenth and eighteenth centuries, luxury and women's

supposedly insatiable cravings for it were sometimes seen as threatening the family. A too ornately dressed woman could easily be accused of the moral failing of overweening vanity or even of the social faux pas of "excessiveness," indicating lack of education or sophistication.[18] In the 1950s, the idea of the self, one's appearance, as work of art peaked. Appearance was deemed important, as was personality, and fashion magazines encouraged women to find their "type" while "being themselves" in their style of dress.[19] Again, it was all about the difficult balance of "looking different" within limits. It could be just as damning to follow fashion too slavishly as to dismiss its dictates too lightly. Skirt lengths entailed risks and challenges.

In his studies of power, philosopher Michel Foucault has described the shift in expressions of power that occurred with the transition to modern society. Power previously depended on authority and threats of violence; in the modern era, however, power is decentralized, relying on self-discipline among those subject to it, so that they adapt to prevailing norms. In attempting to create better lives, people do not violate these norms of their own accord.[20] Such self-regulation is applicable not least to bodies, and especially women's bodies, according to feminist scholars who have criticized Foucault for failing to properly highlight the importance of gender in these "normalization processes."[21] The fact that women and their reputations are judged based on appearance—clothes and body—means that women judge and appraise their own bodies and adapt to current standards. Applied to fashion, the expectation in its simplest form is: here are the trends of spring—follow them and you will be happier.

Fashion companies and media have of course capitalized on this desire to be "right." Even if a woman is uninterested in fashion, there is still, because of the link between femininity and fashion, an expectation that she should stay reasonably informed about "what's in." When trends are changeable and short-lived, "what's in" is more difficult to identify, hence the desire for the lecturing tone that some fashion journalists and readers dislike so strongly. Women find it impossible to defend themselves against fashion by falling back on a uniform, the way fashion-agnostic men can rely on a dark suit or a blazer. The suit can be criticized as out of style but it still signals, as social anthropologist Fanny Ambjörnsson observes, power, adherence to rules as well as suppressed individuality.[22]

In light of the normalization process Foucault has described, it is not strange that women continue to care about their fashions being "right." The ability to dress right can also be seen as a competence that is largely constructed as feminine. Several informants spoke of receiving questions from readers, friends and clients about what colors are trendy and how to dress in fairly ordinary situations such as job interviews, birthday parties and first dates. When I worked for Filippa K one summer in the mid-1990s, women called to ask if they could wear a white blouse with a red skirt, or requested tips on what to wear at the midsummer party. Everyone affected by the fashion field knows, more or less,

who can guide them through the landscape of trends—that is, who possesses fashion capital.

Erving Goffman's studies of everyday interactions demonstrate that people in modern society present themselves in a way that is consistent with what is expected of them in whatever situations they find themselves and in whatever roles they play, in accordance with the norms and informal rules of interaction.[23] Women remain concerned with how their bodies and clothes look and are incorporated from an early age into a gender order in which clothes, colors and aesthetics are vital to self-presentation. Goffman often refers to advice columns and books on etiquette, which he says reveal norms in the clearest possible way. By the same token, fashion editorials with their clear trend directives preserve norms by contributing to an ongoing sense that it is important to be "right"— although the expression of what is right is constantly changing.

In addition, there is a prevailing idea of femininity that presents women as shopping machines driven by uncontrollable impulses that make them spend vast sums of money on an ever-increasing number of belongings. Cultural theorist Rita Felski argues that what makes this desire "modern," that is, born of modernity, is that it is presumed to be controlled and manipulated by calculated, rational consideration of profit. The construction of femininity as passive, emotional and susceptible to persuasion has turned women into ideal subjects for an ideology of consumption that builds on the commercialization of pleasure.[24]

This should not be read as dismissing the importance of menswear. As several informants point out, many men dedicate considerable time to fashion and there is often an expectation that men should be "right" in their dress—or at least not "off trend." The long-standing "fickleness" of femininity combined with the lingering need to be "right" help explain why trends are so closely linked to women's fashion.

Trends need not be perceived as only oppressive and limiting. Trends also enable change: they can make it easier to try new "looks" and have a liberating influence on individuals.

Fashion and trends: power and freedom

Designer Carin Rodebjer considers fashion to be largely about gender and development. She thinks that the changeability of fashion makes it fun to work with, allowing the wearers to evolve and express various things.

Trends constantly suggest new opportunities for individuals to restage themselves, representing occasions for change. To understand how trends can ultimately give individuals power and freedom, one must first discuss fashion's importance as a basis for change. The most common explanation offered by my informants as to why fashion is so appealing is that it constitutes a kind of theatrical costumery. Clothes are part of how people present themselves to the world, and fashion locates them in the present, relative to what is happening in society and to fashion's own history. As a form of expression, fashion contains a host of ambiguities, enabling individuals to recreate the meanings associated with specific pieces of clothing. Fashion is among the simplest and cheapest methods of self-expression: clothes can be inexpensively purchased while making it easy to convey notions of wealth, intellectual stature, relaxation or environmental consciousness, even if none of these is true. Fashion can also strengthen agency in various ways, opening up space for action.

One head of trends at a major trend-forecasting agency reflects on hats, which were once used as social markers communicating concrete things, identifying whether their wearers were bakers, farmers, nobility, etc. Hats communicated even more subtly how wearers related to others *within* their class. Although the rules are no longer as rigid, the same tendency persists. Through our clothing, we project images for others, enabling us to move socially.

People who work in fashion often refer to "tribes." Many informants think that we seek community through tribes and that there is still a social need to be "right" within a specific social context, whether one looks for affirmation in an "urban tribe," such as hipsters, or in a particular profession. The tension between individuality and group identity, highlighted by Georg Simmel, among others, is one explanation for the movements of fashion mentioned in Chapter 3.

Pierre Bourdieu has written about how class is recreated through taste,[25] noting that taste follows very clear social patterns and is determined by the amount of economic, social and cultural capital a person has. When it comes to cultural consumption, class is evidenced in the type of art people like, the travel destinations they choose, the restaurants they frequent, the music they listen to and how they dress. This means that one's style of dress is also an expression of class. Fashion, in other words, is not just about individual choice but is largely a kind of identity construction project, although this process can be unconscious. With fashion, one can distinguish oneself from some people and show belonging with others.

How a person follows trends can also be understood in terms of class and social belonging, especially given that trends, or rather a certain way of talking about them, have come to be associated primarily with mass-market fashion, that is, economic capital. Following trends "slavishly" is not considered very sophisticated, though it is difficult to draw an exact line between appropriate and slavish trend awareness. Neomania, accelerated by the internet, constantly offers new trend labels to consider. Being too late in adopting a well-defined, prepackaged trend is not the way to attain high status; on the other hand, people can distinguish themselves within their groups or against other groups by adopting certain trends and not others. Navigating this fashion landscape can be difficult, but since trends and fashion movements are often internalized by consumers, the process of adoption is rarely conscious—one might simply go out intending to "buy something nice."

Fashion is largely about tension, that is, meeting existing expectations while finding an acceptably individual style. There are additional, related tensions between the private and the public self (e.g., at home and at work) and between the artificial and the authentic (referring to the romantic notion that fashion disguises the authentic person).[26] There might not be any significance to one's outfit beyond the expression of fashion itself, which may refer solely to its own history. Fashion is often justified by the presumption that it says something about the outside world (exemplified in the old maxim that short skirts are trendy when the economy is good), which is indicative of fashion's low status as a field of cultural production. However, for the independence of the fashion field, fashion for fashion's sake is crucial.

Consumption's potential to empower people's independent choices and give them greater control over their lives should not be underestimated, especially not in cases in which people have been excluded from consumer society. Some scholars have identified democratizing aspects of consumer society, pointing to a form of abstract equality between people as consumers. Although consumer society has not destroyed gender and ethnicity structures, it has at least had a liberating effect, they say: individual wishes are heeded and women are permitted to articulate wishes and desires. Other critics argue that consumer society has reinforced ideas of essential gender differences and that the nascent possibility of self-determination has been stifled by new restrictions on gendered identities and calls to "buy more stuff."[27] Although women's gender bending in terms of their clothing is due to their subordinate position as women, the fact remains that fashion gives women a freedom of expression that men lack. Women, unlike men, can dress extravagantly or plainly, dress to take up a lot of space or stay in the background.

Some informants describe actively working to reduce the oppressive aspects of fashion. Jane Shepherdson, CEO of Whistles, talks about the gender structures in the fashion industry. She finds the industry still incredibly sexist: there are hardly any women in management or on boards of directors, even though industry employees in the UK are approximately 80 percent women. Under Shepherdson's direction, Whistles and the Penguin Group publishing house (which views Whistles as "the thinking woman's brand") have hosted a number of feminist dinners. At the first dinner, over 200 women attended to hear speeches by women from various industries, including a film director, an advertising guru and a naval officer. Whistles organized similar regional dinners in the autumn of 2012. Shepherdson considers it important to engage women in the public debate, since it is commonly believed that feminism and fashion are mutually exclusive, an assumption that Miuccia Prada—nowadays profiled as a feminist—held in her youth.[28]

Another way a person can feel empowered as a subject in the fashion field is to follow the creation of incipient taste (see p. 50) from close range. With plentiful information about fashion readily available, an interested consumer can view and comment on shows, read fashion news at the same time as everyone else, view fashion pictures and observe fashion movements. The tacit knowledge collected in this way by consumers allows the internalization of fashion logic so that consumers can discover "the new" simultaneously with those in power positions in the fashion field. A desire for something new may ostensibly happen to coincide with "the new" that others seek. The individual consumer does not feel pushed in a particular direction, however, but feels both included in the fashion community and, like the tastemakers, apparently independent of it as well.

Amanda Palmer, the fashion director of *Lauren*, casts some light on fashion and age. Although her mother had "a superb sense of style," Palmer's mother never dressed like her daughter does at age fifty-one: "I wear my hair as if I were thirty-five years old, but I stopped going to Topshop five years ago. It's not relevant for me anymore, it's too young." Palmer thinks there is an entire group of women, aged forty to sixty years, who feel much younger than their mothers, but who are wary of looking silly, whose knees are not great and to whom the fashion companies do not cater. For fashion to function as an enabler, for it to be liberating, the fashion on offer cannot discriminate against certain groups.

Many informants comment on the current diversity of womenswear. The 1950s, 1960s and 1970s all had very specific "looks" and very few alternatives. In the words of one trend analyst, the attitude was: "This is the look of the season, and this is how you wear it." She sees only advantages to the great variety available today: "Pumps, platforms, cowboy boots or biker boots—everything goes." Palmer agrees. The rapid speed and high turnover of the trends characterizing fashion in recent years have made it possible to be much more individualistic: "It's fantastic. You can like prints, color, jewelry, uniform, minimalism, without being out of fashion. You are not necessarily going to be massively in fashion all the time, but the choices are infinite. In that way, our times are certainly not fashion fascist." The paradox, she says, is that this diversity in itself breeds insecurity, and many women are still more concerned with getting it "right" than with whether black is still trendy or whether beige is the new black.

*

In the 2010s, the fashion world will tell you that most things are acceptable. The great diversity of current fashion means that there are many ways for people to strengthen their agency and self-expression and to lift themselves out of subordinate positions with the help of fashion. At the same time, in practice many people seek belonging through fashion or just want to know what is right.

Most people know that a certain approach to fashion and trends confers status and that fashion, for better or worse, categorizes a person. No one can extract themselves from the trend discourse by opposing it. A lack of interest in talking about trends does not mean that trends have lost their relevance. People still desire to situate themselves in time, to relate to the world around them, to the evolution of fashion, to what it means to be a woman or man today or to whatever meaning is ascribed to the expressions of fashion—including an interest in the next new thing.

Women's relationship with fashion and trends is characterized by both subordination and freedom. The prevailing link between femininity, the body and fashion, coupled with the lingering notion of the importance of being "right," can, in this allegedly tolerant landscape, confuse and create uncertainty for some women. This disorientation might be part of the reason that a desire for trends persists. Women are expected to dress well regardless of whether they have great or negligible interest in fashion and regardless of whether they love to keep up to date or have no time for it. For many people, well-defined trends and clear advice can help, but advisors who adopt a lecturing tone are not highly regarded in the fashion field.

Unlike menswear, womenswear offers more variability and room for individual expression, a freedom that can strengthen individual agency. Female fashion consumers are viewed as more open to change and experimentation, according to my informants, than are men. More women are enamored by fashion as an expression of culture and more women take pleasure in learning about trends—the prepackaged form of fashion—as presented in the fashion media and in stores, without necessarily dressing exactly according to trend. The belief in a tolerant fashion scene could be interpreted as a result of female fashion consumers' becoming more equal, free and individualistic and thus less inclined than before to follow trends. Many women might relate only to what they see in stores, choosing from that. There is evidence to the contrary, however, and many informants claim that consumers do wish to be "right." Perhaps the industry, which packages trends, is driving this development because it has vested interests in providing news, organizing its production and product flow and, ultimately, selling more. As in cultural production in general, fashion actors are more likely to monitor how other producers and actors, in this case trend agencies, meet demand, than to consider the desires of consumers.[29]

6 DESIGNS, BRANDS AND TRENDS — TO LEAVE A MARK

In a glass cage reminiscent of those used in television game shows, I met with Margareta van den Bosch of H&M in Stockholm. Colorful samples from H&M's current Marni collaboration are mixed with Italian lamps and furniture. Van den Bosch has worked at H&M for twenty-five years, first as head of design and now as senior creative advisor, heading a part of the group's designer collaborations. I ask van den Bosch if she can think of anything that is out of style in today's fashion scene.

Though she has responded fairly quickly thus far, after a long and thoughtful pause, she says it is difficult to think of anything that is truly out of style: "On and off trend—I have never liked that kind of stuff. I think that people should be allowed to dress however they want. I don't like criticizing other people's style of dress and I think you should look the way you want to look."

Is this hesitation symptomatic of the current fashion scene? The fashion industry, based on change, should surely phase out certain styles, garments or silhouettes at the same time as it highlights new ones. Or is it that the individual style, in which nothing is in or out, really has taken root? Are there well-defined trends that should not be called trends? How do designers and, in turn, brands relate to trends?

In the first chapter, I presented the idea that trends can function as an organizing principle, and this has been confirmed by my informants. Buyers, manufacturers, designers and journalists gather around trends and agree on a general direction for the future. Without trends, there might be a complete mismatch between supply and demand. The chapter on tastemakers demonstrated that trends often function as news material for these actors, that trends exude an aura of economic capital because they are commercial endeavors and that people talk about fashion in a way that emphasizes personal style over dictatorial trends. The latter can be interpreted as partly due to neoliberalism's focus on the individual and partly due to the internet's opening up of the fashion field. As more people become interested in fashion, and as fashion ideas spread with increasing rapidity, the inner circle of fashion is less interested in what is or is not trendy.

In this chapter, we hear from designers who represent various fashion companies and who operate between the cultural and the economic logics. Unlike journalists and bloggers, these actors must boost fashion sales.

Trend-forecasting agencies often have confidentiality agreements with designers. The latter have an interest in downplaying the importance of those services, sometimes even denying that they use them. However, some information I gained through informal channels from other informants contradicts such denials. Whether or not it is true, it is clear that designers and fashion companies wish to present themselves as self-sufficient, independent of the need for such services.

Mass-market fashion brands

The 1990s and 2000s were characterized by the emergence of "fast fashion." With more efficient buying and distribution processes, mass-market fashion chains, such as the pioneering Spanish firm Zara, could get their clothes into their stores much more quickly than ever before. Fast-fashion chains broke with the seasonal model that had earlier dominated the industry, offering new goods every week. By transferring production to low-cost countries, primarily in Asia, where labor was often exploited, and taking advantage of favorable exchange rates, the mass-market fashion chains were able to price competitively. Both consumers and chains had unprecedented, timely access to fashion information and could keep themselves updated at all times.

In his famous essay on fashion, sociologist Georg Simmel argued that "the more an article becomes subject to rapid changes of fashion, the greater the demand for cheap products of its kind."[1] Elizabeth Cline, author of *Overdressed: The Shockingly High Cost of Cheap Fashion*, believed he was right: trends move so quickly that it is not worth "investing," for example, in high-quality shoes, as they will be hopelessly out of style next season.[2]

H&M

Why, then, is Margareta van den Bosch unable to think of anything that is out of style? When she became H&M's head of design in 1987, the department employed seven people; in 2012, more than 150 people worked in design. H&M now takes great pride in using its own designs. In the 1980s, however, van den Bosch says the process was altogether different:

> The few designers who worked here then—they threw together some patterns, some color charts and some trends, and travelled around the world and tried to find some trendy pieces… At that time we didn't have our own production offices, but instead worked with agents in the regions where we had production.

When she first started with H&M, the designers might have had a few old Promostyl trend books, but van den Bosch is behind much of the company's work with trend books and trend-forecasting agencies. Trend books, she says, used to be far more exacting: "They even talked about hem lengths in centimeters, whether sixty-two or sixty-seven centimeters was right. You would never do that today, that's not what's important." Drawing a specific jacket or making a pattern is something a designer should be able to do, says van den Bosch. She thinks that the trend-forecasting agencies have evolved in step with the times and that their services reflect their expanded target groups, which now include actors from fabric manufacturers to car manufacturers. Trend-forecasting agencies now primarily function as tools for coordination, providing inspiration to a certain extent. A large company such as H&M needs as much information as possible, and all personnel in its head office have access to WGSN.

H&M also uses the services of Promostyl, NellyRodi, Trend Union, the Future Laboratory and LSN Global, Scout, ESP Edit and others. Van den Bosch finds

Lidewij Edelkoort's presentations inspiring, especially Lidewij's unique taste. Van den Bosch has also been an active force in creating H&M's internal library, containing books about everything from art and photography to film and fashion. H&M's designers often take inspirational trips, visiting fairs such as Première Vision, Pitti Filati and Bread & Butter.

Catarina Midby is H&M's trend manager. Her background is in publishing—she has worked, for example, as fashion editor at *Swedish Elle*—and she is also responsible for the company's communications on sustainability issues. Trend work at H&M is carried out collectively. Midby works with H&M's head of design, a color map manager, a materials manager and designers from the divisions "Women," "Men," "Kids," "Cosmetics" and the youth line "Divided." One designer, previously a member of the trend group, is now based in Shanghai and works on trends from there. Midby considers trends absolutely vital to H&M's success and has no difficulty identifying what trends are in. This is easy, she thinks, because everyone has the same frame of reference and information is readily available: "It's more a question of which key pieces within these trends you absolutely can't miss." Successful trend identification involves gut feeling, sales history and customer response. H&M serves a varied clientele with concept segments such as "Trend," "&Denim," "Mama," "Divided," "L.O.G.G." and "H&M+." The trend is translated to fit each concept, so the key pieces for a trend look different across the segments. "We can't just say that everyone has to wear a poncho, for example, because it's likely that only our trend and youth customers are interested in that," Midby says; L.O.G.G.'s interpretation of the same trend might result in a cable-knit cardigan.

When Midby started with H&M in 2004, all departments identified their own trends. With her hiring, and the widespread availability of trend information on the internet, H&M saw a long-term advantage in thinking about trends company-wide, even though they had loosened and morphed into new expressions. Midby explains:

People started shopping more according to their personal taste and style than according to whatever trend was in. But they still wanted to be up to date. So we thought that we could compartmentalize these tendencies, which almost always exist. There is almost always something romantic, something tailored, something sporty and something ethnic. That sporty tendency often includes something slightly futurist as well.

The fashion scene came to be dominated by a more glamorous expression, which somewhat sidelined H&M's solid trend categories. The system of compartmentalizing has now been abandoned, but the strategy of seeking "common trends" remains to some extent. A wide product range ensures that

H&M can provide something for everyone. Today's flexible fashion world involves less risk, according to Midby:

> You can lean on your customers, and it's possible to have a completely different kind of communication with them today, thanks to technology and the flow of information. For someone who is responsive, I think it's far easier today.

Despite the importance of personal style, Midby, like Amanda Palmer, sees that many people do not have a style sense of their own. There is always room for inspiration and for information about how to dress, but the tone should not be lecturing. Midby says the most important thing is to teach people to build a wardrobe that is functional and sustainable, in which fashion essentials, that is, pieces considered necessary for a fashionable look, occupy a central place.

Midby frequently accesses WGSN. Though some of WGSN's offerings are superfluous, since H&M has its own designers who have H&M customers in mind, she appreciates WGSN's reports from exhibitions and catwalks. The analyses of key pieces, however, are "way too late for us, because at that point we definitely can't do anything new, even if we wanted to." H&M tried Stylesight for a while, Midby says, but concluded that the tool was not as useful and that there were technical problems: "They're just so terribly complicated, these sites, you don't have so much time to spend on them. You almost need to dedicate a week to get to know them. And to then learn a new version."

Midby is not interested in the larger issues of dominance or competition in the trend-forecasting services but considers the trend publications sufficiently interesting. Someone in her trend group looks through all the services' books on trends, materials and colors and summarizes their commonalities.

> After that, we look through it in the trend groups … we tease out these tendencies and look at them from different angles, and then we try to find pictures and words, so it becomes a kind of raw material. But then that needs to ferment for a while, so we leave it and return, add and subtract things. We meet every other week to do that. Then it's up to each division to translate what it means for their concept. But they need to follow the tendencies that we have decided on.

As an example of choosing a trend, one year a trend group member who had seen *American Gigolo* persuaded the group that this film had the "right look," and everything fell into place using that style reference. "So you look partly to your intuition, and partly to the facts, which we think these trend books provide."

H&M is careful to ensure that trends do not put too much pressure on production. The planning "evens out" the production process to make it more sustainable, but the production structure means no last-minute orders, for example, as Zara can accommodate, to exploit inspirations from current shows. The desire for trends must be balanced against sustainability requirements, which can in turn lead to "trend misses." Midby notes that H&M was slightly too early with vibrant colors in the spring of 2011; when H&M then launched its white trend, colors were more in vogue and Zara's stores were full of vibrant trend colors. Midby cites another miss in 2009, when H&M chose fake fur jackets as key pieces across all lines, and the trend only gained strength the following year. According to Midby, small mistakes always happen, but for H&M, the margin of error is 20 percent, not 100 percent.

Margareta van den Bosch observes that one aspect of having less-exacting and less-well-defined trends is that several trends can coexist side by side, so silhouettes change more slowly:

> I can say that wide trousers are in. But it takes some time before you see them on everyone. I think people like these skinny trousers quite a lot. And then some things are a bit too difficult to become a major trend. The jumpsuit is one example, or very tight, high waists. The kind of stuff you know a lot of people think is an effort to wear.

On the senior management floor at H&M's head office, where outsiders are not permitted, the top-ten boards are posted and updated each week with the ten best-selling H&M pieces. For a long time, about half the pieces were black, though color has been everywhere in the fashion world for a few years. Only in the spring of 2012 did both prints and color truly feature on the boards. Van den Bosch notes that it takes a long time for something to have a wide impact.

This time lag might be related to how marketing is handled. In her book *The End of Fashion*, journalist Teri Agins argued that marketing had killed fashion as we knew it.[3] The book was published in 2000 before the breakthroughs of the internet's fast fashion, blogs and Web-based trend-forecasting agencies. Some of Agins' explanations for this evolution may have lost their relevance or are specific to the United States (e.g., the shift toward casual dress in the 1980s, women's widespread entrance into the labor market and the consequent demand for business clothes). One of her suggestions warrants a closer look: that fashion was pulled off its pedestal when the sharp divisions between high and low fashion became blurred. *Mix-and-match*, for example, combining Gucci with H&M, became more accepted. In the United States, low-price giants such as Sears, Target and K-Mart started selling fashion under their own brand names. Consumers took the first steps on the road to becoming the bargain hunters that Elizabeth Cline wrote about a decade later in *Overdressed*.[4] The emergence of low-price chains on the serious fashion scene was also facilitated by the simplicity of fashion itself in the 1990s: minimalism, classics and simple chic were the rage and were easy to reproduce on a large scale.

Information technology and new production processes have ensured that the mass-market chains have retained their positions, even though the minimalist and classic "anti-fashion" that Gap, among others, represents now has competition from other styles. The desire to be more demand-driven remains among fashion brands. Where Agins described department stores as trend testers that acted quickly based on sales statistics and removed trends that did not sell, mass-market fashion companies are now flexible enough to sense quickly how well any trend resonates with shoppers and can increase the presence of certain trends while downplaying others. This explains why silhouettes change so slowly and why multiple trends live on side by side.

H&M's sales statistics go back to 1963. Van den Bosch notes that business controllers have a tendency to want to rely on statistics:

> But you can't repeat a success in that way … In my opinion, if you are going to lose money, you might as well do it using new ideas as old ones. Very often you repeat something because you're more "certain" of it, but that's not so certain either. Of course there's endless talk about this. Controllers, designers and CEOs are not equally bold.

While it is important to dare to try new things, this should not be done recklessly but "always with an eye to the customer—you always need to reinvent yourself" and not, van den Bosch suggests, fixate on numbers.

The area of the fashion field where H&M operates is undeniably commercial. To garner additional fashion appeal or fashion capital, since 2004 H&M has initiated collaborations with well-known designer brands, Karl Lagerfeld being the first. These collections are also a way of creating news. Van den Bosch reiterates the importance of always offering something new. Does the constant flow of news always represent true news, though?

> It's hard to say. I suppose that it's the mixture that's new. Most things have been done before. Clothes are things to wear and feel comfortable in—it might be easier to come up with a new lamp. People want to look good and don't like to wear really weird things. It's the combination of materials, silhouettes, colors and prints that bring about the feeling that something is new.

Van den Bosch talks about the increased importance of styling. From my Swedish perspective, H&M embraces all styles, so it is interesting to discover what trends H&M might reject. Van den Bosch lists things that are too expensive or a form of fashion that is too proper and boring, that is, "well-made without really showing it." In H&M's stores, it is vital to present clothes according to themes and "make something out of it." Difficult cuts, deconstructed pieces and the avant-garde are often rejected. H&M's nebulously defined customers look for the best price and quality and yet like being changeable, a bit trendy. Zara's somewhat "ladylike" clothes, she says, are more an expression of southern European style, and their offerings are higher priced. Yet H&M will not call itself a fast-fashion brand: the company rejects the "throw-away" mentality and has invested greatly in CSR (see p. 5) in recent years.

Roland Hjort, design director at the fashion brand Whyred, used to work at H&M, where he went to Promostyl seminars all the time. In his view, the trend-forecasting industry, in particular the internet-based trend services, will grow, since high-fashion brands are dependent on them:

> I know, of course, how big WGSN is at H&M. They use it—it's such an *enormously* important part of their work. But it's there that [the service] should be used, because it's like an H&M. WGSN could almost become a fashion company instead.

Topshop

In the corner room of a floor dominated by open-plan offices, their rows of desks topped with computer screens, Kate Phelan, creative director of the British mass-market fashion chain Topshop, talks about trends. After twenty-five years in the magazine world, including several years as fashion director of *British Vogue*, Phelan wanted to do something different. She had been working closely with Topshop, styling their ads, and brought to the chain a deep knowledge of trends honed through years of analysis. Phelan says that fashion magazines have a double role: to digest what the designers are doing but also to inspire the designers visually, by the way photos are shot or by the use of creative teams, enhancing the reciprocal exchange between designers and publications.

Like the creative leaders at H&M, Phelan is proud of her design department. She describes herself as amazed by the way Topshop broke the rules that everyone assumed applied to a high-street brand:

> I had always assumed that a high-street fashion store would be very reactive to what designers do on the catwalk. But when I got here I realized that they had a very unique, a very parallel way of working to the way that designers work.

The Topshop team of nearly thirty designers works independently of the catwalk, and timing is essential. The designers at Topshop are stimulated by new ideas. While they assess the previous season's collections to find something to take forward into another season, says Phelan, that is not the driving force:

What is so fascinating is that they are taking their inspiration from research trips here and there, from festivals in Texas, shopping trips to Japan, and they come back with amazing pictures of people wearing great clothes. And they then put together these wonderful books of ideas of what people are wearing... Our customers want ideas. They come to Topshop to fall in love with fashion, to develop their style.

The appetite for fashion has changed. We used to work with these very strict seasons—the spring/summer, autumn/winter—and then there was *couture* two times a year. Now designers have to do pre-collections, Christmas collections— the demand from the customers is constant, they want new things all the time... We deliver three hundred new pieces into our stores every week. In the designer market, they now too are feeling that pressure. Their customer wants new things. The advances in e-commerce and the fact that you can have access to these designer clothes on any level, anywhere and by any means, has increased the pace. So the luxury brands are in some ways using the high-street models to service their customer.

In a fashion landscape with many parallel trends, Phelan thinks that customers are less obsessed about trends:

I think they have become more focused on look, style and their choices, rather than being dictated to, which in a way was the case twenty years ago. I think now, as a customer, you have the freedom of choice, which is very empowering. And I think retailers on all levels feel the need to give their customers as much direction as possible. Give them... a relationship with the brand... What we have offered in terms of personal shopping has been incredibly successful, to help people work out what they want to look like, to help people make choices.

At *British Vogue*, Phelan and her colleagues used to laugh at the pashmina scarf, how one minute it was über cool, and the next minute it was over:

It was being sold on aeroplanes and so on. And it's funny because we were saying that it is probably one of the most brilliant things that was ever invented. The fact that you can have this lovely scarf in any color, and it went with anything you wore. And we sort of wanted to throw up because it had become such a mass-market thing.

There is, Phelan thinks, a danger in moving things out too quickly. Asked to name something out of fashion, she answers: "I don't know if I'm right or wrong, but I would say 'no more florals for a while.'" She finds it odd that some people have trouble admitting that something is out but observes that her sense of what is in and out does not always correspond to sales. In a store walkabout, she said, "Oh, no. If I see another tatty torn-off denim short … let's just not do them any more." A staff member showed her the impressive sales figures, and, she said, "I take back what I said." The magazine world is dedicated to bringing in the new, but Phelan knows that it takes time for some trends to be accepted by customers:

> Sometimes, if we put things in too soon, and they don't sell, then others at Topshop say "It didn't sell so we're not going to do it", which makes me really cross. Give it another month and *everybody* is going to want it.

Topshop, Phelan says, is excellent at setting trends for its particular customers, in that the company creates most of its own patterns and designs at the head office on Oxford Street, though others are working with suppliers. Topshop fashion affects how girls dress and look, influencing street style. She does not think most other brands are directly imitating Topshop's designs, with the exception of a few high-street brands:

> You go down into the store in Oxford Circus and you can see people buying an armful of clothes, and you know they are not [going to wear them]. They are buying them to show somebody. That's just the nature of the beast.

Topshop does not use trend services, and this surprised Phelan when she started with the company. She regards it as a sign of the brand's confidence that it can do without such services: "There are enough people with a good eye and skills, people who can interpret the language of fashion very easily." All the real-time information on the internet has made forecasting slightly redundant, and Phelan thinks that the trend services can be quite disabling, pedestrian and obvious.

Not unexpectedly, Phelan and her colleagues love magazines and often use pictures from them when putting together inspiration boards. One example is a large sheet of cardboard one and a half meters high, and about a meter wide, covered with pictures illustrating spring and summer trends that Phelan claims go back to the raves of the 1980s. These boards capture a mood, a casual feeling, in which neon is mixed into the knits without making it "about neon." To Phelan, Topshop's creative process feels innovative in terms of trends, the focus being on the chain's core customer, the girl who goes to summer festivals and on European holidays: "It's all about feeding her needs as opposed to thinking of ourselves with a very serious global image."

As of December 2012, the time of the interview, Topshop was significantly smaller than H&M, having 440 stores compared with H&M's 2,629; as of 2014, Topshop had 500 and H&M 3,300 stores. Phelan feels that H&M offers "a very easy version of everything, a no-brainer"—even if on trend, its clothes are "never going to stop the traffic." It is sometimes difficult to compete with H&M's prices, though, she admits. Phelan and Topshop do not resist the "fast fashion" label: "[Topshop] is fast fashion, but it is absolutely stuffed with ideas. I love that it's like playing styling."

*

H&M and Topshop are eager to appear in fashion magazines but also appreciate the simpler tone of blogs, viewing them as conveying the average person's interpretation of fashion and trends. The popularity of blogs can be understood in light of the increased importance of styling, that is, hands-on tips on successfully combining pieces of clothing. Is it the emergence of blogs in the fashion field that has unmoored the power of tastemakers and designers, eliminating the instructive tone that prevailed earlier? Or did the idea of individual choice come first, with the blogs following? Has the lecturing tone disappeared because the mass-market fashion chains offer a product range more driven by demand? The fact that Margareta van den Bosch cannot point to something that is out of style can be interpreted in light of how demand-driven fashion has meant that all styles coexist, although some are less visible.

Designers with more symbolic capital, and possibly with a history as tastemakers (see Chapter 4), such as Kate Phelan, who are used to determining "the right new," may have a greater interest in distancing themselves from the idea that anything goes.

Although they are located in the most commercial part of that field, companies such as H&M and Topshop are still subject to the force of the double logics, where fashion capital is the currency of the realm. Producing—and emphasizing—their own designs while downplaying the role of trend-forecasting agencies can of course be understood in terms of the cultural logic of the fashion world. Kate Phelan's remarks about the ubiquitous pashmina shawl indicate an awareness of the status mechanisms of the fashion field. The battle between H&M and Topshop over which company is the most directional, or trendiest, is typical of a field of cultural production: in the fashion field, actors compete for fashion capital. This contest involves not just the companies themselves (e.g., Phelan's characterization of H&M as selling "no-brainer" clothes) but also tastemakers such as Daniel Linderoth who conversely describe H&M as "trailblazing." All actors draw symbolic boundaries[5] between different brands and designers, and the relationships are never completely stable. Positioning at the top of the hierarchy is constantly negotiated. Individuals as well as companies differently define what is, for example, fast fashion.

Copying another's designs is considered low status. While many European mass-market fashion companies invest in their own design departments, many American chains still do as H&M did in the 1980s. The fast-fashion chain Forever 21 does not have its own design department but relies on manufacturers and agents. Like many other fast-fashion companies, Forever 21 is often accused of plagiarism. Several informants commented about Zara "being close to the catwalk"; Elizabeth Cline writes that even though Zara has made versions of others' styles—Céline, Prada, even Jil Sander and Stella McCartney—the chain has not been sued for copyright infringement, at least not in the 2003–2008 period.[6] Some designers encourage copying. Tom Ford, for example, has said that there is hardly anything that makes him happier than seeing copies of his own designs, since designer fashion customers and mass-market fashion customers are different anyway. Guy Trebay, fashion critic for the *New York Times*, has said that fashion would disappear if the fashion industry possessed the copyrights that protect books and movies.

Consistency and change

Mass-market fashion companies operate in a part of the fashion field where a broad range of styles is offered. It could be said that some of these companies embrace most expressions under one brand name or a few different brand names.

A brand can be understood as a method of managing uncertainty, an alternative to trends. Brand names offer a force of attraction that fashion companies can rely on. A brand comprises the stories that various actors—for example, companies, media and customers—tell in relation to the brand. Several different stories may coexist, but the brand emerges when a collective meaning has been established. The companies behind a brand try to control people's perception of the brand, using branding models, often borrowed from psychology, that are of three main types.

1 *Mind-share branding*, where a brand's DNA or essence can be summarized in several "core values" (e.g., Dove Soap is infused with moisturizer and replenishes the skin).

2 *Emotional branding*, based on the idea of core values but focused on how to communicate the brand to create emotional bonds with customers (e.g., Coca-Cola is the proponent of *happiness* while Pepsi champions *joy*).

3 *Viral branding*, based on values the customers themselves create; the task of the marketers is to place the product in the right hands so that these customers do not just adopt the product but also promote its worth as defined in terms of core values and emotions.[7]

These brand models all require that the message be hammered home to consumers in one way or another.[8] The models also emphasize the importance of presenting a consistent message. Although the models have been criticized,[9] many fashion companies likely market using them.

Since fashion has change at its heart, fashion companies cannot completely disregard the forward movement that constitutes trends, resulting in a balancing act between the brand and neomania, that is, what I refer to as the tension between consistency and change. It can be assumed that this tension affects how individual companies translate, ignore or disseminate trends.

For mass-market fashion companies, the brand is usually not very limiting. H&M's limits, for example, on what fits its brand are extremely generous. Kate Phelan of Topshop thinks it is good to be able to focus on the product rather than the image, noting that luxury brands sometimes create so rigid an image that they become trapped:

> It's as if there's no room for them to be different or offer anything different, so in some ways their world becomes smaller and smaller. Whereas we, on the other hand, can go on and on and on—it's like an endless offering.

Phelan is another informant who thinks that the fashion scene has become more tolerant, possibly due to the growth of the fashion industry. Thirty years ago, it was a very small community and only a select few were invited to view a designer's work: "There was a kind of veil over the industry, which really protected it, creating an inaccessible aesthetic around it."

Kate Phelan sees the 1990s' emergence of strong brands, especially in the United States, as a result of the fashion industry's past insularity. Ralph Lauren, Tommy Hilfiger and Calvin Klein, among others, grew into big brands and developed products that appealed to a much wider consumer base than previously. Teri Agins argues in *The End of Fashion* that these brands were usually run by designers with no portfolio and no education in design—they had hardly designed.[10] Agins claims that these brands attracted millions of customers by being untrendy and by creating a form of antifashion. These brands did not speculate in fashion, becoming instead risk-minimizing lifestyle business groups that circumvented the industry's tastemakers and trends via their own marketing campaigns. Similarly, Gap's success came from offering "classics" without any important updates, its advertising campaign being branded "Individuals of Style." For Gap, fashion was presented as about the individual, not clothes. Gap mostly ignored the movements of fashion, its biggest change being a new color scheme every six months. Gap's pieces did not go out of style, and the company turned a profit year after year in the 1990s. With the increased importance of such brands, there was a new focus on the "red carpet" as opposed to the catwalk in marketing efforts.

Although the success of the mass-market fashion companies during the first decade of this century came from their adherence to neomania, the idea of more consistent, and sometimes marketing-driven, brand names lives on in the fashion industry.

Brands in the mid-range segment

As we leave the mass-market fashion brands and move upward in the fashion field, the creator becomes increasingly important. The mid-range segment is often viewed as a difficult range for fashion companies, as they are caught between the luster of the luxury brands and the lure of mass-market fashion bargains.

Whistles

Jane Shepherdson has been the CEO of Whistles since 2008. She, and some colleagues from the management of Topshop, where she had worked as brand manager for ten years, bought Whistles. At the time, Whistles' clothing was awash with frills, bows and extra buttons. "It wasn't an aesthetic that we understood," Shepherdson has admitted.[11] Whistles was founded in the 1980s by Lucille Lewin and soon became known for its tailoring and prints. The first store in Marylebone, London, offered an interesting mix of brands: In addition to its own line of clothing, Whistles carried the designs of Dries van Noten (who was encouraged by Lewin to design womenswear) and Martin Margiela. Shepherdson and her colleagues wanted to recreate excitement and aspiration at Whistles. The brand is positioned above high-street but below designer fashion, at a level that harbors many brands profiling themselves with classic or niche products. In its reinvented version, Whistles would still be fashionable and still follow trends. "A completely relevant contemporary fashion brand, effortlessly stylish, cool, laidback, subtle. Slightly minimalist, but not completely. Maybe you could call it a 'Topshop for grownups," Shepherdson explains. Whistles has achieved great success and by 2012 had eighty stores and was planning to open another twenty. Currently, it is the best-selling brand on the e-commerce site ASOS. Whistles' main market is the UK, but there are plans to expand into other parts of Europe, Australia and the United States.

> Your success depends on how clever you are at interpreting the trends for your specific market. You don't necessarily have to care about the micro trends—it's usually the macro trends that are more essential. The change in the silhouette over time, the change in a color palette. A move into print and away from a more plain color palette, the move from minimalism to maximalism—those changes are the most important.

On the macro level, Shepherdson says, almost all designers on the catwalk have worked with a certain theme, perhaps military. Nobody would ever say that these designers are copying one another; they just happen to be exposed to the same influences. Designers must interpret these influences and make them their own. Whistles fashion is not overly pretty, Shepherdson says, but lace was very successful in the previous season, in the simple clean shapes typical of Whistles. Printed trousers have also done well:

> They are quite cool and easy, but if you are paying a hundred pounds, you don't want to chuck it away at the end of the season, like you would do with something from a cheap high-street store, so it has to be something that can last for a few seasons.

Whistles makes sure its own prints acknowledge the overriding print trends but in its own way. For example, Whistles' British competitor Reiss, while roughly in the same segment, is slightly blingy and more glamorous, and its trend interpretations will always be completely different and less subtle.

> Some of the more mainstream brands find it difficult to interpret a trend, they get it all wrong. One major UK fashion retailer had taken what was effectively a graphic Peter Pilotto-style print, and they had put it on a draped jersey dress. It did not work! It was a total misunderstanding of everything about that trend—of Peter Pilotto's prints, of structure and form, of technology, of digitalizing, and of the future. And here is an old frumpy dress ... it's just so wrong. That's an example of how you shouldn't work.

Whistles subscribes to publications from the trend forecaster Peclers Paris, primarily because the design director loves the books:

> [The trend book] is gorgeous. It's very well done. I guess you use something that you like, that you feel mirrors your own thoughts a bit ... They give you an opinion, and an aesthetic, and if you like it, then you use it or use it in a way that works. It's different from someone like WGSN, who makes sketches and says "these are the five trousers you want to do". It's just so horribly homogenous, isn't it?

Shepherdson liked WGSN at the start: "We used WGSN at Topshop, but now it seems to me as if WGSN has just become a tool to help Chinese manufacturers knock off designs. I think [the service] has lost its edge." On a recent visit to China, she heard a lot about WGSN's development there. She believes that WGSN has become more "commercial" since Marc Worth sold it and that it has lost its significance. Finances play into this: as a small company, Whistles cannot waste money and trend services are "phenomenally expensive." Shepherdson believes that many big organizations use WGSN or Stylesight simply because everyone else does; large firms do not have the same freedom to say "no" as do smaller firms. She also thinks the trend services are here to stay, since there will always be emerging markets in need of information:

> Then there are places like Première Vision. Everyone goes there, everyone looks there, that's where it starts. We were talking about [that fair] recently, actually, because we are going to make a little presentation at fashion week in February, and you need to get the samples here in time. One of our designers then said, "That means that you are asking me to do them before Première Vision? You know I find it really hard to do that before I've seen the fabrics. Seeing the fabrics helps me crystallize my thoughts better."

Does Shepherdson think today's fashion scene is more tolerant than before? "In a way, everything is acceptable today, but there will always be things that suddenly make people say 'I want that!'" Shepherdson thinks customers are becoming more impatient, seeing something and immediately wanting it. At Whistles it takes six months for an item to go from catwalk to store, a lag that will need to be shortened at some point. She easily identifies what's out of fashion at the time of the interview:

> Very short shorts and knee-length skirts are ok, but short skirts are not particularly in fashion at the moment. You can still wear a short skirt and you wouldn't look ridiculous, but they're not really *the big thing*. But if you looked at the catwalk five years ago, designers like Versace and Cavalli had thigh-high skinny skirts. Now they're all knee length.

According to Shepherdson, this change can be traced to the age of most Whistles customers, who are in their forties. They think, "Everyone else can wear whatever they want, but I know that *this* is the right thing, this is what I'm going to wear." The difficult times are when nothing obvious, commercial and wearable is coming through, so a lot of people go back to wearing classics. There are some seasons when "it's all about the white shirt." There are always new things, she says later. Retro is always remixed retro, with different materials or silhouettes. Something has been added to make it interesting. Color and print provide more variation: the item can be produced in different colors over the seasons, giving customers more possibilities to interpret pieces of clothing in their own ways.

Shepherdson delights in the fact that the British fashion scene is experimental. The English are a bit eccentric, very creative, and not particularly commercial in their outlook. A designer can almost do anything, and the English will try it.

Shepherdson thinks the tension between continuity and change is the most exciting part of running a fashion business:

> To maintain a consistency that is always contemporary and that is always new in a way, by making constant, very slight changes that people don't even

notice, but within which your core values are still maintained. If you don't keep changing it slightly, you'll just end up being a yesterday's brand. And the best person at this is Karl Lagerfeld. Not for his Karl collections, but for what he does at Chanel. Every year he creates something that is absolutely contemporary, and yet absolutely within the guideline of the brand.

"[Miuccia Prada] is fantastic, incredibly clever, amazing, every season totally different, totally contemporary, exciting, and yet, absolutely Prada." In contrast, Shepherdson believes that Chloé was too dependent on its former creative director. When Phoebe Philo held the position, everybody knew what Chloé stood for; is there anyone who now knows what Chloé is all about?

Shepherdson sees no signs that the relationship between the celebrity world and the fashion industry is weakening. For Whistles, fashion magazines such as *Vogue*, *Elle*, *Harper's Bazaar* and *Grazia UK* and blogs such as *Style Bubble* are very important. Whistles does not pay celebrities to wear Whistles' designs: it would affect the integrity of the brand, says Shepherdson, and the company cannot afford it. Whistles, however, can ask someone like Olivia Palermo to pop in when she is in town to find something she wants and circulate the photographs widely: "Of course we do that, we would be stupid not to. We pick people we think represent the brand." When Andy Murray beat Roger Federer in the Wimbledon final 2012, Murray's girlfriend was wearing a Whistles dress, which then got enormous media coverage.

The mutual dependency among the organizations in the fashion field becomes obvious in the discussion of media exposure and favorable associations with celebrities. At the same time, the hierarchies of the fashion field are always present. *Buying* celebrity exposure is out of the question; climbing the ladder of fashion based on one's own merits is imperative—it is how fashion capital is preserved.

When describing the importance of translating trends, of interpreting them on behalf of one's brand, Shepherdson echoes the words of the trend forecasters, agreeing with them that the key to a successful translation is an excellent understanding of one's brand. She also emphasizes knowledge of the origins of trends, criticizing some fashion retailers' inability to interpret trends, which she suggests indicates their ignorance, what one could refer to as their lack of fashion capital.

The role of trends as an organizing principle is tacitly understood by Shepherdson. She understands that big companies cannot let go of trend services because "everyone else has them" and that Whistles goes to Première Vision because everyone goes there; it is the place where "it starts."

Filippa K

At Filippa K's head offices in Stockholm, in yet another white-painted conference room with shoes and accessories on display along the walls, Nina Bogstedt, the company's collection manager, describes how she came to the brand. She had just graduated from design school in Copenhagen when she met an acquaintance who suggested applying to Filippa K, because "you and Filippa have similar values." This turned out to be true. Bogstedt is responsible for all the products in the men's and women's collections and heads the design and construction team, ensuring everything comes together in a unified whole. Outside of Sweden, Filippa K's biggest markets are Norway, Denmark, Germany, Belgium and the Netherlands.

It is early summer 2012 and the design department is busy creating the spring 2013 collection for an internal presentation. Such long-term planning means that the design team avoids delving too deep into any particular trend, says Bogstedt, as it could be outdated by the time the collection is launched:

> We don't see ourselves as a trendy brand name, but we represent a certain style that's pretty ageless, viable in the sense that you can combine the products in a lot of different ways and find your personal style. We try to find something that's sustainable over time. A trend is often something that's extremely popular during a short period, after which it might more or less disappear. But then there are some trends that last longer.

For Bogstedt, fashion comes from styling, rather than trendy products. A pink mohair sweater with red pants constitutes a rather specific look, but the same pieces can be toned down when combined differently. The task of the design department is to know what is going on and to strain their impressions through a "Filippa K filter." Whatever is too sexy or too difficult to wear is rejected. Design should not, Bogstedt remarks, make a person feel as though she is out walking her dress.

Filippa K's style remains the same, while its collections vary in terms of colors, prints and silhouettes. The risk of having a brand associated with a particular style is that this style can be more or less on trend during different periods. When minimalism was trendy at the end of the 2000s, journalists were interested in Filippa K, since the brand has been doing minimalism since 1992. About 30 percent of the collections consist of solid products that transcend the seasons, and the rest are specific to the season, Bogstedt explains. "If you have a great jacket, it will look great for another year, so why fiddle with it?" Filippa K knows that many customers return for the staples or to find "the perfect top." The customers are quick to comment if a favorite piece is discontinued: "You're going to continue making these pants, right?" In this sense, the customers sometimes have an inhibiting effect on brand evolution.

Filippa K's design team often looks "at themselves" when creating the next collection, Bogstedt explains:

> "Don't we want trousers that are slightly wider this year?" "Yeah, we do." And so we make trousers that are a bit wider. It's not more scientific than that. And that can make it a bit pompous to sit there and talk about the "wide trousers trend" just because we've made a pair of them. It's more like "We've made wide trousers."

Bogstedt agrees with other informants that the fashion landscape is now more tolerant:

> There are not many things where you'd say "but that's something I'd never…" It's more like you catch up with yourself all the time, it's like some kind of circle, and in that craziness you can also feel a great need to step to the side and take a look, okay, what do I feel like? … Because this thing with chasing a trend, also as a consumer, this uncertainty—am I on trend or not—it's a bit tiresome.

Bogstedt is uninterested in dictating what colors and clothes people should wear. Consumers are independent because of the abundant brand and fashion information available today.

At the same time, uncertainty remains. Bogstedt understands that the *possibility* of being off trend, or of wearing the wrong clothes, can be stressful. Even though the best strategy is to find what one likes and to continue wearing that, she realizes that not everyone has reflected on what they like. Many people have no idea what pleases them. It is for those customers that Filippa K can be a style underwriter: "If you buy our products, you'll never be in the wrong." This is comforting to many customers. Filippa K's position in the fashion field allows it to be a style underwriter. However, Bogstedt stresses that Filippa K is not trying to give its brand an aura that cannot be realized in the products.

Filippa K uses no trend service, either in book form or on the internet, partly for budgetary reasons and also because the design department has the competence to read trends without such aids. Occasionally Filippa K's designers examine Lidewij Edelkoort's smorgasbord of trends; Bogstedt finds Edelkoort's presentations less "anxious" than others: "There, the white, the black, the green, and the red trend get to coexist." Filippa K's collections are a team effort. Like many others, the design team goes on inspirational trips, some to art galleries and others checking out vintage boutiques.

> Trends don't always have to be negative. But today it's almost always used in the sense of something impermanent. Use it and lose it. Something uncertain. You just "pick a trend". But trend can also mean evolution. So it's probably more a question of speed in this case. And I think that our customers appreciate that things don't happen this fast.

Filippa K offers new items to inspire and surprise and create a feeling of "must have" in the customer. Bogstedt describes the excitement engendered by the new:

> You know, you can get that feeling when that sample comes in. "Oh my God, this is amazing!" Everyone wants it, everyone goes to look at it … Because it also makes you happy to find something new. It doesn't work to always have

the same thing all the time. We talk a lot about the balance between classics and fashion, and between renewal and continuity.

Neomania, the constant chase for the new, is also reflected in fashion journalists' search for new brands and new designers rather than new trends. Bogstedt describes an imaginary interest curve, where a small new actor might get a lot of attention because he or she represents something new that everyone thinks incredibly exciting. It is not certain that this interest will translate into customers, but careful nurturing of such media interest can build a brand name, says Nina. Many designers cannot create anything substantial, anything with continuity, before the fleeting interest dies.

In the mid-range segment, and especially among niche brands, designers commonly claim that they are creating the kind of fashion that they themselves like.[12] Many Swedish brands have claimed this over the years. Acne, for example, takes pride in making clothes "from the inside out," "clothes we ourselves want to wear."[13] The logic of "from the inside out" expresses a cultural logic in which a supply-driven relationship with the market is considered better[14] than an "outside–in" perspective that makes clothes that are in demand. The expression "from the inside out" indicates Acne's way of safeguarding its artistic integrity and fashion know-how and as an assurance that Acne does not allow the market to control its fashions.

Filippa K, according to Bogstedt, distances itself from trends—"we don't think of ourselves as a trend brand name"—which is another sign that trends in and of themselves are associated with economic capital, mass-market fashion and "uncertainty." It also means that Filippa K has chosen to emphasize brand consistency over keeping up with the neomania that trends exemplify. While Teri Agins in *The End of Fashion* described how US brand names created lifestyle empires around themselves in the 1990s,[15] Bogstedt is careful to point out that Filippa K is not trying to create some sort of aura around itself: all its promises are fulfilled in its products. While Whistles stresses the importance of translating trends, that is, neomania, Filippa K emphasizes consistency within its own brand, presenting a certain type of personal style.

Exter

The Swedish firm Exter,[16] half of whose market is overseas, in Northern Europe, the United States, and Japan, in that order, makes fashion with a Scandinavian heritage. Cecilia Björk, head of design for the women's collection, describes Exter's clothes as pieces one can easily move about in, pieces that have a function. Exter has a high artistic aim: "We work with creating our own fashion," Björk says, "our own style, and our own trends":

We create trends. We are at the core of what others use in their work later. What the department stores buy and what the trend agencies later use to create their material. As a designer, you're the first to sense what's in. And then, of course, there are those who are better or worse at it. And you can also position yourself closer to the front or further back, depending on your vision. And for Exter, our vision and ambition is to create our own trends, and to tie these closely to our core values. So we have a kind of a style epicentre that we circle around, and through which we interpret our surroundings... Fashion doesn't mean anything to me unless I locate it in a contemporary context and interpret my surroundings through it.

My ability to see what's next, it came really early. I tried different things. I lived in a small town, but I took stock of what I had, and then I started experimenting. What happens if I change this seam? What happens if I put this on? What kinds of reactions will I get? So for me, fashion was very much from the inside out, and it still is. Our work with Exter comes from the inside—what's the feeling of these pieces—and out—what do I want to say. Everything starts with us.

Björk says that the desire to create a new collection for the next season is inexhaustible: "It feels like it just gets better and better. It's a time of the year when you feel that you're the queen of yourself, that it's so darn good." She dislikes the fashion industry's hankering for news and would prefer things to be longer lived. On the other hand, trends are important for Exter's customers because clothes are a simple method of self-renewal, offering a chance to "change your skin" to try something new even if an individual has already found their style or brand. Trends therefore serve as important guidelines.

Trends used to be more rigorously defined, Björk notes, and the current multitude of parallel trend messages makes it more difficult for customers to orient themselves: "This whole personal thing, which is in the air right now, is quite difficult for customers." Like many other informants, Björk confirms the increased demand for styling tips, noting that customers are very open to being told what works.

Björk's concentration on how Exter "creates trends" indicates an ambition to move up in the hierarchy of the fashion field. Fashion capital can be attained and consolidated by letting the artistic flag fly high, stressing that things are done "from the inside out." Employees who join Exter from other fashion companies appreciate how much Exter cares about artistry: "We like craftsmanship and that you are able to see the hand that's made the product. Even if the stitches are machine-sewn, we like details that are derived from craftsmanship." Björk does not feel the need to use a trend service: "I could sell them material. If I wasn't doing this I could have a trend-analysis company and sell lots of trend reports for a pretty penny."

Exter is often too early with trends, Björk says. This is problematic: as a small company, it has difficulties holding products for a long time and requires good product turnover. Though Exter makes constant assessments about where to "position" the brand, mistakes happen, as with the change from jeans to pants, for which Exter was out of step. Björk finds it difficult to know how people perceive the brand's offerings.

> The process is so long. When we have experienced a piece for four years, the customer might have seen it for one year. It's hard to know. At the same time, it's a question of finding a balance in terms of PR and press, which pushes the desire for news. To deal with this within the framework of one's style ... It's easy to be drawn into this thing where everything has to be new. And I also like other niches very much, where a product has a long life cycle.

Here we see defined the balance between change and stability, neomania and brand. While Björk herself advocates a subtle, low-key style with a longer life cycle, she thinks that the focus on trends will persist because key industry elements—the designers, collections, shows and media—want it that way.

Björk directly challenges the work of trend agencies by stating that designers are still the source. To *create* trends is important for her as a designer and for her brand, and it is less important to *follow* trends. The preference is instead "from the inside out." Like other designers in the mid-range segment, she emphasizes that trend-forecasting agencies' primary role is in mass-market fashion.

Antipodium

Antipodium started out as a combined wholesaler, PR agency and retail store for Australian brands in the UK. Creative Director Geoffrey Finch and a colleague identified a gap in the market that they believed Antipodium could exploit, providing a fairly priced brand with a design edge, originality paired with staples. Finch describes Antipodium—which has abandoned its wholesale business to focus on its own-designed clothes—as a "contemporary fashion brand for creative minds, where its confident simplicity and capricious nature are unapologetically addictive." Antipodium clothes are sold in prestigious stores such as Barneys New York, Liberty in London and Opening Ceremony in Tokyo and through e-commerce sites such as ASOS and Shopbop. Antipodium has no bricks-and-mortar stores of its own but sells through its Web site.

Antipodium is well aware of trends but not driven by them:

> Ideas are in the air and we'll often be on a trend before we realize that it is a trend, or realize how big the trend is going to be. I think we are probably

most aware of trends to make sure that we are off a trend at the right time. For example, we've been doing peplums, which are massive now, for a couple of years. In our resort collection last year we had this peplum t-shirt with a georgette back which just kept selling out. And we do repeats and it keeps on selling out. It's tempting to keep on going with things like that.

Antipodium does not use trend services, because it is a niche brand focused on being "very much us" in everything it does: "I guess 'what's us' is probably 'what's me' and what I see and where I am. So that's our trend service," Finch laughs. He spends a lot of time in East London, which he loves, especially the busy area around Bethnal Green, where many designers' studios, like Antipodium's, are located. The busy street life often catches his attention. He observes:

> I'm very interested in meta-modernist theory. In an increasingly standardized world, the search for irregularities becomes more attractive. And I think there is a lot of blandness. I hope that is to the benefit of little businesses like ours. Our ability to deliver personality, that's our biggest asset.

In the designer fashion segment, Finch thinks a designer needs to be picky and willing to gamble on where trends are going, since lead times are so long. Over time, the designer develops an instinct for trends. Like many other designers I talked to, Finch thinks that major trends have almost disappeared, being replaced with micro trends, a result of the speed of change and the development of street style:

> If there was more of a trend thing going on, you would probably have bigger waves to ride for longer and thus you could make more money out of it. Looking at it now it is very difficult to repeat things, even from a very commercial angle. I'm not saying that we reinvent the wheel, but we spend a lot of money on developing things to have that refined element of newness that our customer likes.

"New" mainly entails combining influences at the right time and presenting them in a new *way*, according to Finch:

> Everyone has just hailed Raf Simons' Dior collection. It was really lovely and grand, it was an important moment. What made it new though was the combination of elements, the dig through the archives and Raf's slant.

Finch believes that the recession has made customers smarter: they expect more value and take advantage of the greater choice. Finch accordingly thinks carefully about what each piece is doing in the collection: "If we add a bit of contrast color on there, how does that affect the pullover's wearability and desirability, and what [else] is available in the market at that price?" While the mystery surrounding brands has diminished, the direct customer–designer relationship, facilitated by social media, has great potential. "The consumer is a great teacher," he notes. Finch visits Liberty of London, asking customers what they do or do not like about particular items. He imagines developing relationships with customers through events and other get-togethers, "but not in a 'we're going to sell you something' way." Quality retailers have, according to Finch, become extremely influential. Antipodium incorporates feedback from Barneys, the fashionable department store chain that was interested in Finch's collections three seasons before it actually bought; visits to New York also help Finch get a better feel for what works. He thinks neomania and brand consistency can be married by careful merchandize planning about where to take risks and where to earn generous margins. Some people complain about being located in the middle segment of the fashion market, but Finch says that being positioned at the entry level of the luxury end is very strategic. Antipodium does very well with its higher-priced items, as long, Finch notes, as it offers value in everything it sells.

Finch finds talk about the "democratization of fashion" slightly problematic when it concerns the big high-street brands' claim to be spreading fashion to the people:

I get entirely red now, but if you get a dress there for eight pounds—Have you ever sat down to make a dress? How are you going to make a dress for eight pounds? How are you ever going to get the fabric, cut the fabric, cut the threads, get the machine, have the electricity, sew, ship it and mark it up? There is something dreadfully, dreadfully wrong about that. So democracy, yes to a certain level.

Finch notes that several high-street brands have copied Antipodium items. Just after he started designing, he discovered that a very big designer brand had copied one of Antipodium's shirt dresses, with a distinctive pleated sleeve and a curved yoke at the back. "It was *that* dress. There was no denying it. But I thought: That's a compliment! That's nice, maybe I'm not such an idiot after all." This echoes a common theme, that designers are not usually concerned about being copied, though Finch admits he would be extremely annoyed if one of Antipodium's prints were produced by a competitor *before* Antipodium's own collection was presented.

Antipodium started using fur in the fall/winter 2011 collection as it was becoming trendy. In the UK, where many department stores have anti-fur policies, not a single item sold, but the items were far more popular in Russia and the United States. Antipodium has a number of retailers in Hong Kong and

China, and many of the brand's customers in London and New York are travelers from abroad. He also knows that certain palettes and cuts do not work as well on all markets.

Geoffrey Finch does not speak in terms of "inside out." He does not shy away from customer opinions and is open to designing based on customer feedback. Antipodium is sold by prestige retailers, boutiques and department stores that he uses for spontaneous market surveys. It may be precisely because the brand is offered by retailers rich in fashion capital that Antipodium can afford to be so customer-oriented without losing its own fashion capital.

Rodebjer

Swedish designer Carin Rodebjer's brand was launched in New York, where it is sold in a small number of select boutiques. Rodebjer is determined to retain control over sales to ensure the collection is shown to its full advantage. Sweden still constitutes the brand's biggest market though.

Rodebjer thinks of trends as manifesting evolution: the forward movement makes fashion fun, allowing the designer to comment on the era. She envisions the Rodebjer brand as a hub or platform from which a woman can move freely in any direction—the country or the city—and be both authoritative and sexy.

Rodebjer is also aware that trends can be restrictive and dictatorial: "Pointing out what's right and wrong isn't very fun. It's the opposite of that." Rodebjer long felt that fashion had marginalized her and she still opposes the fashion industry's desire to categorize people, the proliferation of ever-faster trends and increasing "chatter" about fashion.

There are signs that consumers are reacting against this high speed and that some production is returning to Europe from China, manifesting a yearning to return to craft. Rodebjer sees two parallel movements: one toward global fashion and the other toward something more local. China has become a natural market for fashion brands, since its population is so big and the West wants to profit from this. In response to a question about whether fashion companies will be influenced by Chinese culture, Rodebjer says that the constant lack of time in the fashion world would make it hard for a designer to immerse herself in a new culture and be influenced by it. Stepping into Chinese tradition requires knowledge and craftsmanship, otherwise one remains a spectator. The fashion world is selective, some things bestowing higher status than others. Some references are "highbrow" and some are "lowbrow." Rodebjer feels that the fashion world is constantly pawing at the same white, Western references, citing Warhol's The Factory as an example.

Using the "right" references is a time-honored way of advancing in a cultural field, as sociologist Pierre Bourdieu has described in detail.[17] References are usually not overtly aimed at advancement. They could be subtle tributes to heroes and predecessors, intertextual hints that only certain actors understand. Designers affect a lack of interest in advancement as such, but the skillful use of particular references can increase one's status. Designers or fashion brands can manage their existing fashion capital well or poorly, depending on the strategies they choose. The act of referencing continually recreates the field and its primarily Western, white hierarchies. This can make even the use of references seem restrictive.

Rodebjer observes that having "trendy pieces" in a collection makes it easier to be featured on the editorial pages of fashion magazines, especially in the United States. Her fall 2011 collection had an outer space theme, useful to those magazines that had adopted a similar theme, though Rodebjer and her team do not intentionally produce "trendy pieces."

Although she is happy about the democratization of fashion, which brings "fashion to everyone," Rodebjer becomes depressed by the trend hysteria at the mass-market fashion companies. Like Filippa K and Exter, Rodebjer's collections are divided into two sections, changeable and classic, helping ensure that Rodebjer's best pieces will have a life beyond the current season.

*

The stylist Daniel Linderoth observes that there is a *via media* that all Swedish clothing companies want to take. Currently, they look to emulate the fashionable style of Acne, since this generates exceptional sales. Such tendencies, where the dominant style of a market revolves around a certain type of expression, have a host of cultural explanations. As an organizational scholar, I like to consider institutional theory, which illustrates how companies seek legitimacy by imitating other companies with good reputations.[18] This imitation concerns not only style but also work procedures and discourse. For example, the word "effortless" occurs in countless fashion companies' discourse, while the popularity of slogans such as "from the inside out" can be understood as signaling that their users are seeking legitimacy. This approach might be rational from the customer perspective as well, provided that the customer in the mid-range segment is seeking integrity and artistry in the brand.

The use of Web-based trend services does not appear to be widespread in the mid-range segment. Cheap Monday, which is owned by H&M, is one company that uses WGSN's services. Ann-Sofie Back works part-time as the brand's creative director. When she first started with Cheap Monday in 2009, she felt WGSN was stressful to use:

When you had been on vacation you had about 100 reports from WGSN. But after a while you understand that it's stuff you've somehow picked up anyway, and [the service] is more like a confirmation. [The sales representatives] can see that I haven't just made this up—but "look here".

One of Back's initial tasks was to make the collections trendier and more universal. The result was that customers and agents no longer recognized the brand. Cheap Monday has since defined its style more clearly for its target market, that is, young people between seventeen and twenty-seven years old who are either linked to or aspire to be linked to a creative industry. "What we look at, trend-wise, might have narrowed—we don't have to do everything," Back states. When developing a collection, the design team does not first refer to WGSN, but certain trends from WGSN can be identified in the collection's themes. Back views WGSN as a guide, as "confirmation central." Cheap Monday is a fairly market-oriented company in the mid-range segment, where credibility is gained by using arguments that resonate with those who work according to the economic logic, for example, in sales. In this milieu, WGSN becomes—echoing Neil Bradford's words—a form of insurance for success.

Roland Hjort at Whyred has somewhat mixed feelings about trend services:

WGSN does it all. It's like five reference books every day. It drives you crazy. They have created their own sketches. We were close to getting WGSN, but the fact that we haven't is 100 per cent due to it being too expensive... It's really great, but it's not *that* great. It's fun to read all the analyses—they have analyses of everything. We would rather put the money on a stylish *lookbook* or something like that.

Hjort suggests that those such as WGSN that create trends simultaneously contribute to erasing the concept of trends: "They don't have just one trend, they have 200 of them and they bake it all together and hack it up like a little cake. In the end it's just all one big [piece of] dough anyway."

Jane Shepherdson of Whistles comments that many brands in the mid-range segment concentrate on niche or classic products. This is in line with the evolution described in *The End of Fashion*, where marketing-focused companies such as Gap, Ralph Lauren, Abercrombie & Fitch and American Apparel pump out lifestyle products—simple pieces in an infinite number of colors—the fashion aspects of which have largely been lost.[19] The products are not legitimized by intermediaries such as tastemakers but reach consumers through enormous marketing efforts. (The strategy of niche brands, in contrast, is not just to increase sales but to reinforce their own identities.[20]) This can lock these big brands into their own "strategies" and visions so that blandness takes over, as Geoffrey Finch notes, where mass-market fashion and mid-segment brands produce almost identical clothes, generating opportunities for other actors such as Antipodium.

Designers in the mid-range segment emphasize the importance of intermediaries or tastemakers. Finch highlights the importance of relationships with "quality retailers" such as Liberty and Barneys. Symbolic products such as fashion clothes are ascribed meaning in the interactions between designers, tastemakers and consumers, making these legitimating institutions incredibly important. Cecilia Björk at Exter views the role of the fashion press as "branding." Magazines borrow the pieces that stand out. These pieces rarely sell very well, but the brand benefits from the increased legitimacy, or fashion capital, such exposure bestows. When Geoffrey Finch talks about significant tastemakers, he mentions a variety of media: *Vogue, Gentlewoman*, the writers Tim Blanks and Suzy Menkes, the site *style.com* and the blog *Style Bubble*. He thinks that the huge flow of information makes it "incredibly important" to appear in certain magazines. In the current fragmented media landscape, individual writers can be seen as increasingly important. Much is said about the blogging phenomenon, but when asked for examples, designers almost exclusively cite blogs tied to fashion magazines, the star blog *Style Bubble* being an exception. Nina Bogstedt at Filippa K gets the same number of requests from finance journalists as from fashion journalists, suggesting that financial viability attracts as much attention as does fashion. Finance journalism does not, however, confer fashion legitimacy. That several fashion designers talk about the central role of tastemakers and fashion magazines indicates that marketing is not supreme, in contradiction to Teri Agins' prediction in the 1990s.

Operating in the mid-range segment means dealing with long lead times while offering products lacking the luster of luxury brands. Trends are a form of risk taking that Antipodium's Geoffrey Finch claims one can get good at or, as Filippa K's Nina Bogstedt claims, one can simply choose to step away from. Cecilia Björk of Exter considers timing critical for small businesses that cannot afford to stick with products that are too "ahead of the curve."

Several fashion brands in the mid-range segment have embraced a model in which certain products, called "evergreens" or "carry-overs," last over the seasons. Designers often justify this, speaking from the perspective of their fashion capital, by saying that it is unnecessary to change something that has already been perfected, just for the sake of change. Pieces that transcend seasons have another advantage: the companies do not have to clear them out at season-end discounts. This economic rationale is notably not mentioned by the designers.

Designer fashion brands

Erdem

I was taking the tube the other night and I was looking at this blouse a woman was wearing. She sat literally in front of me and I realized it was a copy of one of ours. And this got me thinking of this idea of a trend, that it starts somewhere and eventually trickles down to the general public. The idea of a trend can be so many different things: a movement, a mood, a general kind of feeling that people have.

Erdem Moralioğlu, who made the above observation, is the man behind the designer brand Erdem. Growing up in Canada, the son of a British mother and a Turkish father, he attended the Royal College of Art in London, England, and belongs to the wave of younger British designers who made their names near the end of the 2000s. He says it is wonderful and exciting to be part of something totally new, creating something that was not available before. When Moralioğlu sees a copy of an Erdem piece, he sees it as a sign that his work has permeated society and takes it as a compliment. "I'm not sure that I would feel that way if it was an *exact* copy—that's very dangerous."

In speaking of his brand, Moralioğlu uses the word "handwriting," emphasizing that in today's fashion landscape it is important to be distinct. Trends are more relevant to those working in more commercial companies, who want ideas to choose from. Moralioğlu works independently of trends: "I sketch, draw, do research, and create every collection in the same ways that I worked in college." His influences are designers such as Yves Saint Laurent and Cristóbal Balenciaga.

As a designer, I was always intrigued by exploring the codes of femininity. And the idea of garments made with a very human hand. Each garment should feel like there is only one that exists. And that it will make [the woman who wears it] feel very special.

Moralioğlu has never experienced problems combining consistency and change with his brand, because he was clear about his vision when he launched the brand, stressing sincerity and brand integrity:

I always think it's a tremendous compliment when someone says, "Oh that's very Erdem" or "that looks very Erdem". Someone who says that like an observation.

With respect to trends, such as print being generally in fashion, Moralioğlu says, "I design clothes and buyers react … and ultimately women buy the clothes or not. The idea of trends working to one's advantage, that I can't answer." He does not use trend services and has no opinion about them. In a discussion of whether the fashion scene is more tolerant now than formerly, Erdem observes that he finds it difficult to pinpoint:

I'm not sure that the industry is emphasizing tolerance more so than the consumers are demanding more things … There is a group of us that started showing in London, as designers, and we think the atmosphere is wonderful, the landscape is more varied, there are more designers who are showing and have credible businesses that are selling around the world, even if the brands themselves are small. So today, department stores like Barneys and Harrods don't just carry big fashion houses but also have room for smaller brands like Rodarte and Erdem. Maybe there is another word … Maybe it's not "tolerant" but more "hungry for the new"? What women want today is maybe far more different from in the 1970s and 1980s, when it was all about megabrands. I think women now want something that is special and maybe that's why room is created for younger, lesser-known brands like Erdem.

Moralioğlu says that a hundred years ago, people were complaining about "nothing being new." Yves Saint Laurent was inspired by Elsa Schiaparelli, and she, in turn, by someone else. Moralioğlu thinks of fashion as a beast that feeds on its past to move forward. It is a visual, cultural medium, not built on abstractions but based on experience and what has been done before. It should always *feel new*. The attraction of fashion for Moralioğlu is that it is constantly changing, and renewing itself. For him, exploration is essential. He often generates initial inspirations in the pre-collection and explores his ideas more fully in the main collection. He notes that the pre-collections are increasingly important and that department stores are buying more and more from them, especially in North America. Buyers, however, are still excited about the catwalk and budget carefully for the fashion weeks in September and February. Erdem offers four collections a year: one in store, one in production, one in preparation and the oldest on sale.

With respect to whether globalization and emerging markets have contributed to the success of smaller designer brands, Moralioğlu considers that survival as a designer brand is ultimately based on the ability to provide something people want and to offer it in the right places, as customers differ greatly between, for example, Dallas and London. Among the emerging economies, Russia and China are particularly receptive of Erdem designs. His pre-collections do well in Australia, where they better match the antipodean seasons. Fashion designers of Moralioğlu's generation are more business savvy and more independent than earlier generations:

If you create a product, you want to be able to sell it, get it to your customer. For us, it's less about being bought by a larger company and more about doing this alone and independently. I think there is a great sense of independence in London.

Like most informants, Moralioğlu considers the introduction of the internet the biggest change for the fashion industry in the last twenty years. Internet affects how people shop and how they experience fashion. Technology has fundamentally changed the whole process, from manufacturing to purchasing:

"When our buyers come to look at the collection, they bring their iPads, and they take pictures with their iPads and the images go straight to their buying office."

The biggest challenge is maintaining the pace. This makes supplying clothes a challenge for small houses, but at the same time Moralioğlu understands that people want things quickly.

The emphasis on the artistic aspects of the Erdem brand may be seen as a way to help build and consolidate its fashion capital. Since Erdem is a relatively young brand, Moralioğlu may have less freedom in presenting it than do more established designers in the same segment. In the end, the consumers' reaction is the yardstick. The concept of trend does not figure in Moralioğlu's personal professional domain, which is more that of an artist's.

Clements Ribeiro

Inacio Ribeiro and his wife Suzanne Clements started Clements Ribeiro in 1993 after completing their educations at Central Saint Martins. In the UK, Clements Ribeiro does not sell outside of London, but as of 2012, the brand sells in nineteen countries, including Kazakhstan, Russia, Singapore, Japan, the United States, China, Italy and Austria. E-commerce extends the brand's reach even farther. People come to Clements Ribeiro for "user friendly" clothes that are at the same time extremely creative, Ribeiro explains:

> There is a bonus about colors, there is a bonus about proportions, a bonus about the very original choice of fabric, which make our looks and our clothes very distinctive and bold. But effectively, they are very simple. We don't do very restrictive clothing. We work with prints in a unique way, with an inimitable eye, and we play along with the fashion movements and adapt our style. We have a distinctive bohemian style to what we do. Our muse is a woman who is creative, individualistic and confident in the way she dresses. We always say that our ideal customer is someone who buys our piece, puts it in her wardrobe, and it looks as if it has always belonged there … We hate the idea that people would buy into Clements Ribeiro because it was the hot, cool thing.

Clements Ribeiro's designs and products are expensive and appeal only to an elite group. Clements Ribeiro makes two collections a year, unlike many other brands that make more. Some items, prints or fabrics may be carryovers, lingering across seasons. Between collections, the brand offers "upcycling editions," that is, vintage items customized by adding something, such as a vintage scarf, to a Clements Ribeiro dress. In addition to their own brand, Ribeiro and Clements have made several capsule collections for Evans, a British brand that focuses on plus-size clothing. For seven years, the two designers were creative directors for the French fashion house Cacharel.

We don't consciously think about trends. But both Suzanne and I think that trends come out of living in a bubble. You are living and breathing what's going on. As a designer you are always visually and intellectually consuming images and stimulation, but because we all live in this bubble, we are all watching, seeing, consuming the very same things. We all watch the same films, visit the same places, meet the same people. And what makes a difference is our own individual eyes, which work as filters … When we try to be individual, we often come to the same conclusions. At the same time, you can also break from it. We get saturated with it and maybe we feel rebellious. That's what trail-blazers do in fashion, they break the mould and they manage to be a step ahead.

Both Clements and Ribeiro are very confident in their taste and interpretations and are therefore more interested in working within the Clements Ribeiro vocabulary than in expanding or breaking it. "We do things *exactly* how we think that they should be done," Ribeiro asserts. Unlike other designers who speak of "from the inside out," they approach new collections by combining features of the previous collection with newer designs and then considering what their customers will want and only then what the media and the market might expect. Ribeiro admires Miuccia Prada, who always succeeds in surprising within the Prada universe that she has created.

Clements Ribeiro does not use trend services, though in the 1980s Ribeiro would stand in line to attend Lidewij Edelkoort's trend presentations at Première Vision because he found them utterly inspiring. Now, he does not need the information, because he and his wife trust their own "filters" to spot trends relevant to the brand. Like so many other designers, Ribeiro considers trend services more necessary for fashion mass retailers or producers of consumer goods who need to be in touch with cultural movements, where trends can be very divergent and sometimes contradictory. That said, when they visit Evans, they enjoy seeing Peclers Paris' trend books, Ribeiro says: "I love Peclers! We find the books so beautifully put together. They are very inspiring and I think [Peclers] offers a good service. Without a shadow of a doubt, it's a very necessary business and a very useful tool."

In a fashion company, says Ribeiro, it is as much about selecting as it is about discarding trends:

Fashion is incredibly conservative and incredibly slow. For an industry that is known for trading on "the new" and discarding "the new" almost overnight for another newest thing, if you look back you will be surprised at how changes in fashion happen slowly. Because we belong to the industry and we look at it with a magnifying glass, we tend to overstate minute evolutions in fashion. But anyone outside of fashion will have these things just going over their heads. For all this incredible display of pyrotechnics and creativity that we have had in the last few years, you could summarize the last ten years of fashion in one futuristic short, well-sculpted digitally printed dress and, with that, dangerous looking shoes. It could be a Peter Pilotto dress, a Balenciaga dress, an Alexander McQueen dress. It's ten years summarized in a very *Alien*-looking cocktail dress.

Fashion after the 1960s seems to Ribeiro to be more about revival. Even Yves Saint Laurent used references that looked back. The originality and creativity of Nicolas Ghesquière, Balanciaga's former chief designer, is a play on tradition, which is why, Ribeiro suggests, Ghesquière's designs have limited appeal: they make beautiful pictures but have very little true impact. Has it been more difficult to be a fashion designer since the 1960s? Ribeiro says no and that fashion is exactly what we want it to be:

> You can look at painting and think painting is such a waste, such an exhausted medium in art. Why do artists still bother to paint in oil? Maybe you think, first came impressionism, then modernism, then abstract painting—directions of art that revolutionized our way of thinking. Haven't they demolished and deconstructed painting altogether? What's the point of painting? ... However, all this completely falls apart if you visit a good art gallery and see the vigour and energy that you can find in some contemporary painting. I think this is also true for fashion. From an intellectual perspective, very little has changed. But in terms of responding to a humanistic and an aesthetic need, fashion is a living and indispensable expression of human nature. And it doesn't need to change. Because women still want to wear dresses, and there is only so much you can do with a dress ... You can try to make dresses with spikes and feathers or 3D printing. But at the end of the day, what you want is a beautiful silk dress that will make you feel wonderful, that will respect your body and express your mood.

Ribeiro disagrees with the condescending suggestion that if something can be identified as a trend, it is over. Trends are ongoing, always in flux, and he is hard-pressed to think of anything that is absolutely "out":

> It all depends on where you are and what company you work for. Two months ago, I thought the animal print trend was finally over. Because for very long we could never see the end of it. And then, guess what? Did you see the pre-collections for Céline and Chloé? All of a sudden, it's so out of trend, that almost immediately, it's the coolest thing again. And then you think, for

example, Christopher Kane introduced the fluorescent colors four years ago. So it should definitely be over. But no. I still think that fluorescent colors are really cool … honestly, anything goes. Maybe you could call it the globalization of trends.

Though Ribeiro was born and raised in Brazil, he thinks that the conservatism of the fashion industry will ensure that it remains Western:

Fashion as we know it is essentially a Western civilization phenomenon. Maybe over time, it will evolve into something else, but it is essentially a Western civilization product … Just as painting … is basically born out of Western civilization. In the East, for example in Japan, they have ceramics and textiles, in China and in the Muslim world they love scripts, paper and calligraphy— things that have no resonance in the Western world. The Western world is about fashion, painting, cinema. And I think they will survive as Western phenomena … In China they are learning fashion through Western fashion. It's the same in Brazil. Brazilian fashion has its origins in the fact that imported clothes were not available, and therefore fashion designers had to emulate European fashion. Fashion is about European fashion. Even American fashion is about European fashion.

Like Moralioğlu, Erdem's founder and designer, Ribeiro is sanguine about copying.

A print of ours was particularly and insistently copied by the high street a couple of years ago. All the blogs and sites saw it as extremely fabulous for us that Topshop made a version of our print. So it actually gave our print and our brand an incredible "fashion cred" and "street cred."

With the exception of knockoffs of megabrands such as Louis Vuitton and Dior, copies tend to be inferior versions of the original items. The copies become available to many and help spread the value of the brand, reassuring the wearers that the original is much better, according to Ribeiro. Dana Thomas, in *Deluxe: How Luxury Lost Its Luster*, similarly argues that luxury brands gain from being copied: their market simply branches out because the knockoffs and originals appeal to different consumers.[21] The bottom line is that a copied design, by being seen widely, adds to the "street cred" of the original.

Ribeiro considers that information technology has made consumers more informed than ever but just as passionate. The internet's immediacy has benefited fast fashion in particular, but the whole industry profits from consumers with better discernment and more knowledge. With so much information at their disposal, consumers could get lost but for the emergence of "curating sites." He believes that what I call cultural intermediaries or tastemakers—such as Net-A-Porter, which combines retailing and curating, offering an assortment of carefully selected designers, items and trends that guarantees quality—greatly influence the community of fashion consumers. Ribeiro regards Web sites such as *Fashionista* (which mixes fashion news, criticism, and career advice, addressing both influential fashion consumers and fashion companies) and *The Coveteur* (which showcases the wardrobes of various fashion leaders and tastemakers, linking individual items to e-commerce sites) as "curating." He thinks that "curating" social media sites such as Pinterest, Instagram and Twitter will grow in importance, helping engage consumers and organizing material by brand and target audience.[22] Certain department store buyers play a legitimizing role that can be problematic. Their power is rarely acknowledged and they seldom buy what Ribeiro and Clements would wish them to buy from their collection, skewing the offering. E-commerce offers a solution by widening the field of available items so consumers can choose exactly what they want.

People need to identify with others in their fashion choices, Ribeiro claims:

> I know it's pedestrian, and I know it might sound like the opposite of individuality, but I think there is something intrinsically human about looking at someone that one thinks is admirable, who cuts a nice figure, and identifying a common thread. I think it makes us feel empowered. In the same way as we look at someone who is dressed in a way that we find unattractive, it may also serve as confirmation. "God, at least I don't look like him or her"... Freud speaks of "the narcissism of small differences"—that's the essence of taste. Taste is as individual as it is a collective phenomenon. None of us wants to be entirely individual, because in that case we would all go around looking like Isabella Blow, each one trying to be more outrageous than the next.

In delivering his vision, in exploring the codes of femininity, Erdem Moralioğlu is a prime example of the fashion *auteur* who struggles over the definition of the designer—a battle central to the fashion field, according to Pierre Bourdieu. Moralioğlu is an exemplar of the solitary creator in Bourdieu's "charismatic ideology," which ignores the roles that key institutions play in creating the creators.[23] In this charismatic ideology, the role of stylists in creating the designer, to which Jane Burton and Paula Reed at *Grazia UK* draw attention (see Chapter 4), goes unacknowledged. Moralioğlu's belief that trends trickle down from designer brands to mass-market fashion companies through imitation is a traditional fashion theory view that Herbert Blumer criticized as long ago as the 1960s. Inacio Ribeiro, on the other hand, seems very aware that fashion is socially created ("We live in a bubble"), and he and Clements move among various positions in the fashion field in collaborating with Evans and Cacharel. His concern for fashion credibility and, above all, the "street cred" conferred by Topshop's copying of a Clements Ribeiro item illustrate the difference between his view of the fashion field and its mechanisms and that of Moralioğlu. Ribeiro's descriptions resonate with many of the arguments of Bourdieu's critics, who maintain that fashion trends often start off outside the fashion industry or are originated by designers other than reputable or famous ones.[24] Clements and Ribeiro do not use trend services but are very familiar with them and even "love" some of what they see. Ribeiro's account of how he and Clements, through their brand, "play along with the fashion movements and adapt our style" clearly hints that Clements and Ribeiro themselves do not subscribe to the charismatic ideology of the solitary genius/artist.

Imogen Brown

For over eight years, Sarah Jordan, collection director at Imogen Brown,[25] has worked alongside Brown, founder and creative director of the brand, though a luxury conglomerate is now an equal shareholder. Jordan tracks products at every stage of production in almost all categories: ready-to-wear, knitwear, jersey, denim, sunglasses, a capsule collection with a mass-market retailer, kidswear and all the special projects. In addition, she sets the calendar for the whole season and ensures that the budget is followed. When Brown is in, Sarah is her "sidekick." She sits next to her and tries to absorb as much of her "vibe" and her directorship as possible. When Brown is absent, Jordan directs the work and meetings. Working so intimately with the founder, Jordan can ensure that the brand stays true to the Imogen Brown vision of designing modern and exciting fashion for contemporary women. According to Jordan, the brand is a leader in design but cognisant of "the excitement around something that becomes a trend," so it also keeps an eye on fashion's movements. Imogen Brown wants to satisfy the needs of the modern woman:

> The woman who gets up in the morning and gets dressed, drops the kids to school, bikes to work, works until around five, when she meets a friend she hasn't seen for two years, quickly has a drink, then bikes back, picks up the kids from the neighbor and takes them home.

Jordan explains the challenge facing the brand: doing something new while meeting *the same need*—change and continuity exist in parallel.

> Overall I think we are great trendsetters. I think Imogen is amazing in that way … Sometimes I think to myself, and I also tell her, that it's only when she comes and we do a fitting, that something is added. That's why this brand exists and why this business is very successful, that she is who she is. We all try

hard to think how she would have thought. And then Imogen enters and says "That's nice but why don't you do that to it?" and suddenly the item takes on a completely different dimension.

Though Imogen Brown does not use trend-forecasting services, through the brand's collaboration with a mass-market retailer, Jordan learned how that company uses such services in its other collections, for example, suggesting that the theme "running at night in the city," apparently random, probably originated with trend services. Jordan has never seen the need for trend services, for any Imogen Brown collections:

We just don't think about trends. It's not even on the agenda. We just sit here and think: "What can we do this time, that's very cool?" We want to do the best we can, that fits our brand, and then it doesn't really matter if it's trendy or not. It may sound a bit presumptuous, but if we do this, it's cool and it must be a trend.

Imogen Brown is another example of a designer with abundant reserves of fashion capital intending to make a directional mark but without broadcasting that intention. That the brand does not speak explicitly about relating to trends in design can be understood given that trends are increasingly linked to commerce and economic capital rather than to fashion capital. The brand's legitimacy in the fashion field makes it possible for Jordan to state that if they at Imogen Brown create something cool, it is automatically a trend, while acknowledging consumers' interest in trends and the necessity of the brand keeping abreast of "fashion's movements."

Jordan agrees that there are more trends now but prefers to speak about trends in terms of items:

Waves of items that become more relevant, and items that become less relevant. We were talking about it the other day. There was a business discussion about t-shirts ... Nowadays, you don't wear a t-shirt that much. You wear a silk blouse. We've moved on. So much that Zara has them in every color, every print. And that's a good thing because everyone is onto that trend. It's going to move on from that trend again, the next thing might be a knitwear piece. That's how I see trends. It's all about items.

The Imogen Brown products are designed to last—"you would never throw away your Imogen Brown blazer or Imogen Brown shirt"—reducing overconsumption.

The fashion scene has become more tolerant, Jordan thinks, but so has society as a whole: "But I dare you to turn up with cow pants and a clown shirt. People will look at you. Today fashion is so much about individual style, so it can be difficult to point out something that is absolutely out." A Romeo Gigli number from the 1980s is not really out at the moment, but it is not worn by most women. "You might want to wear it in a few years, or maybe there is some goth around who would die to wear it."

Contrasting styles have always existed side by side. When the Yves Saint Laurent Rive Gauche woman strolled down the streets of Paris, there was still a Dior woman out there, Jordan recalls:

> It's just that some brands are at the moment more "on trend"—to use your words. If you think of Balenciaga and Imogen Brown—they are so very different, but I love when Charlotte Gainsbourg wears Balenciaga, she's the coolest chick on the planet. I want to look like her, but I know I'm a real Imogen Brown girl.

Jordan believes that styling is more important today because fashion magazines are more commercial and business driven. Many fashion editors used to style themselves, such as the Italian fashion editors of *Grazia* and Nicoletta Santoro. Styling has become professionalized, and editors such as Alexandra Shulman at *British Vogue* have stylists such as Lucinda Chambers.

Most designer brands target a broader age range today than in the 1960s, 1970s and 1980s, between twenty-five and sixty years of age. Jordan cites the example of a friend of her mother who was described as "a YSL woman": she was very chic and preferred Yves Saint Laurent products. That woman is now a grandmother, and both her daughter and granddaughter now buy Yves Saint Laurent.[26] The fashion house is a source of joy for all of them.

Imogen Brown produces a small "iconic range" in ready-to-wear, mainly bestselling tailored jackets, tailored trousers, jeans and some knitwear. Compared with brands such as Bottega Veneta and Gucci, Imogen Brown has few carryover items. Jordan observes that it is easier to do carryovers with accessories, and Bottega Veneta and Gucci have relatively more accessories than ready-to-wear. This observation constructs clothing as something changeable but bags and accessories as more stable.

The importance of pre-collections is increasing. Imogen Brown's sales currently consist of 60 percent pre-collection and 40 percent main collection items, but Jordan anticipates that the proportion may soon be 70:30. The show is still extremely important, but everybody's pre-collections are presented on *style.com*. Jordan contemplates the industry's timing:

> Fast fashion is wrong. But at the same time, [the fast-fashion companies] do everything at the right time. High fashion has pushed everything too far. Our stuff gets into the store at random times. The spring pre-collection gets into the stores in October. The main collection for spring and summer has to be

in the stores by March. So between October and February is the delivery of Spring/Summer. And then, May until July is the delivery of Autumn/Winter. That is slightly random. And we have somehow been pushed into this. I think the department stores have a big say in that.

Celebrities occasionally ask the design team to create something for a particular event, and from time to time the brand does this. The design team anticipates such requests by offering eveningwear as part of the pre-fall collection (which coincides with "the event season").

> Eveningwear always sells well. It's great for the Middle East market. And we do cool eveningwear that is not classic. We usually start to think about the collection, then we think of a range plan for eveningwear, and then we think about different women that could wear it. In my role, I could, for example, say "This dress would be great for Keira Knightley, and this is really for Anne Hathaway." ... The press department is then asked to contact these people and supply them with sketches to see if they like them.

Imogen Brown personifies how contemporary designers move between different parts of the fashion field and between their own fashion brand and collaborations. The products of a brand can be consumed in "derived versions," in the form of cheaper T-shirts, underwear or sunglasses on which the designer brand bestows an air of luxury, an "auratic appeal."[27]

Of the designer brands discussed above, only Erdem has no relationship with the trend services. The others have come in contact with the services but do not subscribe to them and dismiss the idea of involving them in their design process. They are convinced that trends—or, as Moralioğlu calls them, "news"—are important to their customers and that customers are better informed than ever. This provides a rationale for keeping track of trends, "news" or "movements of fashion," even if, like Jordan at Imogen Brown, these designers consider themselves the *trendmakers*.

The desire to be a trendmaker

Reverence for the designer permeates every fashion organization, from mass-market fashion brands to designer brands. The best-regarded designers are those who leave a mark on the field—*trendmakers* without using the word—and most designers aspire to reach this point. Skillfully interpreting one's surroundings is both inevitable and fun, and the more influential and distinctive the interpretation, the higher its status. Prepackaged trends are *not* high status, so a few designers stress design "from the inside out." Some designers note that their offerings are often too early, recognizing that timing is important to ensure that a relevant trend has taken hold among consumers. Yet customers are more knowledgeable about fashion than ever before, making it more difficult to be "early." Trends often barely run full cycle before returning, as when Inacio Ribeiro notes animal prints being cool again. Styles are scarcely registered as they so quickly pass. The sense that all trends coexist in the tolerant fashion scene is countered by actors such as Jane Shepherdson of Whistles, Kate Phelan of Topshop and Geoffrey Finch of Antipodium who make it clear that things do fall out of style. These three stress the skill involved in interpreting trends correctly. Designer brands pay less attention to timing—understandable given their relatively stronger position in the fashion field. Sarah Jordan explained that even if an Imogen Brown item is exceptionally early, it does not matter as long as Imogen herself believes in it. This can be seen as reflecting how the brand's position in the fashion field greatly depends on its reception among critics and other tastemakers, that is, people with great fashion knowledge who know to appreciate "the early."

The leaders in the hierarchy of the fashion field say little about consumers' uncertainty, perhaps because consumers in their segment have greater interest in fashion or are wealthy and therefore can purchase fashion status. Self-confident customers are emphasized because they bestow status on the brand.

The interviewed designers are open about their high consumption of fashion information. Despite unwillingness to be followers, they all admit to being dependent on the movements of the fashion field, whether they highlight consumer behavior, general fashion evolution, competition in the highest fashion strata or designers' dominant references. They are fully aware that fashion is a field where consumption and production are closely intertwined. They often speak of trends as existing "somewhere else"—among consumers, fast fashion, the industry's structure with its fashion weeks or tastemakers such as buyers and fashion journalists. Though designers long to leave their mark, or create trends, this is coupled with a reluctance to support the trend machinery.

The internet has significantly affected the dissemination of trends and the industry's neomania but, as Inacio Ribeiro suggests, the craving for news and packaging in trends cannot be equated to *major changes*. Trends can be microscopic, mattering only because of "the narcissism of small differences." Trends can be dampened by the new possibilities of demand-driven supply characterized by shorter lead times, more statistics, more distribution channels and novel inventory management. Nina Bogstedt at Filippa K points out that customers are often unwilling to see certain pieces of clothing discontinued. In *The End of Fashion*, Teri Agins recounted how department stores in the 1990s removed clothes representing trends that did not immediately take hold among consumers.[28] Now that mass-market fashion companies have assumed the role of trend testers, this often leads to lingering trends, as H&M's top-ten seller boards attest.

Making one's mark brings high status. As having one's design copied is clear evidence one has made a mark, it is understandable that not everyone views copying as a threat. This tolerance can be understood as indicating a fashion company's status in the field, though Sarah Jordan finds it annoying when fast-fashion companies copy a Imogen Brown design that represents significant work and inspiration.

Trends as organizing principle

Information technology and the internet in particular have undeniably influenced the relationship between designers and trends. Despite technological change and the resulting speed, almost everyone testifies to the central importance of trends in the fashion field. Everyone goes to Première Vision, everyone buys fabrics from manufacturers who are influenced by trends, everyone deals with tastemakers and many have at least some relationship with trend-forecasting agencies. For some companies, trend services are indispensable.

Trends are most useful as an organizing principle to fashion companies in the mid-range segment whose long lead times mean that production is never as demand driven or adaptable as that of the fast-fashion companies. The paradox is that these mid-range companies talk more about the importance of finding a personal style and insist that trends are not as interesting a concept today. These brands are well aware that mass-market fashion companies are always on the lookout to be "inspired" by others' initiatives. While trend-forecasting agencies serve both segments, they are not always as beneficial for mid-range companies with long lead times, so the attitude of these companies is understandable.

The tastemakers' reluctance to issue trend directives and their advocacy of personal style protect their positions of power, which would be threatened if they shared trends in a world where information spreads in seconds. In step with the fashion field's expansion, certain tastemakers have become more guarded in their statements, while others claim that this fashion elite follows very carefully charted rules about what is on or off trend. Designers cannot think in this way because they must reach out to their customers and sell clothes. However, in downplaying the importance of trends, they may be emulating the rhetoric of the tastemakers, given their position in the fashion field, or they may be downplaying trends in order to focus on consistency in their brands.

Trends as personal growth

Although all actors acknowledge the importance of trends for the fashion field as a whole, many designers distance themselves from trends because they recall commerce and low-status fashion and because the idea of trends can seem limiting. Some designers, however, emphasize trends as enabling personal growth: Kate Phelan talks about the fourteen-year-old who does not know who she wants to be; Carin Rodebjer, Nina Bogstedt, Cecilia Björk and Imogen Brown talk about the modern woman with several contrasting roles, about creating opportunities for personal growth through trends; Jane Shepherdson describes the British market as excellent ground for experiments. This understanding of trends and their impact is not particularly widespread among the trend agencies, possibly being neglected because neomania shifts the emphasis to creating news.

Retromania

In the industry's frenzy to deliver news, references to earlier designers, styles, expressions and details result in the retro waves that have recurrently swept through fashion since the 1960s. Some scholars argue that the popularity of retro is primarily about a need to remember, where designers, musicians and filmmakers act as "freelancing historians" who revisit our past and replicate certain styles.[29] In the book *Retromania: Pop Culture's Addiction to Its Own Past*, which examines the retro hype in pop music, author and music critic Simon Reynolds suggests that it is the contemporary facility with which we can access and share information and data that has driven the interest in retro.

Whereas music can be digitalized, clothes are inevitably material[30] and are distributed in a very different way. Nevertheless, the spread of news and impressions is the same in both industries. Some fashion brands, for example Diane von Furstenberg, inspired by the music industry, have reissued older collections and patterns.[31] Retro is a sensitive subject in an industry that seeks "the new." Nina Bogstedt, for example, states that Filippa K is not retro but contemporary. Designers may look for inspiration in vintage stores, finding certain details that they combine with newer ideas to create something unique.

In his book *London: After a Fashion*, about the evolution of fashion in London, Alistair O'Neill settled on 1965 as the year that fashion news and innovation peaked. After this, postmodern pastiches and style recycling took over.[32] British fashion brand and store Biba, founded by Barbara Hulanicki, is often viewed as a pioneer of retro fashion, one of the first brands to surrender completely to the past. Previously, historical fashions had been revived from time to time, for example, classical Greek or Roman, but Biba provided endless flashbacks to and combinations of more recent styles with which people had personal relationships. The flashbacks came increasingly close together. In *Retromania*, Valerie Steele, a professor in fashion studies, noted that designers started referencing the 1980s in 1990. During the remainder of that decade, various elements of 1980s fashion were on trend about every three years. Steele found that these references circulated fairly randomly, disconnected from social meaning in a sphere of "taste and coolness." Her claim is supported by Roland Barthes in his text *The Fashion System*: the movements of fashion, he said, are almost always completely arbitrary.[33] In *Retromania*, Reynolds argued that changes in fashion are not about progress: fashion is not just the opposite of change but also opposes change artistically and politically.[34]

This harsh comment must be understood in relation to fashion's function as a cultural production field. An independent field, according to Bourdieu, is one where there is cultural production for culture's sake—in this case, fashion for fashion's sake. Designers and tastemakers are loyal to the field and create fashion that advances their own positions in it. Ascribing fashion a different meaning from the one that dominates the field would expose a dependency on a different field. A brand that only seeks to sell and has no fashion ambitions belongs in the economic field. If Greenpeace launched a fashion line, it would not likely be taken seriously in the fashion field, as the initiative would be interpreted as aligned with the organization's position in the environmental politics field. If any efforts in the fashion field were designed to effect, for example, political change, the fashion would not be primarily about fashion but would always be subordinate to the political field. None of the designers I spoke with claimed to see their fashion work as primarily intended to earn money or change the world; they instead insisted that they create fashion for fashion's sake.

This is not to say that various positions cannot coexist in the fashion field, where stances supporting the environment, social responsibility, animal rights as well as feminism are common. That so many designers, particularly women, emphasize that trends represent progress and freedom suggests that they perceive a liberating power in fashion. As with all cultural consumption, this meaning emerges in the interaction between clothes, their wearers and the social context. As we have seen in the interviews, many mention fashion as constituting theatrical costumery. Without claiming that fashion itself drives change, we see that fashion can convey political ideas and be used as a tool to identify affiliations or the renunciation of dominant ideas. Happy, and sometimes unfortunate interactions can arise between fashion and politics.[35] Could it be that Reynolds is unable to see the real change for all the small fashion swings?

Simon Reynolds views retro as a given aspect of cultural production when creativity is enmeshed in the market, with its constant fluctuations of mania and nostalgia. Retro is an unavoidable aspect of pop culture. In retro's constant retrospection and self-referencing, the construction of fashion, as Carin Rodebjer and Inacio Ribeiro both noted, is constantly recreated as Western.[36]

Consistency versus change

Designers in the mid-range segment may downplay the importance of trends because they have a bias toward *consistency* (see p. 100). Brands prioritize clarity and consistent style. The public relations machinery of fashion houses, as tastemakers point out, is far more powerful than it used to be. Collections are presented in ready-made looks. Brands give clear directives on how their pieces should be presented in stores and how the brand should be communicated.

Some view this balance between consistency and change as the fun part of the job, while others see it as possibly overwhelming. Ann-Sofie Back, creative director at Cheap Monday and the head of design at her own label Back, is experienced in creating renewal within the context of the brand:

> I take old ideas and recycle them. To be honest, it just goes round and round in a circle, ideas that I've used in the main collection that I bring back and mix up. Right now I'm working with some stuff from 2002 that I've returned to and some things from 2004, and then there's something from last year's collection for [Ann-Sofie Back] *Ateljé*. The theme is myself, kind of into eternity.

Nina Bogstedt illustrates the difficulty of maintaining a consistent style identity as styles themselves go in and out of fashion when she talks about the sudden interest in Filippa K with the return of minimalism at the end of the 2000s. The fashion landscape may be tolerant, but different styles are emphasized at different times, as Jane Shepherdson, Sarah Jordan and Inacio Ribeiro observe.

Although many actors in the fashion field are still focused on brands, the process described in *The End of Fashion*, in which marketing and brands gained power in the fashion field, has halted.[37] Information technology's opening of the innermost rooms of fashion to a broader audience via sites such as *style.com* has only increased interest in fashion information. Intermediaries—whether tastemakers or less legitimate actors such as self-proclaimed fashion bloggers—exploit this, providing the general public with a constant stream of fashion news. As the influence of intermediaries increases and consumers become better informed, marketing apparatuses cannot afford to disregard the powerful intermediaries with their immense fashion capital. The tastemakers are back. The increased importance of "curated sites" and "quality retailers" are signs of this. Moreover, neomania—the hunger for the "right new"—is more prevalent now than ever before.

Tastemakers have great influence on designers and brands. As noted in Chapter 4, one fashion editor claimed to have hinted to designers that they should perhaps not focus solely on prints, a subtle warning to avoid locking themselves into a particular style or defining their brands too narrowly to enable change, to be able to design something new. At the same time, many designers stress the importance of customer recognition and of the brand's representing something that adds value amid the welter of trends.

Consistency versus change and gender

Some tastemakers refer to gender when talking about the tension between consistency and change in a brand. Since fashion is characterized as feminine, women are widely believed to be more competent to judge at least women's fashion. Some informants, mostly Swedish, consider men and women equally skilled in identifying and interpreting trends and in judging fashion collections, perhaps reflecting Swedish beliefs about gender equality. Nevertheless, in the parts of the fashion field where cultural logic prevails, aesthetic decisions are made and taste is important, women are in the majority. Conversely, the higher in the fashion hierarchy one looks, the more likely it is that male designers prevail, which can be understood as expressing the prevailing gender order.

Many informants believe that a designer's gender affects the collections created. With respect to the tension between consistency and change in brands, April Glassborow at Harvey Nichols thinks some female designers are particularly good at developing their brands, for example Donna Karan and Stella McCartney. Donna Karan may no longer appeal to the very young customer—it is often said that her customers have matured with the brand—but Glassborow argues that Donna Karan has kept her brand alive and creative within the framework of its core values. This ability to grow and evolve with one's customers, Glassborow says, is something female designers seem to do better: "With Stella McCartney, it appears as though her collection changes to reflect changes in her lifestyle and she is true to herself rather than to the mood of the season." Women designers wear the clothes they design, which enables them to evolve within their brand DNA, Glassborow observes, while some male designers get stuck in an *ideal*:

> Male designers will have an image in mind, or indeed a muse, whose silhouette they admire, and base their collection on this body image. But it doesn't always mean that it fits or suits all women, sometimes leaving their collections less universal in appeal.

One of the biggest changes in the fashion world in the last thirty years, according to Sarah Jordan, is that women have truly succeeded as designers: "They are good designers, not just designers." In Christian Dior's time, women were not fully emancipated in the fashion industry. In the 1970s and 1980s, when there were few really big brands, the number of women designers slowly increased, with Donna Karan spearheading the movement. Now there are Stella McCartney, Sarah Burton at Alexander McQueen, Phoebe Philo at Céline, Consuelo Castiglioni at Marni and Clare Waight Keller at Chloé. Jordan observes that women in the top designer positions often find that their family life keeps them "grounded": "Imogen will suddenly say, 'Okay, but the kids go to bed at 7.30 pm, I need to go home.'"

A stylist notes that many male designers produce amazing pieces but suspects that these items are intended for very specific women, mentioning Calvin Klein and Ricardo Tisci's collections for Givenchy. She suggests that female designers such as Miuccia Prada, Jil Sander and Consuelo Castiglioni make more wearable clothes with a forgiving aspect and that women designers are more charitable toward other women about clothing. This is true for some male designers who have influential women at their sides, such as Christopher Kane, with his sister, Tammy.

Fashion and economy

That the fashion field is completely intertwined with the economy is obvious in the designer interviews. While the trend-forecasting agents talk about how their services make things easier for the fashion companies from an economic perspective, they do not assume any financial responsibility for realizing the trends they identify. Selection is the primary task of the tastemakers, even though many economic considerations are involved when, for example, a department store places an order. For designers, financial decisions tied to production are central. How can trends be materialized in the most reasonable way and with manageable risk? This is where some companies, particularly mass-market fashion companies, seek flexibility in production, whereas others might "step aside" to avoid becoming too dependent on trends, and still others create an aura around their brand by managing their fashion capital well. It is in the fashion-producing organizations that decisions are made about the trade-offs between fashion and economic constraints. This is also evident in the structuring of collections, where mass-market fashion companies, mid-segment brands and designer brands prefer a basic selection of so-called evergreens, or carryovers, that transcend seasons and are never marked down.

Designers often downplay the importance of trends by pointing to their limiting effects, suggesting that trends cynically exploit people's insecurities. Virtually all designers I spoke with agree that personal style is increasingly important, regardless of the significance ascribed to trends. Furthermore, just as the desire to be "right" continues to be a driving force of trends, this desire has also steered the industry in a direction where energy and resources are devoted to presenting various looks in lookbooks, on Web sites and blogs, in fashion magazines, through personal shoppers, etc.

Sociologist Patrik Aspers argues that the markets of the fashion field are embedded in one another but that they can be understood in terms of status markets and standard markets. Those parts of the market where consumers encounter products through retailers are *status markets*, while those parts where brands engage producers are *standard markets*. On status markets, products attain their value and meaning from social linkages, positions and status, and not, for example, from fabric quality. The pieces are imbued with meaning by their context, not inherent characteristics. Aspers, in other words, speaks of status markets as dealing in symbolic products. So far in this book, I have dealt with status markets. On a standard market, however, buyers and sellers follow set roles organized according to price, quality and delivery contracts, not according to the symbolic value, for example, of fashion. The standard market reflects the power relationships between buyers and sellers, and Aspers would say that buyers' interests have been institutionalized. Though traces of status may be evident also in this section of the fashion field, it is not the principle around which the standard market is organized. Aspers views the "investment market" where financial analysts operate as a standard market organized around accumulated wealth. Companies' identities are established according to how profitable they are or are expected to be. The markets are embedded in one another so that decisions on one market may well have implications for another. Markets keep track of what other markets are doing,[38] as do the financial analysts who monitor fashion companies, who must also consider how trends affect them.

7 FINANCIALIZATION AND TRENDS—TRENDS AS FASHION RISK

I'm completely ignorant. I'm a stock market analyst. I have been to two fashion shows, Burberry and Hugo Boss, and I have no clue if they are going to work, if it's good or not. People around me looked like they were enjoying what they were seeing. No, as an analyst you always look at other things.

At Canary Wharf, one of London's financial districts, I spoke with Robert Gray, a renowned analyst for a major international investment bank whose specialty is luxury brands.[1] I am interested in knowing whether and, if so, how he relates to trends when he evaluates fashion companies. This is the first time I have had to specify that it is fashion trends I am studying, as opposed to the macroeconomic trends of which he and his colleagues are more inclined to speak. Gray explains his reasoning:

As an investor you always think about the DNA of the brand. Obviously, the fashion—the catwalk collections—is such a small part. For Burberry, where the catwalk collection lies under the Burberry Prorsum brand, it represents less than 10 per cent of their total group sales. And that part is certainly not as profitable as the rest of the business.

At the same time, he says that fashion collections are incredibly important: they drive *aspiration*—the mantra for analysts in the luxury segment—and enable companies to charge upward of EUR 80 for T-shirts. In addition to the ready-to-wear collections shown during fashion week, Burberry's monthly collections are displayed in shop windows and on its famous Web site, and these also constitute only a fraction of total sales. Burberry trench coats, overcoats and large bags are intended to be sustainable fashion, salable at full price in coming seasons.

In 1997, Louis Vuitton, currently the strongest luxury brand in the world,[2] launched its very first ready-to-wear collection, designed by Marc Jacobs. Many analysts were skeptical of what they regarded as the introduction of "fashion risk." The profitability of Louis Vuitton's ready-to-wear was significantly lower than that of its bags. Gray explains that investors keep an eye on fashion risk:

> People in my shoes look at these companies as investment propositions. And then what do you want? The faster growth, the higher margins and as little cyclicality or volatility as possible.[3]
>
> What tends to happen with fashion risk is that the company tends to outgrow in years that the collection works, but then it suffers even more during the not-as-good period that follows. So from an investment perspective, you tend to prefer businesses that have more evergreens, more permanent collections.

Does Gray see any companies with high fashion risk among the luxury brands he monitors? The Italian fashion houses, he says, generally have high fashion risk, specifically naming Versace, which is family owned and not listed on the stock exchange, and the German firm Escada, which is controlled by the Mittal family, though a listed company. Several companies have worked hard to find the right balance between new and permanent items in their product range. Since its initial public offering (IPO) in 2002, Burberry, to address its enormous fashion risk, has developed a product range in which almost 50 percent of items are not clothes, while reducing the actual clothing collection to core products and classic pieces. Gray thinks that the collaboration between Head of Design Christopher Bailey and CEO Angela Ahrendts is working well for Burberry. He also mentions Céline and Chloé as brands that have found a good balance between the design team and the CEO.

Louis Vuitton's ready-to-wear collections, initially heavily criticized, proved successful, and I spoke with numerous analysts who cite the "Louis Vuitton model" as ideal for the entire industry. Profitability originates in products with low renewability—that is, that change little in design and can be sold from season to season—such as "evergreen" clothes, bags and accessories, while the company's high-profile ready-to-wear collections are shown during the big fashion weeks create a "buzz" around the brand.

Gray observes that the fashion risk is higher for womenswear. Strong menswear brands such as Hugo Boss and Ralph Lauren might face a constant risk in the selection of cuts and colors, but they have a much more stable core than does womenswear. To reduce the risk in womenswear, higher-margin brand extensions are common, products considered less vulnerable to fashion risk, such as shoes, small leather goods, jewelry, watches and bags. Perfume can function as an invitation to a brand but is the least attractive of all brand-extension categories as perfumes are extremely competitive. The analyst does not read reviews of fashion shows, instead monitoring order books to ensure that the brand continues to generate interest.

The City of London and Canary Wharf are home to investment banks and other financial services companies whose financial analysts and stockbrokers act as another type of fashion field intermediary. They provide institutional investors, pension funds, asset managers and insurance companies with advice on buying, holding or selling shares, providing their customers with ongoing reports often used by others in the analysts' organizations. Analysts and advisors maintain close contact with the investor relations departments[4] of the companies they monitor but also seek an information advantage by using data from other sources, so they can more realistically evaluate the fashion companies' shares. Analysts monitoring the fashion industry specialize in luxury goods and retail, including large mass-market fashion companies such as H&M and Zara. Evaluation concerns future expectations, so financial analysts must track macroeconomic tendencies, industry-specific events, competitors' activities and of course the strengths and weaknesses of specific companies.

Fashion and capitalism

Fashion scholar Elizabeth Wilson has called fashion "the child of capitalism."[5] As previously noted (see p. 18), modernity and industrial capitalism were foundational for the evolution of fashion. It was in the emerging democratic society that the need to indicate one's belonging, to show off oneself and one's group, was born. In the ascendant cities, public life was increasingly prominent, so consciousness of one's self-presentation was greater than before. Fashion has always been linked to urbanism. Sociologist Norbert Elias wrote that during modernity's "civilizing" process, people became *conscious* of civilization, convinced of its superiority over earlier more barbaric or "primitive" societies. This consciousness, as manifested in science, technology and art, came to prevail in the West.[6] Fashion also carries an inherent elitism. When today's Western fashion celebrates its worldwide victory, it is easy to see its imperialist roots. Capitalism's traces in fashion can also be seen in fashion's forward momentum, neomania and constant change. Fashion is a dynamic phenomenon that is equally liberating and limiting. Elizabeth Wilson notes that fashion can appear relativist, a senseless production of styles; she claims that "fashion speaks capitalism," being consistent in an ambiguity also found in capitalism:

> Capitalism maims, kills, appropriates, lays waste. It also creates great wealth and beauty, together with a yearning for lives and opportunities that remain just beyond our reach. It manufactures dreams and images, as well as things, and fashion is as much part of the dream world of capitalism as of its economy.[7]

As addressed in the previous chapter on designers' and brands' attitudes to trends, fashion companies in today's Western market economy must manage the tension between consistency and change. Strong brand names are useful in competition as they raise the entry barriers against others and create loyalty, meaning and attraction for customers. Neomania, the constant pursuit of the new, goes hand in hand with capitalism's need to put new products and dreams on the market. Many fashion companies focus on this tension—although they may not use the words "consistency" and "change"—and so do also stock analysts as they calculate the value of company shares.

Capitalism also provides opportunities for private ownership. Many privately owned fashion companies are family-owned. Some companies in the mid-range segment are privately owned while others are owned by private equity firms. Hoping to expand in Western Europe, the United States and various emerging markets, many fashion companies seek new capital by going public. They enter the financial market where various actors buy and sell financial assets in the form of securities (e.g., shares). This is an intangible market where actors speculate on the future development of various instruments and on the behavior of other actors. The financialization of our economy has increased greatly since the turn of the century and is well defined by Epstein as "the increasing role of financial motives, financial markets, financial actors, and financial institutions in the operation of domestic and international economies."[8] The financial market has become tremendously important for the functioning of the rest of the market economy, to the point where it is even possible to claim that the financial economy creates the conditions for the market economy. A critical factor in this development has been the emergence of large institutional investors such as pension funds, hedge funds and mutual funds. These investors are driven by the financial market logic and compete to attract private savings. Institutional investors often seek to invest in companies whose shares will increase in price relatively rapidly, giving shareholders a good return on their investment. Investment professionals working for these institutional investors are paid bonuses based on certain performance metrics, which may incentivize prudent investment behavior. Investment banks and brokers function as financial market intermediaries between funds and listed companies. They also act as sounding boards, giving advice to institutional investors.

None of the analysts I met legitimized their actions, views or attitudes using a cultural logic. They operate on the fringes of the cultural production field in an area of external, economic logic. Analysts and brokers are tied to the wider business sector and frequently monitor various industries. Their goal is to make good investments, not create good, interesting or innovative fashion. The prefixing of "fashion" to "trends" is only one reflection of the world in which they relate daily to different types of trends: wealth trends, commodity price trends, wage-cost trends and so on. Analysts' ratings, however, have repercussions for the fashion companies and their ability to grow. The actors in the fashion field recognize and are affected by this logic of valuation. So how do luxury-goods analysts relate to fashion trends as such and how can this be understood?

Luxury fashion and trends from the analysts' perspective

Here, the task of analysts is to provide advice to clients on their share portfolios in the luxury segment, which includes not just fashion houses but producers of alcohol, watches, jewelry, bags and accessories. Fashion is changeable at its heart, creating a problem of coordination between supply and demand. How can analysts know that the new collection of a fashion house will be well or poorly received, or whether it will be as well received as previous collections? Do analysts factor in the legitimating structures of the fashion field, the trend-forecasting agencies and tastemakers, to better predict values?

Trend services

Trends and trend services can be seen as helping coordinate supply and demand, organizing principles of the fashion field. Susanna Kempe, CEO of WGSN, describes WGSN's expansion beyond fashion to other clients, including manufacturers of various consumer products incorporating design elements and several British banks. This expansion to banking appears to have happened "through referrals and brand reputation," says Kempe, since WGSN has never marketed itself to that sector. There are two kinds of banking customers: general analysts, interested in luxury goods and retail and who monitor fashion companies, and consultants in mergers and acquisitions departments who must familiarize themselves with specific companies. Consultants disappear once the acquisition process is complete but the growing number of banking customers has prompted consideration of whether WGSN should develop a targeted product such as a "due diligence service."[9] Kempe regards problematic IPOs, like those of Prada and New Look, as instances when WGSN could have provided useful information.

Several analysts spoke of contacting fashion experts and other trend consultants for information and advice. None of the analysts I interviewed has used WGSN, Stylesight or any other Web-based trend service that highlights fashion. Some are familiar with the services and acknowledge that they would be useful, budgets permitting, while others asked me for the names of trend forecasters. (I may unwittingly have given impetus to the trend service "snowball.")

Valuation of stocks in the luxury segment

Analysts have no standard procedure for valuing stocks but consider a wide range of factors on various levels. It is vital to communicate regularly with companies to obtain relevant macrodata as well as industry-specific information. Macroeconomic data cover, for example, economic growth, wealth trends and demographic information, while industry-specific data illuminate how various categories within a sector are developing.

One analyst, who had previously performed competitor analysis at a large European fashion house, says that her current team focuses on the organic growth of the brand (excluding currency effects), including growth through new and existing stores ("like-for-like" growth). This information can be categorized by region and country, but as many purchases are made by traveling customers, such information rarely reflects the *true* buyer. Data must therefore be interpreted in terms of travel flows, which, in turn, depend on currency effects, import duties and taxes. The data must moreover be understood in light of macroeconomic trends, such as economic growth and the increase of disposable income on relevant markets, while incorporating company-specific information, such as the number of new stores and the company's capex budget (i.e., money that can be used to open new stores or expand current ones). Care must be taken, as some growth results from acquisitions. The position of a specific brand in its development phase can determine its potential for expansion or for "brand extensions"[10] (perhaps through licencing agreements), new stores and increased sales at department stores. "If a specific brand isn't sold at Saks, this must of course be viewed as a possibility," says one analyst. When Burberry recently enlarged its spaces at Nordstrom and Saks Fifth Avenue, both well-known American department store chains, this was immediately reflected in sales, notes another analyst.

It can be difficult to obtain accurate figures that allow for comparison of growth through new versus existing stores. To identify growth through existing stores, the usual approach is to undertake closer study of the relationship between price mix and volume increases, identifying how sales are divided between truly high-end products and more basic goods, to clarify what kinds of products drive up profit margins.

In addition to growth in various categories and regions, analysts are also interested in how companies position their brands. According to the analysts, it is impossible to quantify all factors, such as the risk of design piracy and the resulting overexposure: "It [i.e., valuation] is never totally mechanical," says one analyst.

Luxury brands generally have high operating margins. Depending on the company size, these margins might be used for continued expansion, which of course affects earnings per share. Sales growth is often the most relevant indicator in valuing a company, since it reflects what is most important in the luxury segment: the strength of the brand. Margins become a more interesting factor when valuing two companies with the same growth rate.

When stock valuation is discussed, none of the analysts I spoke with even touched on the fact that fashion companies operate in a field of cultural production, where cultural logic prevails and fashion per se is crucial. If a fashion company does not sell products through Saks Fifth Avenue or Nordstrom, analysts view this as an opportunity, not as signaling weak positioning in the fashion field. In other words, analysts view companies such as Saks Fifth Avenue and Nordstrom as economically dominant actors rather than as culturally *legitimizing* actors.

Distinctive features of the luxury industry

Three major luxury conglomerates include fashion in their business lines:

- LVMH Moët Hennessy-Louis Vuitton, which has interests in fashion designers such as Louis Vuitton, Kenzo, Céline, Givenchy, Fendi, Marc Jacobs, Emilio Pucci, Donna Karan and Edun

- PPR (Pinault-Printemps-Redoute, later Kering), which has major interests in Gucci, Yves Saint Laurent, Bottega Veneta, Balenciaga, Stella McCartney and Alexander McQueen

- Richemont, which includes Chloé, Shanghai Tang, Azzedine Alaïa and retailer Net-A-Porter in its portfolio

"The most penetrated" countries,[11] where luxury brands are the most common, are Italy, France and Japan. The most distinctive feature of the luxury goods sector is the enormous strength of its brands, which ultimately gives them superior pricing power. The consumers to whom luxury brands appeal are notably price insensitive: the brand is so enchanting that they are willing to pay for the brand itself, not just the quality that the brand guarantees. All the analysts I spoke with agree that the power of the brand distinguishes the luxury sector from most others.

The significance of existing brands and the emphasis on brand heritage and history raises barriers to the entry of new actors. Some analysts argue that it is still possible to enter the market, citing Dolce & Gabbana and Roberto Cavalli as examples of "new" brands (twenty- and forty-years-old, respectively). Certain designers make names for themselves as heads of design at particular fashion houses and thereafter introduce their own brands, as did Roland Mouret, Alexander McQueen and others. There is a cadre of relatively young fashion designers such as Alexander Wang and Proenza Schouler with their own brands, though some analysts are reluctant to view these as fully developed luxury brands. "They need to be subsumed by a larger group of companies, under an umbrella of other luxury brands, to survive and expand," says one analyst. "If you want to expand, you're bleeding cash from day one. It's expensive to open boutiques, hire staff, produce and communicate." Of the brands examined in the previous chapter, probably only Imogen Brown qualifies as a "true" luxury brand by these analysts' definitions, since a luxury conglomerate owns a major stake of the company.

The barriers to entry are assumed to be increasing as the emerging markets grow in importance. Consumers in those markets are said to be extremely loyal to European and, to some extent, American brands with distinct heritages. The Chinese market is unique in that exposure of these brands is unusually large there, while there is no measurable domestic competition. The promise of expansion and growth permeates the luxury industry.

Some analysts also mention capriciousness and changeability as typical in the luxury goods industry, acknowledging that this is characteristic of the fashion industry generally.

Relationship to trends

Capriciousness and *changeability*—with these concepts we return to trends. The cultural production field that is fashion applies two logics, economic and cultural, seen as each other's opposites. The cultural logic is internal. Those who legitimize their actions with reference to it wish to advance or consolidate their position *within* the fashion field. They learn the cycles of fashion with its self-referential system. Cultural logic dictates that individuals and organizations that fail to legitimize their actions, views and ideas according to this logic will be regarded as not truly interested in fashion. Those who legitimize their actions with reference to economic logic alone will perceive fashion people as uninterested in business— as truly disinterested actors, in Bourdieu's terms—and will dismiss the fashion world as arbitrary and capricious. This characterization is overly sweeping but nonetheless highlights the underlying contradiction between the two logics, which no individuals can change on their own. Despite the presence of the strong cultural logic at the heart of fashion, the field remains absolutely commercial and very capitalist. The rules are well understood by those in the field—the two logics are not separate at all.

In a glass-walled skyscraper near St. Paul's Cathedral, two international investment banking analysts discuss trends and luxury brands. One analyst, Helen White, says that fashion trends are much vaguer than the data they use: the analyst team therefore looks at broader trends, such as the importance of heritage. When fashion companies "return to their roots," sort through their archives and reintroduce new variations of some items, brands with well-defined and explicit heritages have a better chance of selling well. White and her team also follow trends in goods such as handbags to analyze which brands offer the very best:

> But it's very subjective and you can get caught up in something that is only a tiny portion of what drives the numbers. So it's qualitative, definitely, but we do look at different surveys and what the department stores identify as the top-ten must-haves, to get a sense of what's going on. There are also conversations with families and friends. We ask people on the ground about what they are seeing, what they are hearing, what brands are doing well. The department stores won't comment on it, but we try to talk around it. But it's difficult. We look at what the fashion critics say after the runways, but the runways are ultimately a tiny, tiny part.

While many informants emphasize the importance of "checking out the store," White is somewhat skeptical about the merits of this method: how a store looks on a particular day can deviate so widely from the norm that the visit is meaningless. The companies like to reduce analysts' expectations of sales growth and profit margins so that these can be surpassed to create positive surprises. Sales data from retailers and brands' own stores are often confidential for competitive reasons: no outsider should know the sales of a brand on a detailed level, for example, in particular regions or product categories.

In addition to the seasonal top-ten lists of the major department stores, White likes to read blogs and fashion magazines to learn what clothes and objects are highlighted as trendy. "Reading fashion magazines is part of my job," she says, identifying the most credible fashion magazines as *Elle, Vogue, InStyle* and *Harper's Bazaar*. "That [i.e., trendiness] can be an indication, but it's only a part of it." Trendiness does not always translate into sales, since a single clothing item is a minute part of total sales for any luxury brand. It is more significant when one of these major fashion magazines defines a bag or shoes as the season's "must-have," as these will have a greater sales potential. White clearly comprehends the commercial side of the fashion scene.

In the fall of 2010, Gucci's 1973 handbag line was featured on several such seasonal trend lists, which was picked up by White's analyst team in report on the fashion conglomerate PPR. In addition to fashion magazine coverage, public relations (PR) has become increasingly vital, says White. For example, many brands that had no close connections to the Los Angeles film industry are making concerted efforts to establish themselves with parties and complimentary items: "Tod's is one example—all of a sudden everyone wears the shoes!"

Another analyst says that they do not look closely at fashion when evaluating fashion company shares but concentrate instead on how much the company invests in advertising campaigns and building stores and, more generally, on how the whole luxury sector is performing. Fashion factors are considered by analysts when assessing whether shares are under- or overvalued. An analyst might, for example, consider whether "a brand has lost its head of design, or if the product doesn't seem to be popular, or if the ad campaign is not getting good reviews."

The changeable heart of fashion is recognized as problematic by luxury analysts. Fashion has become *fashion risk*. The proportion of luxury-brand sales that constitutes real fashion (that is renewed and that is characterized by or creates trends) is such a small percentage of total sales that it has little relevance for the valuation of the company's stock.

Many male analysts agree that womenswear is more variable and therefore more difficult to judge. This view might be partly attributable to the two logics being constructed as opposites, which means these analysts view fashion as a meaningless flow of shifting styles. The analyst who bluntly stated that he is totally ignorant about fashion is embedded in the economic logic. It would be interesting to know if an auto industry analyst could safely and confidently make a similar statement about being ignorant of cars.

The tension between consistency and change

Many luxury brands have adopted a business model similar to Louis Vuitton's, in which a small proportion of sales consists of new products (featured on catwalks, in the media and in store windows) and most sales consist of carryovers or evergreens that are not marked down at the end of each season because they will sell equally well next year. This model "gives the impression of change, but actually, not much is changing. It's primarily the runway show, which is a tiny sliver of the whole range and always a bit artistic, that represents this change. There is always that 'show factor' that doesn't necessarily translate into sales," one analyst observes.

The few new products in each season consist of limited editions; when they are sold out, there are no more. The luxury fashion houses have abandoned the two-season system, instead introducing products in frequent releases, "capsule collections"[12] and special collections that exploit the fast-fashion approach. The changeable portion is not what drives their business, but it does help brands attract attention—free advertising, as it were—for their message, or "news," to be heard. One analyst I spoke with observed that the significant expense of advertising a product, versus the cost of its creation, illustrates the absolutely central role of communication.

Growth in the luxury industry

Financial analysts claim that luxury brands must also master the balance between exclusivity and growth. The well-known investment bank Goldman Sachs estimates that the world will have an additional 600 million luxury product consumers by 2025.[13]

The listed luxury brands or company groups often have single controlling owners, PPR, LVMH and Hermès being good examples of this structure. Burberry is the foremost fashion company with a complete "free float," the controlling owner being expected to trade in the stock. Analysts believe that the luxury brands would prefer to avoid the stock market were it not for the necessary capital that can be raised from it; in fact, some analysts stated it would be easier for fashion brands to work out long-term strategies outside the market.

Shareholders seek growth, but growth can lead to overexposure, which in turn devalues the aura of luxury. Most big brands strive for total control over production, distribution, trade, communication and pricing, cutting back on wholesalers, running their own stores and obtaining concessions in preferred department stores. There is always a concern that wholesalers and independent distributors with priorities other than safeguarding the integrity of the brand might deeply discount products to clear their stock and cover costs.

Compared with mass-market fashion brands, luxury brands have relatively few stores, Louis Vuitton taking the lead with 460 stores in sixty countries. The analysts I spoke with expect that most luxury brands will eventually each have

around one hundred boutiques in China. Of course, growth in China depends on successful boutique locations and staffing and on expansion into second- and third-tier cities[14] having large enough populations of wealthy customers.

Though the insistent economic logic may seem to have little to do with trends, it profoundly affects the space given to changeable fashion, and hence trends. Against the promise of multiyear expansion and growth in emerging markets, luxury brands target aspirational consumers in their product marketing. Fashion houses, too, adapt to this logic, giving neomania, which is fashion's heart, a less prominent role.

Mass-market fashion and trends from the stock analysts' perspective

In her book *Overdressed: The Shockingly High Cost of Cheap Fashion*, Elizabeth Cline outlined how customers' expectations of constant price cuts now inform much of the fashion industry, particularly the low-price chains. In 1900, average American families spent 15 percent of their income on clothes. The most common items purchased in stores were ready-to-wear suits, which cost on average USD 15 (USD 380 in today's prices).[15] In 2011, by comparison, the average individual American spent USD 1,100 and the average family spent USD 1,740 per year on clothes. In other words, under 3 percent of the average 2011 household budget was spent on clothes.[16] With the proportion of personal budgets spent on clothes being lower than ever, Cline noted that clothing money has never before gone as far as it does today.[17] *The relative price* of clothes has, in other words, decreased significantly.

H&M

In 2004, Swedish mass-market fashion company Lindex's fashion miss, the "mountain of trousers," was widely covered in Swedish media. The company was said to have interpreted the current mood so badly that trousers worth EUR 2.65 million were left in stores.[18] In my interviews with the Stockholm-based analysts who specialize in mass-market fashion retail firms, the terms "fashion miss" and "fashion risk" were common. Nils Vinge, H&M's head of investor relations, says that the company's head of design sometimes participates in quarterly meetings with financial analysts in an effort to educate them about fashion, about the unique aspects of the industry. As of February 2013, H&M has a market capitalization of EUR 45 billion, making it the biggest company on the Stockholm stock exchange and several times larger than all other companies in its sector together. All the Swedish analysts I met with estimated that they spent half of their time on H&M, so it is unsurprising that conversations about financial analysis and fashion trends largely concerned H&M.

The analysts appreciate that H&M's head of design attends the quarterly financial meetings. As one analyst puts it, "An analyst's strength is not assessing collections, but assessing the growth potential, estimating profitability." He admits that during the presentation of quarterly reports, analysts are often so focused on numbers and financial questions that the head of design's words pass almost unnoticed, seeming to target the media more than analysts. Another analyst says of the head of design's participation:

> It adds some *flavor*... you get to meet someone else and hear something else. But to put it bluntly, it's not something that's going to change your view. I mean, of course if she was a disaster ... that would probably make you a little concerned.

Several analysts do not even remember the head of design's participation and think that she usually does not receive many questions: "The thing is that the financial industry is so incredibly trained to focus on what the EPS is, what the result is going to be."[19] One analyst says he and his colleagues have given up hope of being able to assess a collection, leaving "that factor" to H&M and only monitoring how H&M "manages" it and that discounting is not "too extensive."

"Essentially, the activity of a fashion company is to purchase a stock and then sell it. And this involves a gigantic fashion risk that the company must manage in various ways," says one Stockholm analyst. Until 2000, H&M had "fashion misses" approximately every five years, when the collection was out of step with the times. The last time was at the turn of the century, when H&M's offering had too much color while customers preferred gray, black and blue. The historiographies of several analysts are remarkably consistent in this; many others also got it wrong at the time—global fashion was generally off, one analyst adds. They all agree that major changes have occurred since 2000.

Nils Vinge, who has held several positions at H&M, describes H&M's business model, which is based on the "fashion triangle." At the apex, Vinge explains, are the latest trends, in the middle the season's fashion and at the bottom the "modern basics"—for example, simple socks and sweaters that everyone needs in their wardrobe. The large sales volumes occur in the lower parts of the pyramid. The higher in the pyramid an item appears, the more volatile (i.e., changeable) the fashion. Only a limited number of stores in large cities carry top-of-pyramid garments, as fashion "early adopters" are not as common in smaller cities. H&M also incorporates the "Boston matrix," a model familiar to business students, which is used to categorize a company's products according to their position on the market and how much they contribute to profitability. The four categories in this matrix are "stars," "cash cows," "question marks" and "dogs." The very latest trends are question marks: the company "flings them out," initially selling these items in limited quantities in select stores in big cities. If the trend catches on, perhaps even sells out on the first day, H&M orders much more of similar goods. The company must not, however, stay with one trend for too long, lest it become a "dog."

H&M's fashion pyramid and Boston matrix have been well communicated, because all Swedish analysts refer to them. They recognize the shortened lead times required for this business model to function well, so that the company can quickly sense the market's reception and put in extra orders. "H&M has created a model that removes the fashion risk," says one analyst. As H&M stopped using the two-season system and instead began to sell several smaller collections that continuously feature new pieces, its ability to adapt gradually increased: "One collection can be a bit off—there might have been too many polka dots or too much color—but then you fix it quickly." This means the fashion risk has decreased. It is quite easy for mass-market fashion companies to look at their mail-order and online sales numbers to gain a preliminary idea of what customers want. The global fashion companies have also managed to significantly reduce their inventories, which further lessens the risk. In 2000, in conjunction with H&M's color "fashion miss," the company's inventory to sales ratio was 15 to 16 percent; currently, it is 9 to 10 percent. Much more is bought "in season," enabled by short lead times and increased productivity. Customers know that the range changes quickly and that they need to buy when the coveted piece is in store. Mass-market fashion companies reserve options on production capacity at factories, placing immense demands on suppliers' flexibility. This points to the institutionalization of buyers' interests, which the sociologist Patrik Aspers has noted as typical of a standard market (see p. 136).[20]

Analysts speak with admiration of H&M's confidential database of statistics dating back to 1963 covering how various clothing items, broken down by their attributes, have sold. This information facilitates the company's risk management, they say.

Not everyone believes that the fashion risk has been completely eliminated. In spring 2012, one analyst said: "[H&M] has pretty good stuff in the stores—you can see it in the sales, things are happening." The year before was more dubious, but it is difficult to capture these variations in an Excel spreadsheet model, he noted. Another analyst points to the possible problem with fashion companies' use of the expression "fashion miss." It can be a convenient explanation for a fashion industry CEO who blames the buyers, when it is a problem that is perhaps rooted in targeted market segment and leadership.

The risk of not taking risks

Risk management was often discussed in the interviews with mass-market fashion analysts. All of them agree that companies must dare to take risks. If companies concentrate only on securing gross margins, operating margins, financial rewards, etc., they will eventually die. One of H&M's success factors is that its buyers take risks. The company has created a culture in which failure is acceptable, for example, when a buyer chooses an extreme fashion that then does not sell well. One analyst sees mass-market fashion companies as taking fewer risks during economic booms, when underlying demand is strong, and greater risks during recessions, when the supply must stand out more: "You won't [just] buy a white t-shirt if you're hurting for cash. You must really want the piece you purchase." For this reason, many mass-market fashion companies raise their fashion levels during recessions: H&M, for example, intensifies its designer collaborations, entering into them more frequently.

None of the mass-market fashion analysts that I interviewed admitted to using the large Web-based trend services, though some of them took note of the names WGSN and Stylesight when I mentioned them. Many analysts have invited bloggers and trend analysts to give presentations in order to better understand their relevance to the mass market. However, the analysts seem to have reached the conclusion that blogs are often "too personal." The analysts want answers to such questions as: What do people buy in Jönköping, Braunschweig and the suburbs of Chicago? Do the shopping behaviors differ between these places? Is the trend-conscious big city woman more into mix-and-match? They have also consulted local trend scouts, such as fashion journalists, as well as H&M's head of design to learn how people involved in fashion work.

One analyst team has often consulted trend analysts, engaging them to talk to investors and appraise collections:

> But it's impossible! I mean, we have really tried to do what you ask about, but the conclusion has always been—it's not possible. I'm sure it's doable if you break it down, but we have to look at our daily activities and how much time we can spend on it.

As for analysts potentially using trend-forecasting services for more detailed information to help them predict the success of a company's collections, one analyst observes, "[the trend concept] is super interesting, but we can't evaluate it. And we don't dare to bet on it. I don't think anyone dares to bet on it." However, I explain that it is unlikely that a mass-market fashion chain's collections would ever starkly contrast to the big trend services' forecasts. Their prognoses are, so to speak, already "baked" into the collections. Since some mass-market fashion companies have long lead times for some parts of their collections, the services' close-to-the-season forecasts might be more useful to analysts. One analyst thinks that the corporate finance departments that deal with mergers and acquisitions use trend services more frequently and that luxury-brand analysts would have more use for their information (interestingly, luxury-brand analysts said the opposite). No analyst considers it particularly significant that the mass-market fashion companies use these services to minimize risk. At the suggestion that fashion companies' subscribing to trend services could be a safety factor for investors, analysts indicate that they trust the companies to deal with risk management. The analysts' job is to interpret the outcome by examining sales levels.

Several analysts described visiting stores around the world, studying the range of goods and potential sales, even taking pictures and questioning sometimes reluctant sales staff. Not all stores are reticent: "at H&M on Hamngatan, they're used to analysts, they have finance people going in and out all the time." One analyst explains:

> The area where many analysts could probably improve is understanding fashion better. But at the same time, fashion is so terribly subjective and difficult. When H&M releases a collection, they don't know themselves if it's going to work—you hope it's going to work, but it's anybody's guess. If analysts are going to go out to the stores and assess whether this fashion is good or not, it's going to be so subjective, and they will probably only get it right every other time.

Here again, we see that the financial analysts view the cultural logic of fashion as arbitrary and capricious.

Valuation of fashion stock from the perspective of Swedish analysts

Mass-market fashion analysts also look at GDP forecasts, private consumption forecasts and other macrodata, but it seems more difficult to draw conclusions about the growth of mass-market fashion companies than about luxury brands based on such data. In markets that H&M has fully "penetrated," for example, in the Nordic countries and Germany, sales are lower during serious recessions. In some markets, companies can negotiate better terms during recessions, for things such as leases. Recessions can also mean that companies gain new customers seeking more "bang for their buck." H&M's risk is viewed as mitigated since, as a global retailer, it is simultaneously exposed to so many quite different markets.

By studying H&M's catalogs over time, analysts estimate price trends, especially for basics. Several analysts consider that H&M's long-term strategy means that it behaves more like an unlisted company in many ways. The company is said to be willing to lower prices for two years, for example, if it believes that this will produce the desired effect in five years, even though this affects the short-term financial results.

A mass-market fashion company needs a market capitalization of just under SEK 1 million to interest most analysts. Just as in the luxury goods segment, for a company to be worth monitoring, it is important that its free float of shares be large enough to trade. This means that some Swedish fashion companies, such as Odd Molly and WESC, are too small. Given that some listed companies are extremely secretive, analysts may contact smaller unlisted companies, which are normally more open, to learn about industry tendencies (e.g., whether purchase prices in Asia are rising or falling) that could affect larger companies. Analysts stay current with the industry by maintaining regular contact with senior personnel, reading unmonitored companies' quarterly reports, reading industry media such as Swedish *Habit*, American *Women's Wear Daily* and German *Textil Wirtschaft*, participating in and arranging seminars and meetings with representatives of corporations and institutions, and visiting companies and suppliers in various countries. Analysts often visit smaller companies that share suppliers with larger firms, since bigger corporations are often less willing to cater to analysts.

Valuation of fashion stock from the perspective of British analysts

Most British analysts I met do not monitor companies with market capitalizations of under GBP 1 billion. They monitor retail firms such as Marks & Spencer, Debenhams, H&M, Inditex, Primark (part of AB Foods) and Next, as well as retail segments such as electronics and home furnishings.

Fashion trends are more important than people think, says one analyst for an independent stockbroker in London's City. Financial analyst teams in the City attach different priorities to fashion trends depending on the subsector monitored, he says—a familiar claim among British mass-market analysts. Some analysts monitor both mass-market fashion companies and luxury brands. Fashion trends are more meaningful when monitoring young fashion retailers:

> If you are covering Marks & Spencer or Next, then price and quality are more important. But in the case of H&M and Inditex, if the fashion trends are not right, then it could affect the figures considerably.

One team of women analysts at a large international bank claims that they sometimes have a different perspective from that of most financial analysts. "Because of course we think about where we shop, [my boss] thinks about where she buys her kids' clothes, things like that. So it [i.e., the perspective] tends to be a bit different from that of a middle-aged man," says Lisa Brown. Many of the companies monitored by this team have young people as their target market. The team includes a young woman just out of university who provides valuable information about where she and her friends shop. Brown emphasizes the importance of seeing the consumers' side, not just weighing financial data.

Because it is difficult to assess demand in fashion, the all-woman team starts by studying demand over the previous six months and previous year, considering campaigns and collaborations that might affect sales and price trends. The catalogs of the fashion chain Next are published quarterly and offer some guidance as to price trends on fashionable pieces. Brown says that it is unhelpful to assess the future more than three to six months ahead:

> My boss has fifteen years of experience and has a feeling, an intuition, about what is going to work—probably a little similar to a buyer who follows trends very carefully. And you make a sort of guess, an estimate. You can be totally wrong, and sometimes it is difficult when your figure is very different from everyone else's.

Weather and the dates of particular holidays can also affect the success of collections. Brown's team studies the collections and the team members divide the top fashion magazines among themselves to discern whether a particular brand is especially prominent. They often contact companies of interest to ask about their collections, though listed fashion companies are reluctant to share such information. In that case, the team makes its own estimates, though "we're not fashion people, we are just out looking," Brown adds.

No British analyst I spoke with uses trend services because of lack of time and staff. Like the Stockholm analysts, they think that these services would be of more use to luxury goods analysts. One analyst from a large international bank finds the services too expensive but understands why people use them:

> It's all about minimizing markdown. With these services you can make sure that you have the right product at the right price and maximize the returns, get a better return on capital employed in that business by earning more profit per pound of sales.

Several analysts I spoke with have access to various databases of industry statistics, industry journals such as *Drapers* and magazines from internet retailers such as ASOS. There are much clearer links to tastemakers in Britain than in Sweden. One analyst is friendly with a style director at Selfridges, and some editors-in-chief of fashion magazines have also become personal friends.

All of the British analysts speak of fashion magazines as a source of information about the season, especially regarding the frequency a particular brand is mentioned in the editorial pages.

"*Cosmopolitan* is my favourite magazine," says one young analyst who, in addition to working a large London bank, runs a private-equity firm investing in fashion companies. He knows that editors feature certain products in such magazines not because these products are good but because their producers pay well but realizes that such mentions are crucial to success, even more than advertising is. One way onto the editorial pages is via celebrity endorsement of an accessory or piece of clothing. Social media constitute the only promotional channel equivalent in importance to such feature coverage.

At a time when both raw-material and labor costs are high, many mass-market fashion actors have chosen factories and suppliers with longer lead times, which according to one British analyst reintroduces fashion risk. If a style produced eight months before does not become popular, the company can be in trouble. It is equally tricky to increase production of an item if demand increases.

When analysts meet with a company, they typically ask, "Have you increased the amount of high fashion relative to basics?" rather than get too specific. A big retailer might reply, quite specifically, "We were on trend, because we had a lot of neon, a lot of jumpsuits, a lot of sportwear, the right shoes."

One British analyst who specializes in retail companies for a large international bank says that the fashion sector is incredibly "subjective": everyone has an opinion and everyone has had shopping experience. When it comes to evaluating a fashion brand specifically, in addition to determining what added value the brand offers its target audience, he also looks at whether it has appeal across borders, to understand its global potential. He might need to examine each season in isolation, as growth of 4–5 percent during spring and summer does not necessarily guarantee the same growth the next season. There are many factors to consider: collections, design and consumers.

> H&M is not what I would call high fashion. A proportion of what they sell comes from the high-fashion line, but the largest part comes from the commodity sector. Then it's more about those items being in line with the seasonal trends, that they have the right colors, the right key looks, at the key entry price points. But if you are someone like Zara, you build far more on your fashion credentials than you do on your basics credentials. Zara has a very sophisticated design and feedback process which allows them to minimize fashion risk within their offering. So they focus far more on maximizing their sales through a fashion offer at a right price, whereas H&M is slightly more volume-driven and based on a lower-fashion garment.

Some fashion companies succeed in their activities without following trends, such as Desigual, which is quite off trend, he says, and consequently could never have as many stores as, say, H&M.

Analysts define companies in the mass fashion market very differently, for example, some viewing H&M as high fashion, others not. These differing understandings should not be confused with the struggle for fashion capital in the fashion field (see p. 99). From the perspective of financial analysts, value has nothing to do with prestige or fashion capital but with how companies, based on their fashion profile ("Are they *high fashion* or not?"), manage risk. The reasoning is based on economic logic.

Companies sometimes manage fashion risk by expanding. If a fashion company expands its retail space by 10–15 percent, entering new markets where the brand is not yet established, it matters less that the brand is not fully in line with local trends. Consumers will buy simply because the brand is new.

Analysts are inundated every day with information on consumer sentiment, the housing market, retail sales, consumer spending, GDP growth, interest rates, tax levels, oil spills, material shortages and car sales, which are all considered important indicators of future consumption. They all claim that what happens to consumer sentiment and activity is absolutely central to their valuation of fashion stocks.

The tension between consistency and change

The brands in the mass-market segment differ from those in the luxury goods industry. They are often well known but not always as defined by their aesthetic as are luxury brands, and no analyst spoke of the pricing powers of these mass-market brands.

When it is suggested that H&M as a company "embraces everything" and is not defined or limited by a certain style and is in a way *not* a brand, Nils Vinge observes:

> It's interesting. We want to appeal to everyone, we talk about democratic fashion and so on. Everyone can find something at H&M, which is a strength. But it can also be a weakness. Because we can do everything pretty well, but we can't be the best at everything. If you have more of a niche, you can be the world's best in what you are doing for a while. But the risk is that if that trend disappears, then the brand becomes boring.

Interbrand's annual ranking of the best global brands placed H&M as number 21 in 2011 and number one among fashion retailers. In contrast, Louis Vuitton was number 16 that year and first in the luxury brands category. Nils Vinge was asked by a financial analyst, "Is H&M a brand or not? Because if you are, that would be great. You can charge more for the same product; the customer is willing to pay more for the brand." Another analyst remarked, "I don't think that you're a brand. The risk of being a brand is that it has a product life cycle, and from that follows the risk that it may go out of style. Then the company as a whole would be uninteresting."[21]

Since H&M is being copied and the company has made inroads into emerging markets, it is increasingly evident that H&M is viewed as a brand, though its business model remains that of providing fashion and quality at the best price. All the analysts I talked to view H&M as a brand. As a British analyst notes, "the tag at the back of the shirt means that it's a brand." One analyst says that he regards it as a brand "with a strong fashion character"; according to the same analyst, H&M and Inditex both feed on trends, which means that they do not lack opportunities for renewal and that the brand does not restrain them. He goes on to say that brands in the mid-range segment usually have periods when they are very successful and their style fits the current fashion, but eventually they run out of luck. Mid-segment brands, which are fairly narrow in their niches and may have no evergreen products, often run a high risk, says another analyst. Odd Molly's cardigans and Björn Borgs's colorful print briefs are examples: such distinctive items can help a company do very well, but if consumers lose interest in the cardigans or briefs, for example, the brand rarely has anything else to offer. Analysts agree that the fashion brands in the mid-range segment range are too *binary*: "they're either really trendy, or completely out of style and then they die," failing to remain attractive to customers who seek something new.

The London analysts are very aware of the difficulties inherent in the mid-range segment. Analyst John Smith explains that service, quality and execution must be balanced to assure the right amount of profit. These companies must be far more engaged with and focused on their target market. It is a difficult position in a market increasingly polarized between exclusive design and high prices and lack of design and low prices, he notes. Mid-range brands need to offer customers a trade-up to convince them to leave the low-range segment while offering high enough quality to attract customers who normally shop in higher ranges.

The mid-range segment is shrinking because, analyst Smith claims, some companies have made the mistake of not following trends:

> You have to move with seasonal trends. Very few brands can get away with selling the same products year in, year out, products that don't change at all. But you can't afford to stray so far from your brand identity that you alienate your present customers.

A common way to manage the tension between consistency and change, says Smith, is to launch additional versions, lines or special collections, as does the British brand Barbour:

> A Barbour jacket is still a Barbour jacket. It doesn't change. But the brand now has a quilted version and a waxed version. They have different colors, they have a Steve McQueen collection. They have capsule collections and diffusion lines. Launching new collections, that's what you can do to make it more attractive and relevant to the customer base without alienating them.

Many designer brands have *diffusion lines*, that is, sublines in a lower price range that retain the characteristics of the brand and its aura but have a wider appeal, such as Marc by Marc Jacobs and Jil Sander Navy. It can be dangerously tempting just to keep doing what already works, Smith cautions. French Connection had one of the fashion industry's best campaigns in England with the FCUK clothing line, but the company continued it one season too many. Wholesalers could not sell their inventory and store sales collapsed. There was not enough that was new—the range consisted of repetitions ("retail-by-numbers")—and it was clear that the company had lost touch with its creativity. "If your brand collapses, if you deviate from the trends, it may take years to re-establish the credibility of the brand," Smith concludes.

The analysts who monitor retail are, like their luxury-brand counterparts, dubious about their own influence on the industry. Their short-term view means that a high share price is emphasized, often at the expense of building a sustainable brand. The time that companies must dedicate to informing the analysts is another drawback. Ownership is a key consideration in the assessment process. A fashion company owned by a private equity firm, whose capital market goal is to build company value for three years and then sell, will develop differently from a privately owned company, whose goal is to develop sustainably for decades.

Expansion and growth

All analysts of mass-market fashion companies see remarkable potential for expansion. British Topshop has entered the North American market and is expected to establish itself on the emerging markets as well. Inditex, which controls the Zara brand, among others, now has over 6,000 stores worldwide[22] and more than 400 stores in China, where it can expect to expand over the next twenty years. Since 85 percent of H&M's sales are European and 12 percent from the United States, "H&M's exposure to the emerging markets is … completely underdeveloped—so that's a great opportunity," says one British analyst. For a large company such as H&M, massive economies of scale are available in advertising, supplier contracts and leases.

In the developed world, e-commerce will be the major contributor to further growth, but the BRIC countries are the number one growth opportunity, says one British analyst specializing in retail at a large banking corporation at Canary Wharf:

What you have is a rapidly emerging middle class population in these emerging markets [with] disposable income and aspirations to own and increasingly aware of global fashion trends and global fashion brands. That's the key driver. When people talk about the globalization of the fashion industry, they're actually talking about the *Westernizing* of the fashion industry. They're not talking about Latin American fashion growing in isolation and being exported to the rest of the world. They are talking about Western fashion being exported to the emerging markets.

*

When financial analysts relate to fashion trends, they are aware of aspects that other fashion professionals ignore, such as the price of raw materials, labor costs, wealth trends, taxes as well as share price.

Many analysts, regardless of their specialty, speak of fashion as subjective and capricious, ultimately beyond rational understanding. While mass-market fashion analysts can use friends, family and customers as informal research subjects, this is more difficult for luxury goods analysts who do not "get" the logic of fashion, womenswear in particular.

As noted above, in the fashion field the two logics, economic and cultural, are constructed as each other's opposites. For those governed by an economic logic, the internal, cultural logic that prevails in the fashion field seems arbitrary and subjective, and it is often gendered as female. Even if people respect this logic, and understand the importance of renewal, they still find it difficult to approach. Male analysts often do not engage with fashion professionals, for example, the head of design present at the quarterly meetings. Some analysts, especially women, have slightly fewer reservations about the "capriciousness" and subjectivity of the fashion industry. This may be because these women are more used to the field and more familiar with its aesthetic knowledge base: one senior female analyst, with fifteen years of experience, has developed an intuition and a feeling for what works. It may still be that analysts find it difficult to predict, for example, how well a collection will sell, because they do not participate in creating the incipient taste (see p. 50).

It became evident to me that many analysts, both those analyzing luxury fashion and those addressing mass-market fashion, do not see the need to assess actual collections, simply leaving the "fashion risk" to the fashion companies themselves. Yet the companies manage this risk by creating business models that minimize these risks, adapting to the financial market. Luxury brands as well as mass-market fashion brands adopt fashion pyramids like that of H&M, with a base of enduring goods and a small portion of trendy fashion. They seek not only financial stability but also legitimacy in the eyes of the financial market through the structure of a trusted product range.

British analysts, unlike Swedish ones, seem more aware of fashion as a field of cultural production reliant on tastemakers such as magazines and department stores. One interpretation is that UK tastemakers have a larger influence on the global fashion scene than do Swedish ones (although there is nothing that prevents Swedish analysts from reading international magazines). Another possible interpretation is that British analysts monitor a range of British mass-market fashion companies such as Next and Marks & Spencer that have a relatively large home-country customer base and for which British tastemakers are crucial. In contrast, the Swedish domestic market and tastemakers are less decisive for H&M, whose expansion ensures less "fashion risk," since the brand is globally attractive.

Dana Thomas remarked in *Deluxe: How Luxury Lost Its Luster* that luxury fashion's dependence on capital markets has resulted in reduced quality because of the focus on high margins and earnings per share.[23] Sean Cormier, professor of marketing and textile development at FIT, told Elizabeth Cline that the pressure to produce cheaper clothing comes both from consumers and from fashion companies that demand better margins and cannot survive if consumers shop only during sales.[24]

Simultaneously, in the mid-range segment, many brands have increased their prices by 8–10 percent over the last few years to compensate for higher material prices and wage inflation abroad. The current societal trends opposing overconsumption and favoring greater social and environmental responsibility mean that many fashion companies expect to sell fewer items but at higher prices in the future. One British analyst thinks that the mass-market fashion companies will likely follow the mid-range lead:

> The whole fashion industry was supported by a decade of what I call "the cheap US dollar–Far East carry trade". We were all going out to the Far East and sourcing product cheaper, thus taking advantage of a weak US dollar since all the Far East currencies are pegged to the US dollar. Buying that product much cheaper allowed me to sell my garments back in Europe at ever cheaper prices, year after year, and still make more money on the margin. I could use my volume gains to source cheaper and cheaper.

This disinflationary dynamic has now been reversed, he says:

> [But] the cost of labor in the Far East is going up at 15 to 20 per cent every year, commodity prices—for example cotton—are rising year by year. We are now starting to reach a level where some of the entry-price-point retailers like H&M or Primark in the UK are so big that they can start to set the agenda for the industry as a whole. If Primark or H&M decided to put up their prices by a couple per cent, the rest would follow. Because it's not in anyone's interest not to follow. Because if you try to undercut Primark and H&M on price, you will eventually go out of business. After all, they are the biggest players around.

Such price increases can have consequences for what financial analysts refer to as "fashion risk." The mutual embeddedness of the status and standard markets (see Patrik Aspers's concepts on p. 136) is illustrated in the British analyst's comment on mass-market fashion companies' reintroduction of fashion risk. As costs increase in the standard market where manufacturing occurs, the resulting longer lead times (e.g., it may be necessary to switch to factories with less efficient processes) engender greater uncertainty, which has repercussions for the status market, where garments obtain symbolic value as on or off trend. An increased CSR focus in production can create higher "fashion risk" if improvements in working conditions and sustainable processes extend lead times.

Expansion into emerging markets gives rise to further risk minimizing, as a result of fashion companies being forced to submit to financial market logic to attain needed capital. Fashion, which is rooted in modernity and capitalism, is closely connected to Western culture. As pointed out above, the globalization of the fashion industry is really the expansion of Western fashion. The following chapters therefore concentrate on the emerging BRIC countries, not to fully map their fashion fields but to capture certain discourses that complement the Eurocentric/Western image of fashion.

8 THE BRIC COUNTRIES AND TRENDS

India

Vogue India's Trend Report appendix for May 2012: The predominately European fashions are sorted into the categories "Loud and Proud," "Sugar Rush" and "Citrus Punsch." One startling article features the kurta, a typically Indian garment like a long shirt or tunic, worn by both women and men: "The Indian classic has gone global. International runways showed various versions of the kurta, a must-have for all shapes." The pictures from Céline, Anna Sui, Junya Watanabe, Louis Vuitton and Dries van Noten are indicative of not just the global success of the kurta, with its Indian origin, but of how fashion and trends are viewed by fashion professionals in that country.

India's potential as a fashion market is gigantic. Informants in both London and New York spoke about the total dominance of menswear and the success of denimwear, especially for men, in India. The market is growing at enormous speed, and India's former import restrictions, lifted only in the 1990s, still lend some Western brands a certain cachet. "In India, it's all about denim," says Susanna Kempe, the CEO of WGSN, which in 2011 bought Denimhead, an American Web-based trend agency focused on denim, to better support their Indian market, where at the time Denimhead lacked customers.

Harleen Sabharwal is a trend analyst who describes the Indian fashion market as undynamic but budding. Indian fashion designers do not renew themselves but find one form of expression that they keep repeating, neither creating nor following trends: "You can't have more than one Manish Arora bag." My own anecdotal experience confirms this: the Manish Arora shawl I purchased one year was still for sale a year later, though it would not be considered a staple or basic. Manish Arora, however, has been lauded by Western cultural institutions such as the Victoria & Albert Museum, where his work has been exhibited; he has been named best Indian designer and has shown several collections at London Fashion Week. In 2011–2012, he was the creative director of Paco Rabanne— an unmistakeable sign that the emerging markets are now fashion nations to be reckoned with.

According to Sabharwal, the Indian fashion market consists of 80 percent menswear, 10 percent denim, 7 percent children's clothes and 3 percent womenswear. The Indian middle class was estimated at 160 million people in 2014 and is expected to quadruple by 2030.[1] At the same time, 75 percent of the urban population lives on INR 80 (approximately EUR 1) per day. The enormous urbanization and shift to affluence that is occurring offers possibilities for business. To understand the meaning of trends for India, India must be seen both as a fashion market and as an emerging economy.

The office of Reliance Brands is in Cuffe Parade, an upscale business area. Reliance Brands is part of the Indian industrial group Reliance Industries founded by Dhirubhai Ambani in the 1960s and still one of India's largest companies, operating in everything from petrochemicals, oil and textiles to retail and telecom. Reliance Brands began with thirty staff in 2010 and reached a thousand employees in 2014. In total, the company has about 150 points of sale. Reliance Brands is recognized for its joint ventures with well-known brands such as Diesel, Paul & Shark and Ermenegildo Zegna. Reliance Brands is both a private equity company creating value and a genuine fashion company. Reliance Brands CEO Darshan Mehta considers it essential that any collaboration be long term— "We don't want to be a corporate escort service"—and draws a parallel to the Hindu marriage which is supposed to be everlasting.

Darshan Mehta has a longer-term view of the dominance of menswear and denim in particular: "Levi's has been in India for twenty years—of course you are going to find jeans here." (Levi Strauss established itself in India in 1992, roughly the same time as Lee and a year after Pepe.)

India, like many emerging economies, is characterized by supply constraints. Future demand cannot be determined from present consumption; that is, people wear jeans simply because jeans are available. Mehta explains that growth is more about market creation than competition: "Western people often come from demand-starved economies and don't realize that it's not about taking pizza slices from each other, but about enlarging the overall pizza size itself." For example, about 200,000 new cars were sold in India in 2000; in 2010, 2.3 million new cars were sold, reflecting not increased demand but improved supply. Interestingly, Mehta believes, as does Harleen Sabharwal, that domestic designers largely lack a business vision.

Despite certain commonalities shared by the BRIC countries, such as their being emergent economies with a growing middle class,[2] it is important to keep in mind that their economies differ significantly in certain respects, for example, natural resources, agriculture, manufacturing and demographic development.

Although the interviews I conducted in the BRIC countries also concerned trends, the informants tended to bring up the institutional provisions for fashion production and consumption, such as laws and regulations, trade barriers, currency effects and corruption, often to shed light on how their situation differs from that in the West.

At one time, the Indian government required all foreign companies intending to establish monobrand stores[3] to form joint ventures with Indian partners, with a foreign direct investment ceiling of 51 percent.[4] Inditex and Zara, for example, partnered with Trent, the retailing branch of Indian corporate giant Tata, to a maximum of 49 percent. This policy has strongly benefited Reliance Brands.

Mehta's company is interested in collaborating with well-known brands that have positive associations and high brand recognition in the Indian market. For example, at the inauguration of the first Diesel store, Renzo Rosso, the founder began by thanking everyone "for coming to the launch of Diesel." One woman interrupted: "I just want to correct you. You are not here to launch the brand … You are here to launch the store. Everybody already knows about Diesel."

Reliance Brands does not use a trend service "because we typically buy the product, we don't design the product," Darshan Mehta explains. When he was CEO of Arvind Brands (which works with Western brands and also has two brands of its own), that company used both WGSN and Stylesight. According to Mehta, India used to be two seasons late with fashions, but no longer, as "the world has become flat." He says that Indians generally follow European fashion much more closely than Asian fashion, in terms of both phase and design, because the historical link to the UK makes India more culturally aligned to Europe than to Asian countries such as Malaysia, Thailand, Singapore, China, Taiwan and Korea. Mehta insists that "India is not an oriental country." Fast-fashion chains such as Zara and Mango carry the same trend-oriented selection as in the West, he says.

It is impossible to open stores at the same pace at which the customer base is growing, Mehta observes, partly due to distribution channel constraints, but mostly because of the rapid growth of the middle-class market. High-street shops, department stores, e-commerce and malls do not yet exist. A monobrand store needs a neighborhood, and building shopping malls is totally different from building brands. Mehta is optimistic: the luxury-focused Palladium Mall was recently opened in Bombay, and several of his partner brands are represented in monobrand shops. In 2011 there were only ten modern malls in India; Mehta expects there will soon be fifty. Malls provide an entirely different shopping experience for the whole family: no more hot streets and a wide selection ensure shoppers will not have to leave their comfort zone.

India is unusual because it is home to both new and old money, says Mehta; in fact, excluding China, India is one of the largest economies based on new money. He explains: "New money wants to demonstrate its arrival. A car is always in your front yard, never in your back yard. The money changes the caste to which you belong—the new caste is the car in front of the house." Indians trade up in the categories of consumption in which they are highly involved, while trading down in others.

Mehta anticipates that the second decade of this century will see fashion undergo the same shift in India already experienced by the automotive and home electronics industries in the early 2000s. Fashion is becoming a category that is traded up, and Mehta sees this as reflecting women's changed position. Most foreign brands currently available in India are either menswear or unisex, with the exception of a few high-street brands such as Zara, Vero Moda and Mango. When the *new* money first arrives, men spend it on themselves. Families with double incomes have only been a reality during the last decade in India, since cultural norms dictate that few women work and then only transiently between marriage and having children.

"The luxury brands will tell you that Indian women want to wear traditional clothes, and for special occasions they might wear a Gucci bag, while the ready-to-wear has to be more traditional. I disagree completely! There are just not enough brands here," Mehta exclaims. As Indian women enter the workforce and mature as consumers, they will demand more, as did one 37-year-old woman from an enormously rich family who longed for the launch of the Steven Madden brand "despite the fact that she could afford more than twenty Jimmy Choos." Mehta sees a challenge in balancing between local adaptation and maintaining the international aura that makes foreign brands appealing and aspirational. The MTV television channel, for example, was instantly successful, until it introduced a "Hinglish" version combining Hindi and English. The channel came to be seen as Indian and lost its aspirational quality. Other international brands launched in India, such as Nike and Reebok, are nowadays seen as Indian, but not always in a favorable way.

The effect of the Bollywood stars—Mehta calls them "market accelerators"—on fashion trends must not be underestimated, and what they wear on screen has an enormous impact. Marketing communications must also appeal to the new Indian mind-set, says Mehta. The newfound confidence resulting from the rapid development of the country from an overwhelmingly agricultural country to a well-known information technology and knowledge society makes Indians relate to fashion in a new way. Some brands acknowledge that sense of confidence. The window displays of Louis Vuitton stores exhibited a theme inspired by Diwali, the festival of lights celebrated in India between mid-October and mid-November. Zegna has a collection whose suits and jackets have "Nehru collars," an Indian feature that recalls the Chinese mandarin collar, and photographed the campaign in Rajasthan.

One woman professor at the elite Indian Institute of Management in Bangalore says she could never dress in a colorful sari: "I would not be taken seriously." She uses her brown-beige sari to teach me how to read trends in the embroidery and the pattern on its edges.[5] She is convinced that both her daughters, as professional women, will wear Western clothing.

Darshan Mehta's descriptions of the Indian fashion market's potential are perhaps to be expected given his company's position. However, Western companies are clearly inclined to interpret markets and act based on the workings of the mature Western fashion markets. While the global luxury conglomerates look to the burgeoning Indian luxury market, Reliance Brands identifies its greatest opportunities in the mid-range segment. The financial analysts' contention that expansion may mitigate fashion risk is illustrated through the attraction of mid-segment Western brands such as Diesel and Steve Madden. As trends play an empowering role in the West, as described in Chapter 5, the potential in India for women's fashion beyond the focus on brands could be substantial, though offerings are currently limited even for young women.

With insufficient competition, some Indian designers may end up on the beaten track, part of their sales made to customers for whom lack of innovation goes unnoticed. The framing of trend reports, as noted at the beginning of this chapter, where items from European and American fashion houses are being interpreted from an obvious Indian viewpoint, exemplifies how an unequivocally Western perspective gives way even in such a Western publication as Indian *Vogue*.

China

The luxury market is absolutely booming. It's all about conspicuous consumption, it's all about wearing a brand. So you will see head-to-toe LV, head-to-toe Chanel, head-to-toe Gucci. We have busloads of mainland Chinese coming into Hong Kong and buying five Louis Vuitton handbags with cash … Shopping is a national sport here. People shop, shop, shop if it's a day out. People are constantly consuming. And those fast-fashion brands that have entered here have done incredibly well, because they feed that constant fix of I'm shopping, I'm shopping, I'm shopping. (Rosie Baker, Trend Consultant, WGSN Asia-Pacific)

Tsim Sha Tsui in Kowloon is a well-known and gigantic "shopping zone" containing at least 450 shops—and the offices of WGSN Asia-Pacific. Rosie Baker,[6] after working in the UK fashion industry, is trend consultant here. WGSN Asia-Pacific has 520 customers in Asia; 40 percent of its revenues are from Chinese clients.

Rosie Baker describes the market as immature: the Chinese have not yet developed the sense of *how* to wear it—it is just about *wearing* it. One sees a luxury brand-led group of people who distinguish themselves by wearing head-to-toe luxury brands, essentially wearing their wealth. Clothes, bags and cars are prioritized, much more than the home—people tend to entertain outside the home. The logo is crucial. But Baker observes that this is beginning to shift. The mix-and-match style typical of Europe and the United States, in which people mix designer clothing with vintage or high-street brands and develop their own style depending on their age, where they live and what bands they like, is starting to develop in China, too, especially among Chinese youth more exposed to the rest of the world.

WGSN has had offices in Asia since the early 2000s, but its business has taken off since 2008. The company now has offices in Hong Kong, Melbourne, Singapore, New Delhi, Shanghai, Taiwan, Tokyo and Seoul. WGSN's Asia-Pacific section has forty-three employees and many freelancers, who mostly provide trend reporting and business intelligence. Since 2008, the business has also taken a new direction. In the early 2000s, it was focused on trend reporting from Tokyo, but after "a bit of education in the market," the business is now centered on the Chinese market. Baker finds it fascinating that the Chinese are so keen to learn and to grow their businesses. As soon as they understand how the trend service works and its uses, they are very quick to adopt it, she says. For long, however, the site was available only in English. The biggest change that WGSN has noted is that Chinese manufacturing companies want to create their own brands in their own immense domestic market. Baker explains:

> With the service, customers can not only understand what's going on globally, but … can see what all the other brands around the world are doing. They can look at different shapes, colors and materials, prints and graphics that are copyright free, downloadable CADs that they can use themselves. It can make their transition from … what historically would have been a copier to being a designer, feeding the export markets and now moving into the domestic markets and providing their own designs. With the information from WGSN, that is a much easier shift for them, which is fantastic. And for us … I think we will never in my lifetime run out of potential customers.

In 2011, in the Chinese market, 75 percent of WGSN's customers are made up of domestic-brand retailers and about 40 percent are manufacturers. In WGSN's "Share the love" campaign, existing WGSN customers, buyers at brands and retailers with manufacturing in China were offered trial subscriptions for their suppliers to encourage them to purchase the service. Baker points out that retailers, buyers and brand representatives often prefer the manufacturers to "be on the same page." In its marketing, WGSN emphasizes that its service offers a "stamp of approval" of the companies that subscribe to it. Manufacturers can use the WGSN logo in their promotional material, which Baker says signals to buyers that "these manufacturers are investing in themselves and have global knowledge." In emerging economies, WGSN is sometimes flexible on the subscription pricing so that new small businesses can afford to access at least a specific product area, such as menswear or accessories. Baker says that the company also offers discounts to schools and institutions, as is done in other parts of the world:

> We think it's really important that students grow up understanding global trends, particularly in Asia where historically they've had a domestic view ... The goal is for their students to come out of college and be very successful in their domestic markets, and then turn to export overseas.

The information is widely disseminated, and not only through WGSN's Web site. There are also innumerable "knock-off" sites, where unrelated companies pirate (and often translate) information from the WGSN and Stylesight Web sites, as well as from trend books. Several interviewees that I meet with mention this problem. One informant notes that while they usually send cease-and-desist letters, this is only a temporary solution, since the companies pirating its information simply take down their sites and start new companies under different names. There is no effective way of preventing this information theft. Very often, the trend-forecasting companies' marketing and press coverage emphasize the successful history of the companies and the exceptional service they provide. Imitators lack the thirteen years of experience and the highly skilled people who conduct the trend analysis. Says a trend research consultant based in Shanghai:

> It's actually quite difficult to fight them. I know [a large trend-forecasting company] has been successful in taking two companies to court ... But then they pop up again under a different name. It's so prevalent in China. Every brand has the same problem—everybody is sort of ripped-off. We had an extraordinary situation. There is a company called SXXXL, which basically scrapes information from [the large trend-forecasting companies] and sticks it up on its site. They even leave our names in—they don't even try and hide the fact that it's [us]. A while ago we went to a trade fair where we had a booth, and they were next to us. They would tell people to go next door, to us at [the trend-forecasting company], and have a demonstration of the service, and then come back and buy "exactly that information" for a tenth of the price. This was going on throughout the day ... our teams closed our booth, because we'd run out of bags, and we left. Then the SXXXL team moved into our booth and pretended to be [us]! No shame!
>
> We recently had another example where a company calling themselves Pop (in fashion), sends an SMS to our customers saying Pop and [us] together are launching a new Chinese site—this was just before we launched our Chinese

site—that you can sign up for X amount … a quarter of our price. So I phoned them up and I said, … "You have to stop this. You are not allowed to use this. This is fraudulent." So we had to send a message to all our Chinese customers explaining that we are not launching a site with someone else. It takes so much time and effort! And, of course, there can be those who got that message and went "Oh, well, even if it's not endorsed by [the trend-forecasting company], if it's still [their] information, then I'll buy it."

Back in Hong Kong, Baker finds it frustrating that the experience, aesthetic knowledge, robust work process and global perspective that ground WGSN's trend forecasts are entirely disregarded by these actors. It is not, she emphasizes, an industry that can be entered "just like that":

Not everything makes a trend. Just because something is seen on the streets of Japan, doesn't make it a global trend. It doesn't even make it a Japanese trend. It just makes it somebody wearing [certain items] in a street of Japan. It's so much about cross-referencing, and looking at music, art, politics, history, culture, etc., before we surface something that we call a trend. Our people understand, on the basis of their experience as designers, creators and trend forecasters, what makes a trend and what doesn't.

Steve Newbold, managing director of WGSN 2013–2014, emphasizes that most of the companies that wish to be customers and genuinely want the right trend analysis to help them grow their businesses look for the real provider rather than cheaper imitations. According to him, even if some reports are copied, it is increasingly difficult to replicate the service as a whole, thanks to the talented trend experts employed and the advanced technology infrastructure.

The global extension of the trend services is partly due to deliberate marketing and partly due to trend services being copied. The Chinese view of intellectual property rights is often said to be influenced by Confucianism. The saying "to steal a book is an elegant offense" is frequently cited to indicate that copying is not considered wrong in China. Others argue that the ubiquitous copying results from insufficient economic development and a dysfunctional institutional framework.[7]

While Baker decries plagiarizing trend forecasters, WGSN provides manufacturing companies with downloadable patterns for creating "fashion" collections under their own brands even though they lack in-house design departments, thus turning a blind eye to the aesthetic knowledge of designers and mainstreaming selected styles of designers to companies that have not invested in design at all and without always referencing particular designers. For example, some financial analysts regretfully note that the Hong Kong-based logistics and trading company Li & Fung, which coordinates production and distribution for a plethora of Western mass-market retailers, has created its own collections after having "stolen a glance at what other companies have ordered." It is just possible they simply exploited WGSN's offerings.

Harvey Nichols' chief operating officer in Hong Kong, Audrey Sun, confirms that the buyers, marketers and salespeople of Harvey Nichols in Hong Kong actively use WGSN. She does not fear WGSN's information becoming *too* widespread, as the high price of the service means that many companies cannot afford it. In addition, WGSN supplies so much information that no one firm can use it all. The buyers and Sun identify trends during the fashion shows and in the showrooms of various brands, and every night during "the buying season" they have a buyers' meeting to recap what they have seen and to decide what trends and buys are most relevant to their market. From these discussions, the fashion direction of upcoming purchases is determined. Sun knows that Hong Kong customers prefer brighter tones such as pink, coral, fuchsia and yellow to more muted tones such as brown and beige. Long dresses and skirts do not sell. The trends in womenswear are more prominent, multidimensional and eye-catching than those in menswear, where trends are usually reflected in more subtle details. Hong Kong customers are also hungry for "the new," always open, wanting to try something different and not notably brand loyal. Hong Kong fashion customers follow trends more than brands.

All five trend forecasters I met in China have new and different perspectives on trends. Until recently, generally only those Chinese individuals and firms who buy, design and manufacture for the global market, and who need to be up-to-date on trends in foreign markets, have had much interest in trends, but their gaze is now increasingly turned toward the domestic market. Here, an interesting merger of Western and Eastern aesthetics is occurring, says WGSN's Rosie Baker. Many international high-level brands such as Louis Vuitton are taking inspiration from the cultural heritage of China, particularly since the Beijing Olympics. Chinese brands, designers, buyers and manufacturers are interested in trends associated with celebrities and in what is shown in foreign movies, but in a less sophisticated way than in the West, according to Baker. Shops may feature typical Western shapes but in different colors. Baker has noticed a higher demand for consultancy services among WGSN's Asian customers, which Baker predicts will only increase as American and Korean customers want to know how trends generate and spread in China.

Historically, Chinese companies wanting to move into the UK or the United States have served WGSN as an important customer base, and one hot topic concerns which Chinese fashion company will be the first to make it internationally. "Li Ning? Metersbonwe?" Rosie Baker asks rhetorically.

Olivia Linqin[8] is content manager for WGSN Asia-Pacific. Originally from Singapore, Linqin worked for fashion magazines and then in trend forecasting before moving to WGSN in Hong Kong four years ago.

In discussing copying with Linqin, I describe my experiences in Shanghai and Beijing. Copies of designer clothing appear everywhere: in the Silk Market and "fashion department stores" in Beijing and in small boutiques in Shanghai's French Concession. At first glance, these can be mistaken for shops with their own unique selections, but the real purpose of these shops is to sell copied "bargains." Offerings are arbitrary and directionless, without surprise or interest, and some effort is made to convince the customer that the featured small-sized items are "hot off the press," made especially for models and sample collections, and wrapped in plastic "direct from the factory."

Linqin's take is different. The "copying culture" of China has educated the Chinese, especially those who could not afford to purchase international brands:

> The small stores and smaller factory outlets are a very big factor to why China has leapfrogged the fashion factor. You go in there, and a Balenciaga jacket that normally would cost RMB 15–20,000 is available for RMB 600. "Yes, I can dress in today's trends and today's brands, for my developing-country salary." And because they can do that they are able to experiment and develop. It becomes part of the language.

Linqin tells me about a Miu Miu T-shirt with leather trim that was part of the 2011 spring/summer collection and was available under two months later in a Hong Kong shop selling Chinese paraphernalia. The quality and material were not impressive. Shortly thereafter, Linqin saw an unsophisticated but very wealthy woman from a small Chinese city wearing that shirt. Is it the fake version? If she is rich, it could well be the original:

> So here is a woman who by all definitions doesn't have any taste, but she is wearing one of the hottest items from the Miu Miu collection. It's a fascinating conundrum—it's fashion turned completely inside-out, upside-down. You have no idea where anybody stands at the moment.

Whereas fashion and how people relate to trends can reproduce social class in a Western culture (see p. 84), social stratification based on fashion consumption is harder to interpret in a Chinese context. When the Chinese look at themselves today, they now ask "Am I fashionable or not?" says Linqin. Many Chinese are just as fluent in the fashion language as any of their European or American counterparts.

One of Linqin's basic tenets in understanding the Chinese market compared with the rest of the world is that it is a collective-based market, the focus not being on the individual but on the collective, "the family." If others in a group follow a trend, each member does, too. No one wants to stand out too much; no one wants to be the only one in the room looking different. Trends that gain a foothold in

China often become pervasive, though subculture fashions are watered down, as was the Japanese "mori girls" ("forest girls") trend. In Japan, this trend had an ecological ethos, but once it filtered down to Hong Kong and China, it was more about having an item in raffia,[9] losing its cultural context. Chinese consumers experience brands per se as more important than any lifestyle accompanying a trend.

Like Rosie Baker, Linqin believes that the Chinese state is hoping for a Chinese brand to succeed internationally in the 2010s. The People's Republic claims to want to help domestic brands expand globally, but it is less clear exactly what the state is doing to accomplish this. Angelia Bao[10] works as a project leader at a government-owned organization that aims to strengthen the textile industry in the country. For the ten last years, the organization has been the agent for a French trend-forecasting agency that offers trend books and trend consultancy services adapted to specific client companies. The demand for consultancy is especially high among domestic Chinese companies, though the organization, like Stylesight, will not provide statistics about its client base. It also offers its own trend analyses to companies that cannot afford the French agency's trend books. These analyses are very basic, often merely marketing surveys regarding colors and shapes. The organization also provides the French agency with trend information to support its consultancy assignments.

Trends are also important for the domestic market, as more companies build their own brands. Chinese brands cannot be as directive as Zara and H&M because they are not sufficiently global, notes Bao. Chinese business clients often complain that the European trend forecaster's color schemes do not fit the dominant skin tones and that Chinese people have different tastes and preferences. Bao suspects that the dislike for gray tones has less to do with skin tone than with consumers' being unaccustomed to those colors. Still, globalization has created demand for trends, and international celebrities, street pictures and internet trend reports all fuel that demand. In major centers such as Shanghai, international trends reign and these trends will likely replace the obsession with brands, though the situation differs in the second- and third-tier cities (see p. 148). In those cities, women often like "cute" girlish trends from Japan and Korea. Different cities have different views about beauty, says Bao, and some brands even adapt their profiles to specific cities. Chinese versions of all the important European, American and Japanese fashion magazines are readily available, along with a host of television shows about fashion. Like WGSN's Rosie Baker, Bao regards the "pirate" Web sites as a big problem; she believes that the only way to convince customers to stay with the French trend forecaster is to heavily invest in additional services. But then again, as many traditional French trend forecasters, it does not have an extensive online presence.

Olivia Linqin of WGSN finds the Chinese trajectory of the fashion brand JNBY striking and illustrative of China's unique market. JNBY—"Just Naturally

Be Yourself"—was founded in 1994 in China by eleven women, all best friends. It makes sculptural clothing with an organic twist at a premium Zara price point and is available on a small scale in New York City, with its own store on Greene Street and a presence at Scoop, Barneys, Saks Fifth Avenue Online and Shopbop. Previously positioned as mass-market fashion in China, its sales were so poor that the brand was repositioned as more premium, raising its price point by 20–30 percent. The brand is now a success in China, with approximately 600 stores.

Mira Finley,[11] the New York-based brand manager for JNBY in the United States, provides an enthusiastic company-side perspective on the firm. Formerly a buyer for Nordstrom and sales director of wholesale at Juicy Couture, she has vast industry experience and can speak knowledgeably about the relationship between the United States and China, JNBY's target market, how its designs relate to trends and about the company's founders:

> It blows me away that a group of eleven-plus women can work together for so long and remain friends. In the US it's not easy to do that. Everyone is always eager to climb the ladder. So it's this amazing brand that they created a lifestyle out of... Although it reflects and welcomes trends, it always keeps its DNA true.

Finley sees that Chinese brands are not used to thinking globally but also sees that the Chinese are impatient to learn. The Chinese admiration for other countries is one thing, but in reality all they know is the Chinese way: "You and I have been exposed to so many different ways of thinking." Still, she contrasts the Chinese eagerness to learn with the Sinophobia she sees in the United States, where people fear that China is going to take over the world.

"No one in the fashion industry ever has a franchise."[12] Finley's declaration is somewhat countered by the JNBY experience, where, starting with a group of women behind the brand, one friend after another has started JNBY franchise operations in various areas of China. This can be problematic for control of the brand, as it can be difficult to ensure franchisees follow the brand's guidelines. Many of the franchise stores are still run like "mom-and-pop stores,"[13] with no formal controlling structure.

Finley describes JNBY's position as "between Topshop and the designer brands." Competitors are Rag & Bone, Vince and Helmut Lang, but JNBY has a distinctive Chinese–Japanese look and feel that competing brands lack, she says.

A celebrity endorsement is seen as vital for the future of the brand. Such endorsements are very important in China where Chinese brands still carry a stigma. The same is true of the American market. Finley says the first question buyers ask is "Where are your clothes made?" One buyer indicated that her customers would not be willing to purchase JNBY shoes. Finley sees it as key that people understand that just because something is Chinese, it does not mean that "a bunch of underage sweatshop workers are behind it—it can be an amazing group of artistic women."

The JNBY design team uses various trend services, though Finley does not specify further. The design team travels and finds inspiration in exhibitions, art and architecture and even people—the first collection sold in the United States was inspired by Patti Smith, the songwriter, poet and visual artist. The collection for spring 2012, in contrast, is entitled "Chinese culture through clothes," and concepts such as "time," "blue-and-white pottery" (i.e., Chenghua porcelain),[14] "Zen monks," "rock'n'roll ink" and "mood" served as inspiration. She describes how the designers visited manufacturers who produced clothing, not designed in China, for American and European brands. The JNBY designers took all the scraps from the factories and made a collection from it, as a commentary on today's fashion system. The brand initially faced problems when it started to sell in the United States and Europe, partly because of differences in sizing, but more because the collection was perceived to lack color and pattern and the sweaters were considered too heavy. "The design team is very open to feedback, though," says Finley.

While Western mass-market fashion companies have shortened lead times and become more flexible, enabling adaptation to demand on an unprecedented scale, Chinese manufacturing has not kept pace, Finley notes:

> JNBY has ten deliveries of collections a year. One thing that fascinates me is that everyone thinks of China as fast fashion. But we have very long lead times. While the US and Europe can write their Spring 2012 orders through mid-October, we close at the end of September. This is very challenging.

These weeks are not insignificant and her example illustrates the heavy pressure on manufacturing processes in the fashion industry. Chinese factory owners belong to an older generation that is used to doing things the Chinese way, Finley says.

> Honestly, the brand is not very trend-driven. We try to be ahead of the trend. But if wide-legged pants are the trend, you're not going to see JNBY necessarily doing those. Sometimes that hurts us, sometimes it benefits us.

While the manufacturing belt stretches along the east coast of southern China around the cities of Shenzhen and Guangzhou, Olivia Linqin of WGSN considers Hangzhou to be the most interesting city. Near Suzhou in Jiangsu province, China's traditional center for clothing production, Hangzhou is a laboratory for the fashion industry: JNBY got its start there. In Hangzhou's markets are brands never seen elsewhere in China, and many small shops experiment with fashion.

The luxury brands are nowadays well represented in second- and third-tier cities, and Chengdu and Harbin are growing considerably as luxury markets. Luxury retailers use one top brand as a benchmark: according to Olivia Linqin, "There is a market if there is a Louis Vuitton." This international brand is immensely strong: it is the first luxury brand into any city and can therefore negotiate very advantageous conditions, such as paying no rent for the first year. Every city wants a Louis Vuitton store. When the brand opened in Ulan Bator in Mongolia, many wondered if there was even a shopping street, until it was learned that Bottega Veneta and Dior also had outlets there and all in the one modern office block in Ulan Bator. Companies coming into China often do not grow organically but in a more constructed way, possibly due to China's state capitalism, where municipal governments can offer very good terms to the foreign companies they wish to attract.

Olivia Linqin is clear that the Chinese want to be Chinese despite the omnipresent Western influence. China's rapid growth and tremendous global success have made Chinese people very proud and confident. The country's unparalleled economic development means Chinese companies can define success and business models in their own way. She suspects that this confidence will translate into a strong desire, internationally, to buy into the Chinese aesthetic "very, very soon." Linqin notes that catwalk fashions have already been inspired by the Chinese aesthetic and that blue-and-white porcelain has acquired design momentum, but Linqin thinks there needs to be more:

> The biggest challenge is to find more source material. Because historically all traditional Chinese art, books and craft have been wiped out. So in China, they need to find a way to inspire their creative community with what's available. Otherwise the Chinese risks becoming kitsch. As if it's only about blue-and-white porcelain and cheongsam dresses.[15] Now people are looking back to the Qin and Han dynasties. Those designers who do it well are doing their research not in China but in Taiwan, because it's all there. The government needs to find a way to give the big group of fashion people access to history. Because it's not available right now... There is not enough historical material within the design field that people can look at. Look at me, for example, who have been Chinese all my life. If I close my eyes, I can maybe come up with ten examples of what Chinese art looks like, from history. From the Tang Dynasty, from the Song Dynasty, and ten styles. That can't be true! It's a 2000-year-old history, right? So surfacing new types of art and things that nobody has seen is going to be a challenge. A lot of it was destroyed [during the Cultural Revolution]. So you don't know what you can find.

On the other side of the water from Tsim Sha Tsui (TST) in Kowloon, Millicent Lai, chief designer at Shanghai Tang, discusses Chinese luxury fashion. Currently most of Lai's work is with interiors, but she has more than ten years of experience with Shanghai Tang.

Shanghai Tang was started in 1994 by David Tang, a Hong Kong businessman who intended to preserve the best traditions of Chinese design and craftsmanship while expanding into the Western market. Shanghai was well known for its tailoring industry. During the Cultural Revolution, many Shanghai craftsmen fled

to Hong Kong. David Tang contracted these tailors and started a tailoring shop on Pedder Street in Hong Kong, where Shanghai Tang had its flagship store until 2011. Under the name Imperial Tailoring, exclusive Chinese dresses and later a ready-to-wear collection and a gift range were introduced. The company's first signature item was the Tang jacket, silk with a mandarin collar, frog buttons on the front and with a rather loose fit. In the 1970s, during Mao's rule, everybody wore blue, dark green and gray, Lai explains, while Shanghai Tang produced its jacket in very bright colors. Preserving the traditional shape and silhouette of a Chinese garment while modernizing it in color was a new concept, and Shanghai Tang is still famous for its hot pink, turquoise, orange and lime green colors. In 2001, the luxury conglomerate Richemont bought Shanghai Tang and eventually David Tang relinquished control. Richemont's Executive Chairman Raphael le Masne de Chermont is determined to make the brand fashionable and wearable, like a Chinese Gucci: "We keep a little bit of Chineseness, for example, a knot on a dress, the little collar," says Lai. Signature items such as the Tang jacket now populate the Authentics collection. It is updated with different colors and fabrics each season, but every year represents a smaller percentage of the whole line as the company expands its ready-to-wear with trendier seasonal collections.

All Shanghai Tang designers have access to WGSN, and the apparel designers attend Première Vision twice a year to inform themselves about trends in fabrics, shapes and colors, but the main inspiration for the collections is always Chinese, Lai stresses.

When Millicent Lai started working for Shanghai Tang, it had ten stores; now it has over forty. During David Tang's tenure, the brand opened a large store in Manhattan and soon learned that its clothing was considered quirky, iconic and as denoting simple luxury. Some celebrities might wear a Shanghai Tang scarf or jacket, but the New Yorker's conservative preference for black meant that Shanghai Tang designs were unfashionable, says Lai, so the store moved to smaller premises. Even now, European and American visitors are more interested in Shanghai Tang's gifts and home products than fashion, somewhat resistant to the idea of Chinese-style clothing.

By contrast, the brand's next step is into mainland China because "that's where the potential growth is." In the early 2000s, Shanghai Tang had few mainland Chinese customers, but every year since, customer demographics indicate that the number of mainland Chinese customers has doubled, and the Hong Kong market is booming also, mostly because of the many mainland Chinese visitors. Chinese consumers are very interested in high-priced clothing and buy mainly from the seasonal collections. They also purchase a few accessories but hardly any gifts or home products. Lai regards this as a good sign:

> Chinese customers have gone rich for the last ten years. First, they have limited taste—they have been isolated for very long—so they only go for the big names,

Louis Vuitton and Gucci. After a while, they become more sophisticated and also proud of being Chinese, proud of wearing Chinese clothing.

Hong Kong Chinese are still reluctant to wear Chinese clothes, preferring imported goods. Lai thinks there may be prejudice against the typical Chinese style among the Hong Kong Chinese, for political and historical reasons. Lai grew up in Hong Kong; in that colonial environment she was taught that what was modern was from the West:

> But in terms of aesthetics, arts and design, we were never taught about the Chinese … We learnt that to be nice and beautiful and modern is to be Western. So we grew up having this prejudice. But in mainland China, they don't have that. So that's why it's easier to sell to the mainland Chinese—at least when they've got tired of all the big brands. Well, they have not yet got tired of them, but first they just want to show that they have money and taste, and then they go for Western style because it's safe. But after a while they feel more confident about themselves and they start to look back to their own roots.

She considers current developments in the design industry to be much more interesting in mainland China than in Hong Kong.

Today, tailoring represents about 15–17 percent of the sales in Shanghai Tang's flagship store. Shiatzy Chen from Taiwan and New York-based Vivienne Tam are Shanghai Tang's closest competitors, though the latter, Lai feels, has lost focus and over-priced its products, while Shiatzy Chen markets to slightly older women and is

also more expensive. Both brands, however, use Chinese craftsmanship as a source of inspiration. Lai also cites Hermès Shang Xia in Shanghai, Hermès collaboration with the Chinese artist and designer Jiang Qiong'er to create a brand of extreme luxury emphasizing Chinese cultural heritage and craftsmanship. Their products include fashion, jewelry, interior decoration and porcelain, all made in China.

Olivia Linqin of WGSN considers the mid-market segment, between the luxury clothing brands and the mass-market retailers, very crowded. At the low end are mass-market brands such as H&M and Zara, and this is where the major growth is taking place—because the luxury end of the industry is so well established, new actors have a difficult time entering it. Linqin doubts that the Chinese market is ready for bridge brands such as Club Monaco or Reiss, although these brands have established themselves there. Many foreign bridge brands have failed in China because they have pitched themselves as "entry-level luxury." This concept does not appeal to the Chinese: an item is either luxury or it is not—nothing exists between the two, says Linqin. Several luxury brands have adopted a "masstige" (mass + prestige) approach, a downward brand extension in which a luxury brand launches affordable versions of premium products at a price point between the luxury and mid-market segments. Louis Vuitton has been successful in this approach.

The successful mid-market brands are often sports brands. Italian Kappa is popular in China, launched as a fashion brand that is not about performance. Sports brands are often the entry point to the fashion market in China, so domestic sports brands such as Li Ning are targeting the mid-market segment.

Another thriving mid-market brand is the French brand Cache-Cache. The company is a pioneer, establishing a design office in China at the beginning of the century, adapting its designs to the Chinese market and launching a collection of T-shirts with simple graphics, bright colors and ample use of primary colors. Some old Chinese brands from the heyday of the Communist era have been bought by Western firms that intend to capitalize on the aesthetics and the nostalgia. For example, the worker's shoe Liberation was bought by an American firm. The quintessential Chinese running shoe Feiyue was bought by a French entrepreneur who was then sued when he tried to upgrade the shoe and actually convicted because he did not have the rights to manufacture the shoes. His shoes are now regarded as counterfeit, and there is information online to help customers distinguish the French counterfeit from the Chinese original.

By 2012, H&M had been in China five years and opened one hundred shops as part of an ambitious expansion plan. Jon Loman is a designer in H&M's Chinese production office, a pilot project whereby H&M is attempting to create a closer connection with the Chinese market by locating nearer the supplier network. The team includes a pattern constructor and buyer who are well supported by the Swedish head office. Intended to be "the people from the outside who think a bit differently, who may not turn things round as much, may not look at sales statistics, but rather react directly to something that seems hot at the moment," this team will travel widely in the Asian market, primarily in Japan, to absorb inspiration. Thanks to the shorter lead times of China's production network, Loman's team can "fill the gaps" in the collections. They place their orders later than normal so that if they see something apparently missing from the H&M collection, they can write a brief, present reference pictures showing what they intend to create and get approval from H&M's headquarters in Stockholm.

On a trip to Japan in March 2011, the team became hooked on "metallic-coated jeans, pleated skirts and sheer tops," a romantic look that they thought H&M had missed. There was nothing resembling these garments scheduled for production, so they organized a workshop with suppliers in China to see if the idea was viable. They then made some sketches, constructed the patterns and received samples of the items from the supplier network. The sampling process runs very smoothly when one is that close to the suppliers; it took ten to twelve weeks to take the initial idea from inspiration to the shop rack.

Pervasive CSR efforts have led H&M to create more long-term relationships with its suppliers. H&M hopes that, given this assured long-term business, these suppliers will invest in sampling equipment and processes that improve their receptiveness and flexibility to accommodate changes in production arrangements.

While Loman does not consider trend research in China useful at the moment, he believes that development in China will be incredibly rapid. Though it is often assumed that China will simply catch up with the West in fashion, the Chinese might well take an entirely different route of their own making. Given that Western fashion has been dominated by retro fashions for the last ten to fifteen years, the Chinese direction may offer something new. Loman notes that new European fashion in the 1950s and 1960s reflected a confidence about the future—which China now possesses. The Chinese designers that succeed will be those who see a bright and encouraging future.

Western fashion companies are entering China on a massive scale, importing Western fashion, and the Chinese desire for luxury brands in particular is well established. As these brands and their aesthetics expand, with the Western trend-forecasting companies to support them, new seeds of demand are constantly sown. However frustrating the illegal trend-forecasting knockoffs may be, these sites do disseminate content that is indispensable, especially for domestic companies hoping to launch or grow in the fashion field. Several informants believe that the greater Chinese focus on the collective makes trends particularly powerful, perhaps replacing brands—a kind of trend imperialism. On the other hand, the Chinese want to wear fashions that reflect Chinese tastes and heritage, which financial analysts, Western designers and Western tastemakers have not yet grasped. The design heritage of China, however difficult to access, can serve as a new source of fashion inspiration. The only question is whether the Western fashion companies, and the fashion field at large, are ready to accommodate this aesthetic.

Russia

There are no trends in Moscow! That's why there was no point for WGSN to open an office here. (Katia Mossina, Russian fashion designer)

Lesya Olegovna[16] is a trend and fashion business consultant in Paris, who formerly worked for one of the large online trend services as the regional manager for Eastern Europe. She views Russia not as a fashion *leader* when it comes to global trends but as a follower. Trends arrive in Russia at different speeds, some parts of the market being well functioning and others definitely not, which affects how trends are disseminated. The extremely rich segment of Russian society is used to traveling and shopping abroad and to some extent also resides abroad (the families of the economic oligarchs often live in the UK). This means that the disposable income and tastes of the wealthy subset of the population never affect the Russian fashion scene.

Although the Russian fashion scene is not as polarized between rich and poor as many people think, Olegovna finds it difficult to identify the taste of the growing middle class or the trends they adopt. The rich used to choose from a very strict hierarchy of brands, Chanel and Dior being among the few that are widely recognized in Russia. At the highest levels of society, people often wore one brand head-to-toe and brand consciousness was so pervasive that some party invitations stipulated accepted fashion brands. Since then, the rich have perceived the importance of style and trends, and such parties no longer occur, Olegovna believes. Brands, however, continue to be important as people wish to display their wealth.

The poorer Russians want cheap and practical clothing. Trends in this market segment are similar to Western trends, simplified and adapted in features such as pockets, colors and tailoring and using inexpensive materials. According to Olegovna, mass-market chains that want to sell in the Russian market often add shiny elements such as sequins, Ukrainian embroidery and metallic colors, manifestations of Russia's location between Europe and Asia, where many share this fondness for shiny elements.

Katia Mossina is a designer with her own eponymous brand whose tagline is "fun and sexy." Mossina originally studied architecture but changed paths. She studied fashion in the class of Vivienne Westwood at Berlin University of the Arts and later at the Milano Fashion Institute. She divides her time between Berlin and Moscow.

Regarding the adaptation of trends to the Russian market, Mossina says that only Russian designers insist on adaptations. Some claim that "the Russian market is so different" or "Russian women are different," but Dolce & Gabbana is the same everywhere, and it seems to understand the Russian market. Russian consumers learn about fashion and trends via the internet and fashion magazines, as consumers do elsewhere. Mossina suggests that the perceived problems of adaptation may be invoked to hide the unpalatable truth that designers are just not good enough.

While current Russian fashion has no particular style, unlike German, Belgian or Scandinavian fashion, Mossina is not sure it is worth striving for a national fashion concept, because designers may end up simply reiterating clichéd "folk" elements. Russia has no tradition of luxury production, and Mossina intends to design "democratic" and trendy fashion for everyone. At present, Russians are unskilled at mixing expensive high-fashion items with mass-market items, preferring to adopt entire outfits as shown in fashion magazines. It is the younger generation who will learn and experiment. Russian people in general, and women in particular, are not as emancipated as in the West, Mossina observes, perceptively linking fashion, trends and social development (see Chapter 5).

Like many other designers, Mossina considers it unacceptably limiting that "Russian fashion" necessarily implies folkloristic elements, and her brand's slogan rejects that assumption. Lesya Olegovna notes that it is the heritage and the idea of Russia that inspires fashion designers globally, such as the design of the Kremlin, Fabergé, the clothing of the imperial families and old Russian folktales. These features go in and out of fashion while the actual Russian fashion scene has no influence. During the mid-1990s, Russia was "the new" for the European fashion industry, one Russian fashion designer claims, but since then, the industry has looked elsewhere.

After the collapse of the Soviet Union, "the new" was equivalent to "something from the West," according to Lesya Olegovna. The domestic mass-market fashion companies that established themselves took on Western-sounding names such as Taxi, Be Free and Oggi. More recently, some retailers have chosen to embrace their Russian heritage, such as the mass-market brand Tvoe, which combines Soviet nostalgia with the search for the new, although the resulting look may seem slightly dated, says Olegovna. Zarina (a word play on Zara and *tsarina*) is a brand that incorporates some folkloric elements in its collections.

Melon Fashion Group (MFG), one such successful mass-market fashion group, is headquartered in a former sewing factory in St. Petersburg and has about 600 shops in Russia and Ukraine. Its three largest brands are Zarina (targeting adult women, "the wife," with Zara as its prototype), Be Free (targeting young women, "the girlfriend," with H&M as its prototype), and Love Republic (described as "burlesque," it targets "the mistress" and has no obvious European counterpart). MFG's senior managers are all women in their thirties and its employees are 95 percent women. The company puts considerable money and effort into developing its personnel. As St. Petersburg has no equivalent of the Fashion Institute of Technology, MFG must remain attentive to the potential of its employees, and as a result, mass-market fashion offers great possibilities for these young women. "If we note that this girl wants to turn the world upside down, that she has vast fashion knowledge and that she works well in the team, yes, then we give her a chance," explains one brand manager, adding that no one in Russia has more than 15 years of experience in the industry; she herself has exactly that.

The notion of branding is unmistakable at MFG, which uses the Stylesight trend service. A brand manager explains that trends often must be adapted to the local market, as Russian women tend to dress in a more feminine way, almost all wearing high heels and a skirt or dress. Grunge-inspired trends or jeans sometimes pose a problem. The brand Be Free has the strongest trend focus of the three. It targets young women without children who spend a lot of leisure time shopping and offers fast-fashion collections manufactured right after the fashion weeks in Paris and Milan. In 2007, MFG learned from a survey that 70 percent of Russian women dress to appeal to men. Accordingly, Be Free's advertising featured Russia's most famous football player, Andrei Arshavin, and his comments about how Russian girls should look and what they should wear.

Beyond the mass market, original Russian fashion designers have a harder time achieving lasting impact in the fashion field. The Russian arts scene is significantly more advanced and functional than the fashion field. The Moscow arts scene is centered on the Garage Center for Contemporary Culture, founded by the socialite, fashion designer and art collector Daria Zhukova, who is married to the oligarch Roman Abramovich. In the fall of 2011, *Garage Magazine*, which merges fashion and the arts, was launched, with Zhukova as the editor-in-chief. Other Moscow art museums such as the Pushkin and Kremlin museums have recently held exhibits on fashion. Katia Mossina says that fashion critic Olga Mikhailovskaya is Russia's Suzy Menkes and describes her as "uncompromising." Despite their rarity, it appears that national tastemakers do exist in Russia's fashion field.

Not all trends reach Russia, not only because of consumer taste and behavior or the weak legitimizing structure in the domestic fashion field but also because of the country's industrial structure, according to Olegovna. Many parts of the production chain suffer from their communist heritage: inefficiencies, bad planning, poor work ethic, questionable quality and relatively high pay are characteristic. It is extremely costly for a small fashion company to send employees to fashion fairs and shows or on shopping and inspiration trips—there are no cut-price airlines and visa requirements complicate travel—so the Russian fashion industry is slightly insular, Olegovna declares.

Other serious problems are the high costs of importing and exporting, customs charges and taxes, and widespread corruption. Customs officers have enormous power and maintaining good relations with them—whether through outright bribery or developing common cause—is crucial. Many bigger fashion companies, such as MFG, seldom experience delays or problems, customs clearance on average taking one to three weeks for them. Smaller companies routinely complain about problems with importing and exporting. Products can be stopped at the border for up to three months, spelling disaster for small fashion companies, Olegovna says. Smaller manufacturers also have to cope with corruption in matters beyond importing and exporting.

Fashion designers in Russia need partners with business perspective, the ideal being someone with experience in the fashion industry. When Lesya Olegovna began with the trend bureau, it had no customers in Russia and knowledge of the service was almost nonexistent there. Olegovna spread the word about the trend service through advertisements, collaborations with fashion weeks and networking at Russian trade fairs and at Première Vision ("The trade fair that any Russian who could would go to"), but it was only when she made personal contacts with potential customers and explained how the service could help them improve their business that they "fell in love" and signed on. Customers spread the message to others in their network and took the service with them when they changed jobs. It is typical of the market that many Russian trend service subscribers also request consultancy services. Olegovna sees it as a sign that Russian companies are ready to learn from Western corporations.

Donis Pouppis is one half of the Moscow-based designer duo Nina Donis, the other half being Nina Neretina. Although Nina Donis has received considerable international attention, Pouppis is wary of my interest in the company. Though the brand is respected in Russia, he insists that it cannot be regarded as a *business*: "We do collections and then we have a very, very small production." The collections are sold in two well-known and progressive stores in Moscow. The fashion scene, says Pouppis, is full of designers—some of whom are good— and a number of fashion weeks, but everything else is missing: production, well-functioning importing and exporting, cutting specialists, intellectual property rights and accessories. "The problem with the fashion scene in Russia is that it's fake, in my opinion. Because we don't have a fashion industry." The only thing the scene has is an *image* of the designer and of fashion as it appears during the fashion weeks. The mass-market scene is not part of fashion as Pouppis defines it, though he excepts H&M, which does both design and retail. For him, only design is fashion—high fashion.

Pouppis means something different by production problems from what is experienced in, say, Sweden: "No, no. I'm not speaking of us not having production *here*. I am talking about us n�t having *any* production at all. You could be based here and have production in, for example, China. But we don't even have that."

Nina Donis' history since its year 2000 breakthrough is a series of setbacks. In 1987, Pouppis, whose mother is Russian, moved from Greece to the then Soviet Union to study at the Moscow Textile Institute. The Perestroika era and the eight years under the Yeltsin administration were the best times, he says. Although life was tough, there was a belief that things were changing, that people's lives were improving and that the country would become more European. Within a year of his graduation, the new brand Nina Donis showed at one of Moscow's fashion weeks and then went on to win the Mixed Collection Prize at the fashion festival in Hyères. Nina Donis has been named Designer of the Year by Russian *GQ* and *Harper's Bazaar*, has shown at the London Fashion Week several times and had showrooms in Milan. Over the years, the duo has tried to engage business partners and investors, but their experience is that the company is regarded more as a "toy"—something an investor could brag about, especially during a fashion show.

Nina Donis has tried to sell collections to various shops in Italy, France, the United States, the UK and elsewhere, but as each attempt failed, Pouppis and Neretina's despair increased. Importing and exporting legally is nearly impossible for a small company, according to Pouppis. Just registering the company for exporting requires immense work; then each item must be granted an export certificate, which might also entail subsidiary certificates for materials. Each certificate is only good for two years and costs about USD 2,000. A small company simply cannot afford to carry out production. Pouppis provides an example. Early on, the company received an order from Louis Boston, a well-known store in Boston, the United States. The retailer required a bank account. However, in Russia, the State regularly audits the accounts of exporting companies, and the cost of this monitoring was actually double the cost of making the collection. "You cannot work that way!" Lobbying officials to improve conditions for the fashion industry is unlikely to succeed. Pouppis notes that these adverse circumstances are not limited to fashion but apply across the board to Russian industry, making international business impossible for small players.

At one point Nina Donis received an order from a prominent Harrods-like department store in Korea. Since there was no way the company could export legally according to the regulations at the time, it tried to send the products as samples, which in the end failed. Because it is still impossible for Nina Donis to import textiles entirely legally, they have found a procedure where an Italian producer against prepayment delivers fabric to a place in the outskirts of Moscow. "You say a name and receive the stuff, and the guy from this 'logistics company' says 'don't ask me more'," Donis describes.

Katia Mossina sells her collections through retailers in both Berlin and Moscow and has two sets of manufacturers, one for Germany and one for Russia. A trade agreement between Mongolia and Russia has minimized customs duties between the countries. Some of the Russian-earmarked Mongolian production now runs so smoothly that, in the future, a portion of that production could be shipped directly from Mongolia to Berlin. Russia's 2012 entry into the World Trade Organization is expected to further reduce tariff barriers.

The fashion scene in Moscow, with its designers and fashion weeks, is a bubble, Donis Pouppis suggests: there is nothing inside. The fashion weeks are run with good profit margins, all the designers pay to participate, many sponsors are attracted and the media cover them well. Consequently, fashion weeks are increasing in number to the detriment of quality. Their primary purpose seems to be to make people famous, Katia Mossina suggests. Lesya Olegovna argues that the major problem with the Russian fashion weeks is not only their large number but that many of the featured designers are not business-minded, having no idea of marketing to real customers. In addition, few buyers attend the shows.

The woman who produces the Mercedes-Benz Fashion Week Russia (MBFWR) professes herself genuinely tired of the designers who had their breakthroughs in the 1990s, because they seem to regard the fashion weeks as the end goal of their business:

> They are showgirls or showmen. It's like they "do shows," just like Lady Gaga. And therefore they expect us to pay them. They have no interest in building their own businesses. They might sell four dresses a year.

A dress by one of these Russian designers can reportedly cost as much as one by Gucci but in terms of quality, she says, it is the difference "between heaven and hell." In an alternative approach to brand-building, Denis Simachev first participated in the fashion scene, then opened a bar that helped him gain public exposure and finally in other ways capitalized on his celebrity status. MBFWR is more focused on showing younger designers who take a different approach to fashion and display great potential. Again, she acknowledges the immense problems with production and distribution that are beyond the control of any individual company.

At the beginning of our contact, Pouppis stated: "We ignore fashion trends in general."

> We try to make contemporary fashion and design. Doing that means that when we design, when we work on the collection, we don't care about who is going to buy [the clothes], who is going to wear them, where we are going to sell them or if we are going to sell them. We don't think about that at all. The only thing we care about is to express ourselves as designers. To create something that represents the time and the moment we live [in] now, something interesting and new and contemporary. But at the same time, we want them to fit into the meaning of "wearable clothes", that which is not theatrical or historical.

From this starting point it is then possible to make something more commercial and to think about the presentation and sales. There is always the option to start at the other end, he says. If one's purpose is to make a lot of money, one should focus on what trends are "in," what colors are popular, and whether skirts are maxi or mini—"But that's not design."

For Pouppis, anything related to trends is associated with economic capital and the mass market with its customer focus. The companies that survive in the Russian fashion market are, in his view, the mass-market chains.

Some of the Russian mass-market companies were started by the wives and daughters of oligarchs. One example is the daughter of the CEO of the juice and dairy group Wimm-Bill-Dann, Kira Sergeevna Plastinina. She was fourteen years old when her father, Sergei Plastinin, invested substantially in her brand, Kira Plastinina, and opened the first store in Moscow. As of 2013, the company has 120 stores and a ready-to-wear collection, LUBLU Kira Plastinina.

Russian couture makers, who work in the long-established *atelier* segment, survive because of rich customers, for whom highly customized clothing is produced. Those kinds of assignments imply that one has to take into consideration the big hips of the customer or that she perhaps does not like stripes, says Donis. The *couturier* has design in his or her mind but there are many obstacles in the way. Like many Russian designers, Nina Donis tried to extend its business to include private commissions for a while but found that it was not challenging enough from a design perspective: The customers did not request the kind of design that the designer duo wanted to make. In other words, private commissions imply fewer opportunities to build fashion capital as they oppose the notion of the independent designer who does fashion for the sake of fashion.

Despite Pouppis' detailed critiques of the dysfunctional Russian fashion industry or, more accurately, the lack of a fashion industry, he and his partner Nina Neretina keep designing because, according to Pouppis:

> The truth is we love fashion. Fashion as we understand it—not mass market—it's not about trends, not about having certain kinds of bags or shoes. There are a few fashion personalities in the world who are ahead of everyone else. We like that. We believe that we have something to say.

The prerequisites for operating a fashion business in Russia deviate substantially from those in the global fashion industry's center in Western Europe. Trade barriers, corruption and costly auditing must be addressed on a daily basis in Russia. In addition to this complicated framework, the designers themselves often appear to lack business skills. In this context, the trend services could be significant exporters of Western know-how to this emerging market. The fashion field in Russia is not functioning particularly well because of unreliable production processes, challenging importing and exporting conditions and the absence of influential tastemakers. The latter do exist in the form of museums, magazines and buyers at small reputable shops but do not seem to have a noticeable impact on the fashion field. There is a marked gap between the more challenging, "legitimate" designer fashion and the broader mass-market fashion, where the latter employs football players as tastemakers. As in other emerging markets, there are localized conceptions of how trends should be adapted to the domestic market, yet in Russia there is still a close link between trends and mass-market fashion.

Brazil

The trend forecasters I interview almost always mention São Paulo as an exciting fashion city, after Paris, London and New York. The fashion scene is seen as vibrant and young with many domestic designers. For a long time, one of the major attractions was the large-scale boutique Villa Daslù in the Vila Olimpia district.

In 1958, Lucia Piva de Albuquerque began inviting friends and acquaintances to her home to socialize and examine and shop for clothing by domestic designers. She joined forces with a partner, Lourdes Aranha, and they named the resulting boutique Daslù—"by Lu." Daslù could not offer foreign brands until the 1980s, when it became legal to import them to Brazil, though they were heavily marked up because of import duties.

The boutique has moved between various locations, but the informal characteristics of a luxurious home to which the customer is welcomed as a friend have remained, from the comfortable couches to the sumptuous interior design. Dana Thomas thoroughly described the heyday of Daslù in *Deluxe: How Luxury Lost Its Luster*, and many in Brazil refer to the book as significant in introducing Daslù to an international audience.[17] In 2011, the mall operator and competitor Iguatemi bought Villa Daslù (the building) and a private equity firm bought the greater part of the company Daslù, moving it to a mall in a newly built high-rise building.

In 2011, Daslù sold 333 international luxury brands, as well as the house brand, Daslù. The store sees only about a hundred customers a day, compared with the Iguatemi shopping mall, which sees 45,000 people a day. Luciana Marques,[18] Daslù's head buyer, says the difference is that Daslù's customers are transaction-focused: they are not there to window-shop.

In Brazil, where the social class categorizations "A" to "E" (roughly based on monthly household income) are used effortlessly, Marques identifies Daslù's customers as A, AA and AAA. They are fashionable but conservative. The selection of Dolce & Gabbana offered by Daslù is very different from the offerings in Dolce & Gabbana's stores on Avenue Montaigne or Madison Avenue, as Daslù emphasizes the more commercial, attractive and traditional aspects of any collection, the avant-garde being rejected. The staff even offer consultancy services. They know what parties and dinners each customer will attend and can provide advice on appropriate jewelry, clothing and accessories. Daslù capitalizes on fashion as an identity project, as Bourdieu would describe it (see p. 127).

To an exclusive group of Paulistanos, Daslù has played a legitimizing role. When Daslù endorses a trend or a brand, customers will accept it. Daslù has a history of interpreting international trends into "commercial and wearable" versions in the Daslù collection that offer something for everyone from infants to grandmothers. The house brand accounts for 70 percent of sales, while the rest comprises items imported from primarily European designers. Prices are often double or triple those in Europe and the United States because of customs fees, taxes and other costs. Yet despite these protectionist trade policies, during its peak years Daslù sold more Chanel items than anywhere in the world, after Chanel's own store on Rue Cambon in Paris. Customers often bought entire wardrobes at Daslù. Eliana Tranchesi, Piva de Albuquerque's daughter, set the trends. "Whatever was displayed was trendy and was obviously what the social girl in São Paulo was going to wear," says Marques. Tranchesi followed her instincts then, but the trend landscape has changed since. Customers who once trusted Daslù's selection implicitly are now much more informed through various media, and have their own clear ideas of what they *should* be wearing, using Daslù's selection for confirmation: "They wouldn't go straight into Dolce & Gabbana and buy a lime-colored blazer, they would wait until we have it." Trend-educated customers have spurred Daslù's buyers to purchase those items they know will be presented in fashion media such as *Vogue*.

Everyone who works on the creative side of Daslù has access to WGSN online and some trend publications. Using input from WGSN, their travels and buying trips, the creative department presents a trend lecture four times a year for the sales staff and VIP customers. The material also is put to good use in the brand's *Daslù Magazine*. Developing stories about trends is a work in progress, Marques says. Like many department stores in Europe and the United States, Daslù now increasingly buys from the pre-collections, whose offerings are in more tune with local preferences: more wearable, more suitable for the weather, more commercial and more traditional.

Daslù's three new satellite stores cater to a different type of customer, those who might have felt intimidated by the socialite customers and the grandeur of Villa Daslù. Marques considers that these satellite shops "in the city" appeal to customers with more money than before who value brands: a Moschino blouse or a Dolce & Gabbana skirt. Consequently, for these outlets, Daslù buys more of the signature pieces of brands while expanding in new directions, for example, into jewelry, lingerie and contemporary designers. In 2008, Eliana Tranchesis' daughter Marcella and two friends started the fast-fashion brand 284, an accessible and extremely trendy brand that appeals to the economic classes C and D. These classes have traditionally shopped primarily at low-priced department stores. Though many consider the luxury segment one of the fastest growing in Brazil, Marques stresses that the category that is in fact expanding the fastest comprises those who for the first time can afford a fridge, a cooling fan and television.

Vera Lopes, CEO and president of the Luxury Marketing Council Brazil, a member organization for companies in the luxury segment, refers to a study by Cap Gemini that found the luxury market in Brazil to be growing by 15–20 percent each year. In 2011, Brazil had 155,400 USD millionaires.[19] For many years Brazilians suffered from high inflation; during the 1991–1994 period, the average yearly inflation was 2,375 percent[20]—making them, says Lopes, used to living for the moment and spending money. Brazil has since successfully kept its inflation under 10 percent per year during the 2000s,[21] and now that the economy is strong, Brazilians want more.

Being able to pay in instalments has changed the shopping behavior of many people, leveraging them from class E to class AAA. Daslù's Marques suggests that instalment purchasing helps consumers cope with stores' high prices—heavily marked up to cover the high customs fees and taxes on imported luxury goods and other costs of importing into Brazil—that are sometimes double those in Miami, Florida.

One of the Luxury Marketing Council's members is Iguatemi, São Paulo's largest luxury mall. In the competition among malls, international luxury brands often obtain exceptionally favorable business terms. Perhaps those terms are needed: Lopes was amazed by the inflated prices of Christian Louboutin when the brand was launched in the Brazilian market.

Now, as in the previously closed Brazilian economy, the signature items of the big fashion houses serve as *news*, and the big fashion houses are aware of this. "How many Kelly bags or small Chanel bags can you have in your life, if you live in Europe?" Lopes answers her own question: "Two. Then you get tired." In Brazil, the market is underdeveloped, and people have often not had access to luxury brands. In the first month the Diane von Furstenberg store in Iguatemi was open, it was rumored that more was sold there than in the flagship store in New York.

Like Daslù, Iguatemi mall offers an exclusive and luxurious shopping experience. Concierge services provide a space decorated like a living room, offering refreshments, books on fashion, architecture and the arts, with Fashion TV Brasil on the television. Iguatemi's 300 stores are intended to offer everything from luxury to very low-cost items. Flavia Kujawski, the marketing director, explains: "We like to say that we are a democratic mall," a place to experience the joy of shopping and enjoy life. The international brands offer a broad selection: Gucci bags, for example, come in leather, nylon and polyester.

When the signature products of designer brands are news in themselves to many people, what significance do trends have in the Brazilian fashion field? Kujawski thinks that trends have become more important since the end of the 2000s. The younger generation used to focus more on brands, but now that fashion has become global and customers are more educated, very little adaptation to the Brazilian market is required. Only the weather imposes restrictions, some tweed fabrics and boots not being relevant. Iguatemi relies on WGSN, and sometimes the WGSN Brazil office organizes seminars and other activities at the mall.

Brazilian designers are inspired by foreign fashion but are, says Kujawski, utterly creative and excellent at combining art and fashion. Several domestic designers are represented in the Parisian boutique Colette, and it is easy to understand that she regards that shop as a tastemaker. Many informants find that domestic Brazilian design is often expensive. Brazil's protective trade policies are designed to ensure that domestic brands can develop without much competition from foreign brands. Luciana Marques notes that without this protection, domestic brands would have to outsource their production to lower-cost countries in Asia, threatening Brazil's vast textile industry.

Roberto Davidowicz and Raquel Blay Davidowicz are the CEO and creative director, respectively, of Brazil's contemporary ready-to-wear brand Uma. The brand has existed for fifteen years and focuses on women in their thirties and forties in social classes A and B+. Through close collaborations with artists, Blay Davidowicz has made the brand highly identifiable. She gains inspiration from artists, picking up their shapes, patterns and often minimalist aesthetic. The association with the arts feeds symbolic cultural capital so that Uma's collaborations can be also seen as a form of positioning in the fashion field.

Uma has three concept stores in Brazil, a wholesale outlet and minimal exports, generating total sales of 20,000 to 30,000 items a year. Their take on Brazilian fashion consumers provides a sharp contrast to the conservatism of the Daslù customer. Brazilians are hungry for news and something different, Blay Davidowicz claims, because the population is increasingly younger and optimistic. In addition, Brazil is a melting pot of various cultures, and everyone is fascinated by change. Blay Davidowicz stresses the need for design to change constantly, unlike in Europe, where everything is much more traditional and homogenous.

Uma uses WGSN for artistic and global inspiration, though all changes and designs must conform to the framework of the brand, in fabrics, print and color. Following trends has its dangers, though fast-fashion chains such as Zara are also popular. The *telenovelas*—television soap operas—are extremely influential for fashion awareness, and Uma has often provided outfits for typical "Uma characters" on these shows.

Roberto Davidowicz sees three big problems facing Brazilian fashion companies: import tariffs, which prevent designers from outsourcing production to cheaper countries; the strength of the Brazilian real against the US dollar, which makes Brazilian products extremely expensive on the export markets; and high import costs combined with poor transportation and distribution infrastructure.

The designer Inacio Ribeiro (see p. 120), who grew up in Brazil, agrees that many Brazilian brands face unfair competition with international brands but regards globalized *taste* as one of the causes. The domestic brands are losing ground and often respond by choosing a niche strategy.

The Brazilian designer brand Osklen has a store on the Oscar Freire shopping street. Oskar Metsavaht from Rio de Janeiro founded the brand in 1986 when he launched a design for overalls. Educated to become a medical doctor, Metsavaht was also interested in sports and aesthetics. Osklen's Marketing Director Nelson

Camargo believes that the Brazilian fashion landscape has suffered from its colonial heritage. Brazil's fashion has not had a strong identity; instead, designers have long imitated other countries' (i.e., European) fashion. Camargo regards Osklen more as a communication medium than a pure fashion brand. "The DNA of the brand" consists of sustainability, sportswear influences and design and art. Osklen is dedicated to sustainability and invests considerably in research and development, and its team works with researchers to develop more sustainable materials, such as fish skin, for their original designs. Giorgio Armani, for example, made a shoe in salmon skin three seasons after Osklen produced its first. The Osklen collection "Oceans" (Summer 2011) exemplifies the blend of fashion and sustainability, using an environmentally-friendly pigment in the dying process and a recurring color theme of various shades of blue.

While admiring designers such as Rick Owens and Yohji Yamamoto, Camargo describes Osklen's style as "Tropical minimalism." Osklen's minimalism is "sharp, warm, cosy, colorful, simple, elegant but also with a life presence…Oskar is very sensitive, very open-minded. He has a strong feeling for direction. He is a visionary, something of a scientist and an artist."

The brand offers a surf line, a collection line and a leisure line. The brand is not dependent on fashion shows but uses them to demonstrate its artistic vision, says Camargo. Members of the design team do not use Web-based trend services but instead travel and read for inspiration. Occasionally, they check *style.com* to view the international fashion shows. "We would never use trends as a basis. At Osklen it's more about freedom, more about style. Oskar's style," says Camargo. Osklen is clearly imbued with what Bourdieu calls "the charismatic ideology" in which designers are considered solitary *auteurs*. Camargo rarely refers to other fashion designers when discussing Osklen's style, which reveals something about the brand's desired positioning in the global fashion field.

Osklen has its own stores in New York, Miami and Tokyo and franchise stores in Milan, Rome and Sydney. Five percent of Osklen's sales are from outside Brazil. The brand hopes to increase that share, but international expansion requires considerable capital.

Carla Schmitzberger has the irresistible title of Sandal Director. She is responsible for the shoe brand Havaianas that is part of the Alpargatas corporate group. About 184 million pairs of Havaianas are sold each year in Brazil, whose population in 2012 was about 195 million people. Havaianas was launched in 1962 as the "poor people's shoe," that is, focused on classes D and E, but has since become a brand for the entire socioeconomic spectrum. "Our target group is *everybody*," Schmitzberger says. The brand has persuaded celebrities to wear Havaianas, has developed several versions of the famous flip-flop (it even comes in a Swarovski version) and has collaborated with fashion designers such as Céline and Missoni. The flip-flop has gained status, becoming an aspirational product appealing to the middle class.

Schmitzberger has a background in marketing and previously worked with fast-moving consumer goods. She says trends are crucial to Havaianas, so WGSN is an important tool for the brand, along with other trend reports, trade fairs and inspirational trips.

If orange is a hot color this summer and we don't have at least a few orange flip-flops, in different styles, then we're obviously going to lose out on that. Trends for higher or lower heels, more fluorescent colors and so on, are all important to us. We have to make sure we get the trends right.

Do trends need to be translated to the Brazilian market? Schmitzberger believes that there no longer exist any international trends that do not work in Brazil: "The world is so global that the trends are global today." The financial analysts (Alpargatas is listed on the stock exchange in São Paulo) do not care about trends, but "sales are an indirect assessment of whether you got the trends right," says Schmitzberger. Sometimes the tension between consistency and change is difficult to manage, because "[p]eople expect the unexpected of Havaianas." The brand has launched special collections such as Havaianas *slim* (with thinner straps), espadrilles and sneakers. Although the exchange rate is not favorable for exports, 17 percent of sales are from outside Brazil and the company is not letting the strong Brazilian currency hinder its expansion plans.

The interviews from Brazil clearly illustrate the significance of fashion in creating identity. In this country, fashion and social class are closely interlinked, and with a growing middle class, social mobility and hope for personal progress, new spaces for fashion consumption become important, as when Daslù opened its satellite shops and Iguatemi billed itself a "democratic mall." Brands capitalize on people's aspirations to move upward in society, as Havaianas' differentiation of its products evidences. However, an increasingly global fashion field may undermine not only domestic designers competing with internationally renowned brands but also tastemakers such as Daslù, which finds its customers alternatively inspired by international magazines, the catwalk and blogs. Furthermore, Brazilian informants note that the international fashion brands that have enjoyed novelty status, as did Diane von Furstenberg and Christian Louboutin, see intensified competition from trends as people become accustomed to them and to other brands. Neomania, the desire for the new and different, will increasingly be directed toward trends rather than brands.

*

Stories from the BRIC countries repeatedly mention the fact of relatively recent access to European and American fashion products. These products and the shops selling them constitute news in themselves. Some financial analysts are aware that "the fashion risk" of a brand is lower in emerging economies as long as companies are expanding and the brand is a novelty. As fashion becomes more global, certain domestic tastemakers become less relevant. In Brazil, the decline of Daslù as well as the number of informants who claim that nothing needs to be adapted to their specific country market are signs of this development. The trend services, here chiefly represented by WGSN, are now ubiquitous, substantiating the contention that trends serve as an organizing principle even when they are rejected. The demand for trend services, the desire for Western celebrities to endorse domestic brands and the high status of Western brands all indicate that Western-based fashion is conquering the world. The counterbalance to the unbridled demand for all things Western comes not only from representatives of domestic brands in the BRIC countries but also from inside WGSN, as Olivia Linqin notes in describing China's fashion scene. There also appears to be a blurring of the distinction between standard and status markets, as manufacturers, especially in China, launch brands of their own.

Many informants suggested that a focus on trends would follow the focus on brands. When neither the products nor the brands are novelties in their own right, there may be more room for trends and a fashion field rich in nuances, where fashion capital and brands are not equated. The only question is what position the domestic tastemakers will then have in relation to the tastemakers in the dominating faction of the international/Western fashion field.

Some informants in Russia describe the experience of having been part of something—the Russian fashion scene—once identified as "the new," though interest in the scene quickly ebbed. Being constructed as "the other"[22] that complements the norm—that is, Western fashion—can be detrimental since the other never seriously shapes or becomes part of the norm but is always subordinated, always *other*.

9 FINAL DISCUSSION

In New York, I meet with long-time trend forecaster Michael Bennett,[1] who is excited because he believes the world beyond the fashion field will have a greater impact on fashion than ever before, but he is also concerned that the fashion system, as we know it, has collapsed.

> It's my opinion that the fashion industry and the people who run the industry, or are part of it, are not aware of this at all. They're still in a horse and buggy and the world is in a jet plane. They are trying to make the changes conform to their old way of disseminating fashion and excitement. And it just doesn't work, it's failing all over the place... Now we have so many fragmented style tribes that only the biggest kind of messages filter through and it takes so long. Everyone keeps saying that fashion moves faster than ever and I disagree completely. I think fashion is dead in the water! Absolutely! I think finally we may be on the brink of ending this endless retro rehash that is one of the problems... It has been a time of speeding up of fashion and of the birth of the trend system. But it moved so quickly that it was impossible to really have innovation and newness in design or in technology because we were so hungry for the change. So we had to keep going back again and again to the 70s, the 80s, the 50s, the 40s. If I look at one more fashion magazine that tells me that the 70s are back... And in the same magazine it says that the 90s are back, the 80s are back.

He complains about the tendency of many trend forecasters to present trends according to a few fixed categories—always something romantic, casual, athletic, retro and ethnic—similar to the "system of compartmentalizing" that H&M (see p. 92) used for a time:

> All they do is they give each trend a new name for each season, and they often become so oblique that no one can understand what they are talking

about. Then they show the same fabrics and a selection of colors. Hundreds of colors. It means nothing!

Trend forecasting used to be about creating and communicating new ideas, the making of a trend which is not already out there. Nowadays trend forecasters point to a trend which is out there and say "I think it's going to be bigger next year" or "I think you should trade it down a little bit next year." I mean, we often talk about percentages to people. We say "80 per cent of your spring line last year was red, white and blue, and you know, maybe this year you should pare that down to 40 per cent and do 20 per cent blue, white and yellow." So it becomes very pedantic and not what I think of as exciting and fashion conscious.

Fashion people are still excited about fashion, and always will be, but I think they're a shrinking tribe. I liken them to the opera fans. It's a very specialized, inbred, insular group that is madly interested in what is going on in their group, but nobody else is really paying that much attention.

And there is no right or wrong because there is no longer any peer pressure about conforming to fashion. I keep thinking [about] going to a restaurant, a club or a party in the 70s and the 80s, and being able to say "that person is *in fashion*, that person isn't." I don't think you could say that anymore. You can wear anything. It's fun. You can't even laugh at people anymore for being *out* of style. But I think the forecast industry is now so solidly a part of what people think they have to have to run a creative business, so I think it will survive a long time. I liken most forecasts to Latin. It's a dead language. People in fashion speak it to each other and it means nothing to the outside world.

There is so much information and no direction, no opinion. The fashion directors in the past, like Diana Vreeland, were crazily opinionated and would make decrees that were really exciting because they created consumer demand. I don't think we've allowed the consumer to break free of the system. And when fashion became democratic, it was the end of what I think was fashion throughout the twentieth century and a bit into the twenty-first. Fashion as we like to think of it traditionally, is a game of followers and leaders and if everyone is a leader, it's going nowhere.

I see the influence of globalization. It would be wonderful if you could say that Brazil is doing something that is absolutely unique and we can all feed off it. But I don't think you can anymore. All these countries are turning into a fashion melting pot. As soon as a country becomes more fashion conscious and able to buy into the cheap fashion of today, any national identity disappears ... Everyone could come from anywhere. Which I guess is an exciting idea in itself, but again, it seems to be symptomatic of the breakdown of the fashion system.

Bennett does not mince words when he describes the industry of which he was once an integral part. He has every reason to downplay the significance of a certain type of trend-forecasting agency and to insist on his own analysis. In his critique and analysis, Bennett summarizes particular views that were voiced by many of my informants. However, none of these is indisputable.

Are trends, and fashion in general, relevant to fewer or more people than ever before? Does anything go or is being "right" still important? How does globalization affect trends? With Michael Bennett's statements as a backdrop, we return to some of the themes of this book and look not only at the significance of trends as an organizing principle of the fashion field but also at how trends help us understand the fashion field. Sometimes these themes manifest themselves as tensions—hardly surprising given that the fashion field is constituted of opposing logics, with change at its heart.

Trends as organizing principle

I have already suggested that trends historically functioned as an organizing principle in the fashion field, giving producers a clearer idea of what they should produce and consumers a better idea of what they should demand. In this way, insecurity has decreased in the industry because it is organized around trends. Unsold goods and dissatisfied customers, which would otherwise have resulted from mismatch between supply and demand, have probably been reduced as well. For customers to care about what they *should* ask for, they need to care about being on trend. While the cultural and social meanings of fashion are central, trends as a phenomenon interconnect consumption and production practices.

Trend agencies have historically capitalized on the need to reduce uncertainty while being very respectful of the creators in the fashion field and their ideas. While invisible to consumers, they have quietly acquired legitimacy in the field beyond the spotlight. It is in the interest of trend agencies to demonstrate a need to sift through trends and keep up-to-date, as well as to instill faith in the idea that trends come and go. No trend agency actors speak of the dissolution of trends— with the exception of Michael Bennett.

In the same way, many, but not all, fashion companies have an interest in promoting trends, in encouraging people's hunger for the new, in order to sell more of their products. This is the logic of capitalism. Fashion companies' adherence to the trend system is also a result of their adaptation to what they understand as the most suitable or legitimate mode of behavior in the field.[2]

Fashion is one of the most commercial fields of cultural production. Even those designers and brands with the most fashion capital are highly commercial, though their strategies differ from those of the mass-market fashion companies, and while they often take a stance against following trends, they still wish to leave a mark, be trendmakers.

Tastemakers are absolutely crucial to the independence of the field. Stylists, buyers, journalists and others who sense the "incipient taste" also help create it. Tastemakers embrace or dismiss collections, brands and designers, in the process becoming trendmakers. Their active participation in creating trends and designer fame occurs via feedback from fashion editors to designers and via feedback from and collaborative efforts of department store tastemakers seeking to structure designers' collections. Since trend service use is viewed by some corporate boards, for example, as signaling designer weakness, designers must rely on confidentiality agreements with the services. Fashion companies expect designers to have a high trendmaking capacity, and designers in turn satisfy this expectation by minimizing dependence on trend services.

Trends still function as an organizing principle. The mere existence of trend-forecasting agencies is evidence of this. Ann-Sofie Back of Cheap Monday describes how salespeople pay careful attention to whether a trend is described by WGSN, rather than being something that Back has just "made up," confirming the legitimacy of WGSN's outlook. Missing a trend is understood by many to be a disaster. That Première Vision remains so central to many informants, such as the designer at Whistles who wanted to delay making collection sketches until after the fair, indicates its status as an organizing force. WGSN's listing of the names of subscribing Chinese factories on its Web site is also a form of organizing, since the list tells brands where they can turn for production of their goods, with WGSN as a common frame of reference. Several informants note that "everyone else" subscribes to trend services as proof that the services are gaining ground—yet another indication of the role of trends as an organizing principle. The information provided by trend services is understood as somewhat factual. With their increasing popularity in the emerging markets, the trend agencies are assured that the demand for trends will persist. The fashion companies that become their customers are lured into the trends of the dominant field of fashion and especially into embracing its notions of how trends are packaged, translated and disseminated.

In the fashion field, where many actors compete to be trendmakers, the trend-forecasting agencies must lie low while the organizations and individuals with more fashion capital operate openly. This does not rob the trend agencies of their important role as trendmakers, even though they describe their role as "mediators" of trends, acting behind the scenes.

New ways to manage uncertainty

With the advent of the internet, the fashion landscape changed considerably for both brands and consumers. The internet, short lead times, "lean production" and the exploitation of cheap labor, particularly in Asia, made fast fashion possible. As we have seen, mass-market fashion companies can react to all fashion events simultaneously, ideally offering something for everyone. Everything is categorized under trend labels that have become standard, as Michael Bennett notes. The industry's rapid pace, driven by the internet and well-informed consumers who constantly demand news of "the new," has conjured retromania, constant flashbacks that occur parallel to one another. In addition, mass-market fashion has become more demand driven, explaining why all styles linger for so long.

Fashion can be more demand driven because companies and brands have found new ways of dealing with uncertainty. They have started structuring their product ranges so that most now have a base of evergreen goods that last several seasons and are never discounted. Most have a larger set of changeable goods complemented by a subset of trendy pieces produced on a smaller scale. Designer brands produce commercial pre-collections to complement their main collections.

In *The End of Fashion*, Teri Agins declared that marketing was killing fashion. Massive branding efforts enabled many American brands, which were more about lifestyle production than fashion, to circumvent traditional fashion routes.[3] Her book can be read as a tale of the economization of the fashion field, in which brands use marketing, celebrities and the centralization of power in department stores to cut through fashion noise, even while lacking the support of traditional tastemakers with fashion capital. The presence of fashion companies on the stock market is both a cause and an effect of this evolution, according to Agins.

Many fashion companies try to control every detail of their brands—who wears their clothes, who writes about them, where they are sold and even how their garments are folded. The emergence and growth of PR agencies testify to this desire for control. While working on this book, I was taken aback by the PR agencies' role as gatekeepers, especially in Anglo-Saxon countries, which made it nearly impossible to arrange interviews without providing sample questions, information about the book, its publisher and its eventual distribution. One informant from a fashion company says that twenty or thirty years ago PR people would have been called secretaries, that PR is a very vaguely defined profession and that many in the industry are of poor quality. Stories surface of writers who criticized a fashion house's collection and were subsequently banned from showings.[4] Tastemakers do not always seem averse to letting brands purchase editorial space, directly or indirectly (e.g., by running photographs of celebrities wearing their products). This indicates that the position of tastemakers has become somewhat discounted, since these shows and magazines are still taken seriously.

Fashion companies working outside mass-market fashion try to convince customers to put brand loyalty before adherence to trends. The brands accordingly build in unique markers or stylistic traits. Whether it is Paul Smith's, Missoni's or Sonia Rykiel's stripes, or Martin Margiela's four white stitches, these small signs are intended to guide the consumer to quality while guaranteeing clothes that are in sync with the times. As navigating trends is considered risky, brands attempt to build fashion capital in order to attain or maintain good positions in the fashion field. Attracting consumers via the brand can mean that the brand loses touch with the movements of fashion, making each collection an end in itself, disconnected from the larger fashion world. In time, this could mean that the brand loses its fashion capital, as it is no longer embraced by tastemakers. Michael Bennett cites Diane von Furstenberg as an example of this:

> There is no direction. Until you see the label, you cannot know what it is, except the wrap dress. There are long skirts, short skirts, bright colors, dark colors every season. So we're talking about an assortment, from A to Z, that you are offering the consumer and then the consumer creates her own trend story, depending on what she personally likes. No one is guiding her. No one has the courage to say "this is what I'm doing."

Michael Bennett contends that nobody in the fashion field still *creates* demand; rather, trend analysts merely point out trends that already exist. Informants from several French trend-forecasting agencies, whose analysts often criticize the Web-based agencies for reporting trends that are already in circulation, could not agree more. Nowadays, social media offer other ways to interpret demand. Jane Kellock, who, since our meeting, has founded a new trend-forecasting agency, Unique Style Platform (USP), argues that images have overtaken words on the internet.[5] Using Pinterest and Tumblr, consumers can create their own "moodboards," which trend agencies can then analyze. If trend agencies become more demand driven and begin simply reflecting the existing fashion scene, we might see a "short-circuiting" of fashion in which nothing new is added and no trend is allowed to mature.

Fashion appears to have been subjected to economization, with its roots in the financialization discussed in Chapter 7. More companies are going public on the stock market, as they want to expand and need capital to do so. In going public, however, they subject themselves to financial market logic. Financial analysts let the companies themselves manage the "fashion risk" and react only when something goes wrong. According to risk-management scholar Michael Power, uncertainty becomes "risk" when it is subordinated to management systems and must be identified, evaluated and reduced.[6] The financial analysts I spoke with confirmed this view, but many other fashion industry actors, from trend forecasters to fashion companies, also talk about risks rather than uncertainties. This reflects an expectation that people can do something to address dangers and opportunities and affect the outcome of events, rather than abandoning themselves to fate.[7] An event described as a "risk" is situated within a web of expectations where someone is viewed as responsible for its management.

Overall, it is probable that trends as an organizing principle have decreased in importance. Trends are no longer as important when it comes to designers' creative decisions, what fashion companies buy and what consumers demand. This is not to say that trends are now insignificant. Most informants in this book state the contrary: trends are significant but not to the same extent as before.

It is only according to an economic logic that fashion activity is considered a risk. The language of risk belongs to economic logic and its emphasis on control, weighing risks against benefits and, on that basis, choosing the next course of action.[8] Some financial analysts regard risk as greater for womenswear than menswear, an attitude attributable to the greater changeability of womenswear and to most financial analysts' poorer understanding of the world of womenswear. The chapter on financialization shows that only an extremely small part of luxury fashion is exposed to tastemakers and that the mass-market fashion companies can manage fashion capital, for example, by initiating designer collaborations or by embracing all possible trends. If a company emphasizes the brand rather than the designer, it has the option of bringing in new designers if collections are not well received over an extended period. In the economized fashion field, it is most difficult for mid-range brands to assert themselves, at least over time, as they either get stuck in a certain style or renew themselves so much that their "true identity" remains unclear.

Several scholars have drawn attention to the economization of cultural production, noting that the creation of giant corporate conglomerates, the increased importance of financial markets and the greater significance and distribution of management models and terms are common to many cultural fields.[9] The present work demonstrates that even a field of cultural production as commercial as fashion can be described as undergoing economization.

Fashion capital strikes back

Fashion is always contradictory. Societal changes are not necessarily reflected in fashion, and fashion's inherent changeability means that the pendulum will soon swing back. The 1990s, fueled by marketing and "lifestyle brands," was followed by the emergence of fast fashion, which fed on fashion trends. Trends offered mass-market fashion companies legitimacy in the fashion field, often by being inspired by and to some extent plagiarizing designer brands' clothes and at other times by straightforward collaboration in developing capsule collections: fashion for all. When a British mass-market fashion chain produces a dress using a Peter Pilotto print, legitimacy is being sought. Many designers are, after all, flattered to be plagiarized, because this confirms their strong position—

and capital—in the fashion field. Fashion capital matters, as the fashion field functions to a greater or lesser extent on its basis.

In step with the mass-market fashion chains' intensified hunt for trends, the status of trends has decreased in the fashion field. The prevalence of trends in society at large, as well as their exploitation by trend-forecasting agencies, may explain their decreased status—they destroy fashion's magic. Though many designers are hesitant to use the word "trend," most nevertheless wish to leave a mark by creating one. Designers tell stories about how they manage on their own, without the aid of trend-forecasting agencies, seeing themselves as the ones who provide the agencies with material, believing that what they do naturally gives rise to trends. For their part, the trend-forecasting agencies show designers respect by offering confidentiality and making modest claims to be influencing fashion. The fashion weeks are flourishing; they are important for designer and luxury brands, which use the shows to create mystique around their brands to ensure that they sell clothing, bags and accessories. Constantly updated media outlets seek news more hungrily than ever. Although one can argue that the supply of goods is increasingly demand driven, because of the fashion companies' ability to "sense" what sells and to offer classics that transcend seasons, the shows remain vital.

Brands in emerging markets openly rely on trend services because of the fashion legitimacy they bestow; the agencies make available an aesthetic rooted in the West and provide a tangible stamp of quality, that is, the authority of the trend service, whose logo can be used in a company's promotional materials. Trends as an organizing principle prevail and coexist with their increasing importance as legitimators—although they are not always called trends by their creators.

Fashion shows can be seen as *decoupled* from what is sold in stores, being a phenomenon existing solely to create legitimacy. Like all cultural production organizations, fashion companies face contradictory demands from opposing cultural and economic logics. According to organization scholar Nils Brunsson, one way of dealing with incompatible norms is to create two kinds of processes decoupled from each other: one leading to action and another intended to express norms.[10] In the fashion field where the economic logic exerts an increasingly strong influence, fashion companies can act in accordance with an economic logic while claiming to espouse the norms of a cultural logic, since this logic still has a legitimizing value. Cultural logic can create room in which the economic logic can act. Louis Vuitton, for example, invests financially in extravagant shows and advertising campaigns imbued with considerable fashion capital, thereby expressing the norms of a cultural logic, a fashion logic; at the same time, the company leverages this accrued fashion capital to sell a lot of canvas bags, clearly upholding an economic logic. The shows, the "buzz" around them, the designers and the new collaborations all create space in which the company can act efficiently from an economic perspective—a form of "organizational hypocrisy," to borrow a concept from Nils Brunsson.[11]

That certain designers cannot identify anything as being out of style is understandable; they belong to a group in the fashion field that does not subsist purely on trends, unlike the trend-forecasting agencies and the tastemakers. Designers do not relate mainly to trends, since these are lower in status but seek to strengthen their brands or their expression in various ways. Designers still strive to make their mark, that is, to affect trends and create "interesting fashion" and talk a great deal about how exciting, enriching and challenging their work is. Attention can come quite quickly to smaller brands, not just because of the thirst for news and the possibilities of internet commerce but also because of a design expression that initially differs from that of the fashion establishment, before it is absorbed by the trend machinery. As noted in Chapter 6, on designers, brands and trends, plagiarizing is common across the board. The strength of fashion capital is also seen in the self-confidence of tastemakers, who employ their ability to discern what is hottest right now and to identify and create the incipient taste. Legitimizing internet sites—"curated sites," in the words of Inacio Ribeiro— emerged in response to the need for knowledgeable sifting of the A-to-Z range that now characterizes the fashion scene. Some boutiques and department stores in London (e.g., Browns, Liberty and Topshop) present certain collections as "edited," also indicating that the need for tastemakers is not declining. Designers Geoffrey Finch, Erdem Moralioğlu and Inacio Ribeiro confirm the importance of high-quality retailers.

Other initiatives are not easily categorized under the rubric of either fashion capital or economic capital. Information technology has enabled a new form of e-commerce: Moda Operandi allows its customers to buy items directly from the shows during the fashion weeks. Through collaboration with *vogue.com*, the customer can click on the image and be redirected to Moda Operandi's site. Garments that might never have been produced for sale because the buyers deemed them unsellable can be marketed.

Moda Operandi was founded by Aslaug Magnusdottir and Lauren Santo Domingo and is based in New York on Madison Avenue. Magnusdottir previously cofounded an investment company that invested in early-stage fashion brands, such as Matthew Williamson and Rachel Roy, and then at Gilt Group, a discount company focused on fashion. Santo Domingo was and is a contributing editor at *Vogue*. Magnusdottir describes how the idea took root:

[The designers] complained that they would create amazing collections and they would spend all this money on runway shows, that they would get press from it and then no direct sales. Because then the stores would come in and make their selections from their collections. And they would typically buy just a little portion. So the store wouldn't display their full collection, often wouldn't display many of their favorite pieces ... [The designers] felt that they were making the wrong decisions.

The idea of Moda Operandi also sprang from Magnusdottir's frustration. Very often she would want to buy something she had seen on the catwalk only to learn that it would not be produced.

The company, whose average transaction is USD 1,400 per customer, takes a relatively small risk since it does not have inventory. The only costs incurred are for photography, building and maintaining the site and some clothing returns. The one stumbling block is that consumers have to wait three to five months for their items, in a fashion landscape where the culture of instant gratification is pervasive.

Magnusdottir says the idea is working. She notes that mass-market fashion companies have already succeeded in incorporating end-consumer feedback into their processes and that this will eventually happen in designer fashion as well. Brands can use sales data from Moda Operandi in their contacts with traditional retailers to identify demand. The legitimacy created through Moda Operandi's business is both cultural—that is, unique designer items offered directly from the fashion capital-intensive catwalk—and economic—that is, advance sales data from customers. Preconceptions about the future behavior of consumers on which buyers base decisions can be circumvented—or confirmed.

The fashionization of consumer society

That trend agencies sell their entirely fashion-based material to producers of fast-moving consumer goods, car and cell phone manufacturers, furniture companies, advertising companies and banks signals the aestheticization of consumer society. Goods are increasingly valued for their look, especially by the middle class.[12] Ultimately, this aestheticization can be viewed as a process of "fashionization" in which style is not the only thing that is important; it is also crucial that the style never stops changing.

That fashion became available to everyone during the 2000s is often explained with reference to the dissemination of fashion information made possible by the internet, a point also made by many of my informants. The emergence of self-proclaimed fashion intermediaries, especially bloggers, with no special position in the fashion field enables a form of communication that sociologist Manuel Castells calls "mass self-communication." It is a mass medium in which the material is self-generated, creating a composite, interactive hypertext that remixes and combines cultural expressions from many forms of human interaction and communication.[13] This new form of communication may be contributing to the dissolution of the established hierarchies in the fashion field. Fashion information can be disseminated, critiqued and reworked with astonishing speed. The many informants who commented on the well-informed fashion consumers of today identified the potential consequences of such communication. One interpretation of tastemakers' unwillingness to give absolutist advice, highlighted in Chapter 4, is that they would prefer to prevent their power to dictate from becoming even more diluted.

The retromania that disturbs Michael Bennett is fueled by information technology's unending desire for news. The "democratization of fashion," where the very latest is accessible to everyone everywhere, has made fashion relevant to everyone and no one. Nothing is out of style as everything is permitted; clothes are in style again before they have had time to go out. Perhaps we cannot see the fashion forest for all the retro trees. Nevertheless, new things keep appearing on the fashion scene, even though some informants can sum them up in a few words. Wolfe concedes that the "crazy shoes" were an instance of something truly new emerging.

Bourdieu reminds us that the very premise of fashion as an independent field is that there is a belief in fashion for fashion's sake.[14] When fashion has become so ubiquitous as to apply to car interiors, pasta and cell phones, what independence does the field retain? Is it interesting enough in itself? Wolfe is clear that it is *not*; he thinks that fashion will be affected by influences "from the outside" to a much greater degree than before. Science and technology will interact with fashion and make it more interesting, via material development or collaboration between fashion companies and home electronics. The risk is that fashion may lose its meaning as cultural expression, and become a kind of adjunct to the consumption field, bestowing a superficial aesthetic novelty on other goods. This erosion is pushed by trend-forecasting agencies and consumer goods companies. Because the trend-forecasting agencies do not openly participate in the game of the fashion field, but operate backstage, they do not reap the rewards accruing from increased status in the field of fashion and are therefore not troubled by its erosion.

Designers will always be at the top of the fashion hierarchy; they at least still identify with a well-defined cultural hierarchy and are clear about their goal of creating fashion for fashion's sake. Many designers distance themselves from the concept of "lifestyle brand," possibly in reaction to the fashionization of consumer society, where "lifestyle" has come to be associated with the aestheticized consumption of everything from home decoration and food to cars and toys. Trend-forecasting agencies are well aware of this fashion hierarchy; they do not offer fashion companies design information from fast-moving consumer companies, as there is no interest in information from that source. In this context, the fashion field becomes an aesthetic resource to be conveyed to consumer society.

Trend imperialism

The growth of the wealthy and middle classes in many parts of the world means that fashion companies are migrating to those places. Expansion requires capital, so many fashion companies are going public, submitting to the logic of financial markets. Financial analysts claim to leave risk management to the fashion companies themselves, and the companies behave in a way that convinces analysts that risks are low. As the "fashion risk" at the heart of the fashion field is the fashion companies' responsibility, they employ risk-minimizing methods; they create a range structure with a broad base of evergreens and a smaller portion of changing fashion, work with shorter lead times, for example, by contracting lower-cost production (often exploiting workers in developing countries), and strengthen brand appeal to attract aspiring consumers in emerging economies. The culture of risk minimizing created by the financial market logic sees fashion brands in the mid-range segment becoming caught between consistency and change. Some designers and CEOs argue that it is precisely this supposed contradiction that makes the fashion business fun; for them that may well be the case, as tension does create a certain creative challenge. On the capital market it is easier to estimate the sales of brands with high aspirational value, that is, luxury brands, whose fashion level is not as relevant (shows attract attention, but the ready-to-wear collections have little economic value for the brand as a whole), or of mass-market fashion brands that sell in large volume and are demand driven.

Trends sometimes function as fashion news. In the globalized and expansive fashion industry, individual brands also function as news, as the economies in emerging countries have often previously been closed and many people have been unable to afford the brands in question. Fashion companies do not always need to spend much energy on trends themselves, as a newly opened store is news enough. This suits the financial market, which is keen that companies not be exposed to unnecessary risk.

If fashion companies were not as focused on expansion as they currently are, and therefore did not as often subordinate themselves to the logic of the financial market, they probably would not be as likely to present themselves as risk minimizing. Trends might then have greater importance and brands a subtler role. Several informants in the BRIC countries affirm that trends do become more important as the fascination with newly imported Western luxury brands fades.

Fashion has its origins in modernity. As Inacio Ribeiro describes and is evident in the examples from the BRIC countries, fashion is originally a Western cultural expression. As Western fashion companies expand to the emerging markets, accepting an insignificant amount of fashion in return, this gives rise to contemporary cultural imperialism. The many Chinese factories that seek legitimacy for their brands by using online trend services expose the deep roots of the idea that fashion is Western. The increasingly widespread legal and illegal use of trend service Web sites also means that trends will continue to snowball, possibly making it more difficult for other forms of fashion expression to break through. Trend imperialism assures fashion producers in the West of unending demand. In China, informants observed seeds of new types of fashion expression and local trends, but the question is what reception these will have in the world fashion field, especially among the trend-forecasting agencies. Both the fashion field as a whole and its organizations are permeated by hierarchies, and the prerogative of interpretation is not evenly distributed. Michael Bennett, for example, finds globalization depressing since it creates a melting pot of fashion.

Perhaps the solution lies in finding people with the competence to nurture these domestic seeds and ensure that designers, fashion journalists, stylists, buyers and trend analysts also nurture them. As Carin Rodebjer and others point out, the industry allows very little time for immersive research and everyone, including the consumer, is imbued with the notion that white Western references have the highest status.

WGSN's service brochure presents an image of a fashion pyramid. It is strikingly relevant to how people in the industry talk about their range of products: a volume-oriented base constituting 20 percent, a "trend-relevant" commercial portion constituting 50 percent and a directional top constituting 30 percent of offered items. This schema is not unique and seems reasonable but is yet another sign that adaptation to legitimate forms does not just happen organically or in line with financial market expectations. Instead, the trend-forecasting agencies seem to be actively contributing to the organization of the fashion business.

The Eurocentric gaze on fashion in the BRIC countries is noticeable when romantic notions about these countries—often called "ethnic"—serve as inspiration for Western fashion designers, BRIC fashion designers being viewed as complementing the universal, all-encompassing European/American design collective. Once again, this evidences the construction of "the other."

Several informants were concerned about the growing popularity of trend services, especially in China, as if the clients of those services were somehow less than legitimate. Factories in China now launch their own fashion brands, it is said, with the sole intention of "imitating" Western styles and getting their products into the market as quickly as possible. The informants have apparently bought into a belief that trend services care about creativity and do not in themselves contribute to uniformity, which arises only when trend services are available to and "misused" by certain users. Is the concern related to the possession or lack of aesthetic knowledge or fashion capital? Or could it be that when the patterns and information the services provide are used by *non-Western* people, this is to a greater extent seen in the West as plagiarizing, as unoriginal work, while the use of the same patterns and a similar process by producers in the West is more often viewed as taking inspiration?

In fashionified consumer society, it can be difficult to see how fashion and trends could be empowering, or how they could contribute to a greater sense of freedom and well-being. Perhaps we are too preoccupied with news as such, too used to trends changing within a fairly predictable range, to grasp that they can also be empowering for people. For all the talk about Western cultural imperialism, the examples from the BRIC countries also provide instances of people appropriating a trendy Western style of dress to strengthen their position. There is power in the "right" clothes, a clear awareness of the symbolic value of clothes. Of course, this desire for upward mobility can be exploited by Western companies and lead to over-consumption as well as conspicuous consumption.[15] Fashion is still an efficient method to move socially, to control others' responses. Yet the increasing popularity of trends in the BRIC countries could also be interpreted as expressing opportunities for escape and sensual pleasure or as significantly reinforcing the patterns of small change that have been a fundamental aspect of dress since ancient times.[16]

Trends have become low status

The so-called democratization of fashion has meant that the concept of trends has eroded in some parts of the fashion field, becoming associated with mass-market fashion, economic capital, superficiality, commerce and anxiety. Based on my interviews, I interpret this frequently used expression, "democratization of fashion," as alluding to fashion becoming relevant to an increasing number of people through the internet's dissemination of fashion information and through fast-fashion companies' efforts to bring catwalk trends to customers in a matter of weeks.

To justify their own interest, many designers claim a need to follow "the movements of fashion" because consumers often care about and enjoy trends; alternatively, they cherry-pick the trends that suit their own brands. Several designers emphasize their desire to make their mark in the field. However, the indiscriminate adoption of trends is universally seen as a sign of low fashion status. Fashionization creates new business opportunities, and trend services help companies outside the fashion field legitimize business ideas based on aesthetics. Trend agencies, knowing this, naturally emphasize trends even more. Fashionization in larger consumer society uses trends to legitimize phenomena or actions originally based on economic logic, as with sales of laundry detergent, bathroom carpets or hotel stays.

Trends have always been associated with womenswear, which has traditionally been more changeable than menswear. In any society in which women as a group are subordinated, it is unsurprising that phenomena associated with them should be lower in status. It is higher status to step away from trends and speak of "style," not in the sense of "stealing this style" (see p. 71) but style coded as masculine. Positive ideas about style and stability are interlinked and can be understood as reflecting the interests of those in dominant social positions who have no need for upward mobility.

Unchanging style has become associated with sustainable thinking. Several informants highlight men as more exemplary, that is, sustainable, consumers, because their clothes are not as sensitive to trends and last for several seasons. This inevitably raises questions about the relationship between trends and sustainability and about what happens at the meeting point between the cultural and economic logics and the pursuit of sustainability. Is it because of trends that fashion is unsustainable today? Is it because of bad production processes? Is it due to poor quality? Is it due to excessive consumption? Is it the pursuit for profit? Is it the way we use our garments?

The discourse of individuality

The various professions presented here share a pride in "providing inspiration," though they are cautious about being seen to "give direction." This stands in interesting opposition to Michael Bennett's hankering for Diana Vreeland's dogmatic style, whereby she "created demand." The unwillingness to dictate exists both in the relationship between the trend-forecasting agencies and fashion companies, and in the relationship between designers and consumers. The consideration of designers comes mainly from exalted ideas about creators and their positions in the field, while the respect for consumers is imbued with contemporary notions of individual free choice. Nothing should be foisted onto consumers, it is said; they must make their own decisions and choices and find their own style.

Sociologist Zygmunt Bauman wrote in *The Individualized Society* that late modern society casts its members as individuals to an extent far exceeding anything observed in previous cultures. While risks, opportunities, contradictions, structures and conflicts continue to be socially created, as they have always been, the responsibility for dealing with them has shifted to the individual. This individualized culture means we interpret our failures at an individual level. Maybe we did not try hard enough? Perhaps we need to get better at negotiating? Maybe we are not self-confident enough?[17]

The incursion of this individualized culture into the fashion field is significant because fashion is a cultural expression with undeniable social importance, the field being structured by status and hierarchies. Information technology, especially the proliferation of blogs, has allowed individuals without sanctioned positions in the fashion field to proclaim, sometimes to a wide audience, how they relate to fashion, clothes and trends. Designers speak of various *looks* as materializations of personal choice. They, along with journalists, trend analysts and tastemakers, are well aware of the uncertainty characterizing many of today's fashion consumers. In the past, well-defined trends provided safety or self-confidence, depending on when and how they were appropriated. They situated people in their time. The importance of "being right" has long influenced women's relationships with fashion and now, increasingly, those of men as well. Several designers told of store personnel who suggested how to combine pieces to create different looks, a skill that can be communicated through other marketing channels, such as social media and Web sites. Stylists are additional experts on *looks*, while fashion magazines and department stores inspire and suggest, as if they were friends.

April Glassborow and others consider the suggestion that "trends are over" as yet another trend. Karin, the Swedish blogger (see p. 62), calls it disingenuous when designers and fashion people claim they do not give instructions. She believes this is only a tastemaker ploy to keep trend secrets to themselves and notes that not all individual choices are acceptable and that the hierarchy of the fashion field has not been threatened, let alone dismantled. The contradiction between the discourse of individuality ("find your own style") and the power structures of the fashion field exposes the fact that total individual freedom of choice does not exist. Only some individual choices are considered correct.

The discourse of individual freedom of choice and the emphasis on "personal style" could be understood to reflect the need for less risk in the fashion industry. Although tastemakers never admit to it, they can indirectly be influenced by risk-minimizing efforts in the industry and by how the industry manages the tension between consistency and change. This is obvious in the emphasis on "fashion investments" and "classics" that can be combined in almost endless ways and in the encouragement to emulate catwalk offerings by mixing and matching inexpensive fast-fashion items.

Tastemakers are reclaiming their power in the fashion field, for example, by putting greater emphasis on *selection*, both on e-commerce Web sites and in department stores, putting the lie to talk about individual freedom of choice. The tastemakers choose the options from which the individual can choose. No field of cultural production can fully embrace freedom of choice, as there is always symbolic capital that determines what is the most respectable, best, highest quality or most valuable. If this were not so, the field would disintegrate. The tastemakers' and designers' claim not to give overt directives attests to the strong influence of the discourse of individuality. Still, the impact of tastemakers' and designers' subtler directives goes unnoticed.

The relationship between trends and fashion

As I said in the Introduction, I did not want to define the word "trend" but instead allowed my informants to imbue the word with whatever meaning they chose. That no one except the financial analysts asked me what I meant by "trend" speaks to how naturally and unquestioningly the word is used. Trends, it would seem, are usually understood as labels for fashion expressions that can be conveyed, disseminated and communicated and that leave room for interpretation.

Some informants distinguished between micro and macro trends to signal the time horizon, level of analysis or level of precision. Still, the definition is fuzzy. Central to this study is that it is possible to *capitalize* on trends. From the consumer's perspective, a trend can be something that provides direction, dictates or points to a possibility, serving as a source of inspiration. Through various media, consumers can even learn to follow the creation of the "incipient taste." This book, however, has focused on the producers, designers, tastemakers and financial analysts who all participate in shaping the roles of trends in the fashion field, who are *trendmakers*. They might be actors, such as the trend agencies, capitalizing directly on trends, or they might be financial analysts who seek to mitigate "fashion risk" and so shape the impact of trends. The desire to expand in or by emerging markets affects the existence and expression of trends, shaping and defining how the call for individual style is communicated and how the endless desire for fashion news is satisfied.

In examining the significance of trends, I was also able to discern something about the current global fashion field. Fashion cannot be equated with trends, however, but is a larger concept. Inspired by Pierre Bourdieu, I understand fashion as the activities that take place in the fashion field, the tasks and phenomena defined as fashion by its leading actors (see p. 5). Fashion is a cultural expression, an industry and even a scholarly subject that can be examined in infinite ways: fashion in film, sports fashion, sustainable fashion, corporate governance in the fashion industry, the arrival of jeans in the UK, fashion criticism, the valuing of fashion companies, fashion and resistance, Tilda Swinton's relationship with fashion, the design of Yves Saint Laurent, *The New Look*, the role of Daphne Guinness in the fashion industry, hat fashion, fashion and art. Is it then possible to imagine a fashion industry without trends? If fashion revolves around and relies on change, trends will likely continue to exist in some form, given the need to coordinate production and consumption. This book, I hope, shows how the fashion field's creators, production conditions, tastemakers and accessibility cannot be separated from one another, though the role of trends might change.

In Chapter 5 on gender and trends, it is demonstrated that the construction of womenswear as changeable and menswear as more stable is taken for granted. These constructions appear virtually impossible to change. The process whereby socially created ideas appear to exist objectively and independently of people is called "the reification of social reality" by sociologists Peter Berger and Thomas Luckmann.[18] At times, my informants appeared to relate to the fashion field as if its rules and structures were not human creations but eternal verities they must accept and obey: "things just keep moving faster and faster," the insistence on tight schedules and producing four collections a year, the concerns about *lookbooks*, shows and media attention all reflect a belief that fashion's rules and structures are immutable. There are exceptions. Clements Ribeiro's choice to make only two collections per year is a conscious act; according to Inacio Ribeiro, the company feels no compulsion to make more *just because everyone else does it*. Most informants believe they can influence fashion or "the fashion scene," having, to use the words of Pierre Bourdieu, developed a "feel for the game," and can compete, consciously or unconsciously, for reputation and recognition.[19]

Trendification

One obvious feature of my study is that all informants (again, except for the financial analysts) speak only of trends *in fashion*. Trends are part of the language of the field, of its game. Change, the heart of fashion, is conveyed through the categorizable trends. At the same time, trends in the fashion field have a peculiar role since many prominent designers prefer not to use the actual word "trend," seeing it as at odds with their understanding of creativity and creation. They might accept *being* trendmakers, but they will not admit to actively seeking that role. Bourdieu reminds us that, in a cultural field, taste classifies the classifier.

The internet age has seen trends assume even greater prominence, as consumers often use particular trend labels in their online searches, and the internet functions as a platform for disseminating and materializing trends, through trend sites, blogs, social media, internet commerce, Web sites and digital editions of magazines.

Trend labels are significant as they are used as evidence at a later stage, to substantiate trend agency claims of foresight. All-embracing trend labels are, however, met with skepticism among tastemakers and designers, as when Paula Reed of *Grazia UK* mocked "gentleness."

While consumer society is fashionized, there is a concurrent process of trendification extending far beyond consumer society. People talk about trends in all areas: strategy, literature, medicine, IT, technology, marketing, living and education. Without saying that trends are in any way a new phenomenon or concept—the word originates in seventeenth-century English—the presentation of dominant ideologies, movements and ideas specifically as trends, and various trend companies' capitalizing on them, is typical of our time. According to the *Collins Dictionary*'s word counter, the use of the word "trend" in English has increased more than fivefold since 1908.[20]

One way of interpreting the proliferation of trend-forecasting companies is that they express today's penchant for speculating about the future, that is, making decisions based on future expectations. Trends impose a form of order or predictability on the future. They also offer a way to package a message, for example: "blue ocean strategy," "the new novella," "medicinal marijuana," "cloud services," "organic electronics," "gameification," "the new collective living" or "massive open online courses." The future is uncertain—more uncertain than ever, according to Bauman.[21]

Many people speak of "fashions" in various phenomena or of trends in their own industries or spheres of expertise. Trends certainly exist, and the popularity of certain approaches or items comes and goes. The parallel is not exact, for fashion has change, neomania, at its heart and subsists on what are sometimes packaged as trends. The intricate positioning game in the fashion field means that trends are born, legitimized and disseminated in complicated ways. It is not just about popularity.

Martin Raymond is a founder of the trend-forecasting company The Future Laboratory and its subsidiary LSN (Lifestyle News Network) Global. With a background in journalism, including editing a fashion industry magazine in the 1990s, Raymond saw how various industries were interrelated via shared influences and thereby cross-fertilized. He was "not necessarily thinking about trends back then, but [about] patterns, cycles, ways of behaving," noting factors that were often affected by movements outside industry. He observed that while the fashion industry was used to deciphering influences from other industries, that was not the case with architecture, design and other lifestyle sectors. Architecture, for example, is affected by outside influences from fashion, sustainability, design, technology, etc. Raymond saw a gap in the market as, for example, few car manufacturers and cosmetics companies understood how consumer behavior translated into trends. That led to the establishment of The Future Laboratory in 2001. By 2012, the company had 200 customers in the "lifestyle industries," the largest being from the wine and spirits, vehicle and technology sectors. Although fashion companies such as H&M, Burberry, LVMH and Selfridges are also customers, The Future Laboratory does not concern itself explicitly with fashion trends, and Raymond does not consider WGSN, Peclers Paris, Stylus, etc., direct competitors. Instead, The Future Laboratory focuses on consumer behavior with offerings divided into "research," "insight," "strategy" and "implementation." When the concept of trends is used across several fields, and not only in the fashion field, it is not always clear-cut what is to be classified as a trend. Raymond says:

> Trends are like social movements, or a need. If you are a successful business you need to respond to that need. Because it dictates product … As soon as you engage in a decision which is about self-improvement, you are involved in a trend. Or whatever you'd like to call it—it doesn't bother me. But you are becoming part of something. Because by their nature, trends are social patterns that we intentionally or sometimes inadvertently buy into. It might be that everybody is wearing bright green shoes. One day you wake up and want to wear white. And within a month, you will be three. You might not think it's about trends. Religions are trends. Wars are trends. That's what they are.

APPENDIX: CONTRIBUTIONS

This work contributes to several research streams. One stream is the analysis of social phenomena from an organizing perspective. In this context, I examine how trends serve as an organizing principle in general and in the fashion field in particular. The role of trends as an organizing principle is, however, far more complex in the field of fashion than, for example, in a strictly economic field, not only because of fashion's complex logic and legitimization system but also because of fashion's obsession with the new. My book notes the shift from trends being purely an organizing principle to their *also* being a source of legitimacy; in doing so, it joins in the research conversation that treats organizing and legitimacy. The research also contributes to our knowledge of organizations operating in fields subject to parallel but opposing logics. I regard the identification of "backstage legitimacy," which the trend agencies harness, as a contribution to our knowledge of organizational action in such fields. At a more specific level, the book also builds our knowledge of how cultural and economic logics interact in the fashion field to confer significance on trends, at the intersection of production and consumption, contributing to research into cultural production and cultural production organizations.

The book also illustrates how economic and fashion capital interact in the fashion field, resulting in dependencies between mass-market fashion, fashion in the mid-range and designer segments, financial analysts, tastemakers and trend-forecasting agencies, which adds to the research into cultural production and especially fashion production. "The balance between consistency and change" articulates a way of understanding the conditions under which businesses operate in the fashion field. With this work, I join those researchers who have identified the economization of the cultural production field, that is, the ascendancy of the economic over the cultural logic, although this shift is far from unambiguous.

Another contribution to research into cultural production organizations is the identification and analysis of the close intertwining of technology (i.e., the internet and mass self-communication) with both the cultural and the economic material of the fashion field. This, together with the discourses that surfaced in the BRIC interviews, also strengthens our knowledge of the effects of globalization on that part of the fashion field where the symbolic production of fashion occurs.

Yet another contribution to research into cultural production is my examination of how society's individualization affects the construction of such social phenomena as trends in the fashion field, where *looks* can be seen as materializing the construction of "personal choice." Finally, I particularly note the gendering of trends in the fashion field as outlined here, where trends, usually gendered as feminine, have both restrictive and liberating aspects; this examination also contributes to research into cultural production.

NOTES

Preface

1   Elizabeth Wilson, *Adorned in Dreams: Fashion and Modernity* (Berkeley and Los Angeles: University of California Press, 1985), p. 117.

2   Christina Binkley, "What's out: the fashion trend" (*The Wall Street Journal*, January 29, 2010). <http://online.wsj.com/article/SB10001424052748704320104575015141536429662.html> [accessed December 9, 2014].

Chapter 1

1   Lise Skov, "The role of trade fairs in the global fashion business" (*Current Sociology*, vol. 54 no. 5, 2006), pp. 764–783.

2   Please note that different measuring principles may yield different figures; the purpose here is simply to indicate the approximate size of the industry. This figure is from Michael Prest, "Substance and style: the fashion courses that are a cut above" (*The Independent*, April 14, 2011). <http://www.independent.co.uk/student/postgraduate/postgraduate-study/substance-and-style-the-fashion-courses-that-are-a-cut-above-2267507.html> [accessed December 9, 2014]. In his book *Fashion Brands: Branding Style from Armani to Zara* (London: Kogan Page, 2008), Mark Tungate quotes the figure of USD 1,000 billion as the global fashion industry's monetary turnover in 2008. In the UK, the fashion industry's contribution to GDP was GBP 20.9 billion in 2009. Please note that, throughout the book, I use "billion" and "trillion" in the short-scale sense.

3   "Lean" is an approach to production originating in Japanese car manufacturing, where efforts are made to meet demand immediately with perfect quality and no waste; see Nigel Slack and Michael Lewis, *Operations Strategy* (Harlow: Financial Times–Prentice Hall, 2008).

4   Slack and Lewis, *Operations Strategy*.

5   "BRIC" is an acronym coined by Goldman Sachs in 2001, referring to the economies of Brazil, Russia, India and China. The investment bank presented a forecast indicating that the combined GDP of the BRIC countries would surpass that of the G7 countries (i.e., France, the USA, the UK, Germany, Italy, Japan and Canada) by 2050; Jim O'Neill, "Building better global economic BRICs" (Goldman Sachs, Global Economics Paper No: 66, November 30, 2001).

6   Melissa Taylor, "Culture transition: fashion's cultural dialogue between commerce and art" (*Fashion Theory: The Journal of Dress, Body & Culture*, vol. 9 no. 4, 2005), pp. 445–460.

7   Elizabeth Cline, *Overdressed: The Shockingly High Cost of Cheap Fashion* (New York: Penguin Portfolio, 2012); Joanne Entwistle, *The Fashioned Body: Fashion, Dress and Modern Social Theory* (Cambridge: Polity Press, 2000), pp. 208–220; Lucy Siegle, *To Die For: Is Fashion Wearing Out the World?* (London: Fourth Estate, 2011).

8   To understand the concept of "organizing" and "organizing principle," let us assume a situation in which some people meet for the first time. They will initially pay attention to their environment in completely different ways, and often talk at cross purposes, but as they interact, they start making collective sense of what is going on. They begin to develop common behaviors, routines and terms for things and phenomena. Such organizing is a way to reduce the uncertainty that would otherwise prevail. In another example, in the world of fashion, people refer to "fast fashion," "stylist," "spring season" and "pre-collection," and these become concepts that everyone understands in relatively similar ways. People take part in creating the reality that also constrains them, both interpreting and authoring their world. The collective sensemaking that brings about a range of interactive routines and patterns constitutes the process of organizing; see Karl Weick, *Sensemaking in Organizations* (Thousand Oaks: Sage, 1995) and Karl Weick, *The Social Psychology of Organizing* (Thousand Oaks: Sage, 1979). "Organizing principle" refers to something specific, in this case trends, around which organization occurs. Trends can help people in the fashion field focus their attention in roughly the same direction to make collective sense and act upon this sensemaking.

9   Linda Portnoff, *Modebranschen i Sverige: Statistik och analys* (Stockholm: Volante, 2013); The British Fashion Council and Oxford Economics, *The Value of the UK Fashion Industry* (London and Oxford: The British Fashion Council and Oxford Economics, 2010); Datamonitor, *The United States: Clothing Industry Guide 2011* (Dublin: Research and Markets, 2011); N. Panteva, *Trends Outfitting the Fashion Retail Sector* (New York: IBIS World, 2012). The statistics are likely based on different definitions and measurement methods.

10 A common way of approaching fashion in the social sciences is to speak of a fashion system. The word "system" is problematic, however, as it suggests functionalism and cannot be used to explain change. I prefer the concept of "field," a considerably more open-ended notion that, moreover, emphasizes the close connection between my theoretical framework and the field theory of sociologist Pierre Bourdieu; see, for example, Pierre Bourdieu, *Outline of a Theory of Practice* (London: Cambridge University Press, 1977) or Pierre Bourdieu and Loïc Wacquant, *Invitation to Reflexive Sociology* (Chicago: University of Chicago Press, 1992).

11 In other disciplines, such as marketing and the behavioral sciences, people often refer to various "trend theories" and adapt different definitions such as "trend," "fad" and "collective taste." However, since this study takes on a social constructionist approach to the role of trends, I did not want to pre-define "trend" nor to apply any of that kind of categorization as those do not fit my sociologically informed theoretical framework. I deliberately wanted the different voices on trends to materialize and to capture all facets of the trends discourse in the fashion field, and, then, in the final chapter, I discuss the difference between fashion and trend, which is one of the contributions of the book.

12 For a more thorough account of my epistemological position, please see my dissertation: Jenny Lantz, *Taste at Work: On Taste and Organization in the Field of Cultural Production* (Stockholm: Arvinius Förlag, 2005), pp. 29–45.
13 Cf. D. Silverman, *Interpreting Qualitative Data: Methods for Analyzing Talk, Text and Interaction* (London: Sage, 2001).
14 Lantz, *Taste at Work*.
15 Anthony Giddens, *New Rules of Sociological Method* (London: Hutchinson, 1976).

Chapter 2

1   Annette Lynch and Mitchell Strauss, *Changing Fashion: A Critical Introduction to Trend Analysis and Meaning* (New York: Berg, 2007), pp. 1–3.
2   Emma Barnett, "Trend-spotting is the new £36bn growth business" (*The Telegraph*, May 11, 2011) <http://www.telegraph.co.uk/finance/newsbysector/mediatechnologyandtelecoms/8482964/Trend-spotting-is-the-new-36bn-growth-business.html> [accessed December 9, 2014].
3   Ibid.
4   Ibid.
5   Kathryn McKelvey and Janine Munslow, *Fashion Forecasting* (Oxford: Wiley-Blackwell, 2008), pp. 70, 86, 104.
6   Claire Wilcox (ed.), *The Golden Age of Couture: Paris and London 1947–1957* (London: V&A Publications, 2007).
7   Tungate, *Fashion Brands*, p. 85.
8   See Erving Goffman, *Presentation of Self in Everyday Life* (New York: Doubleday, 1959).
9   Yuniya Kawamura, *Fashion-ology: An Introduction to Fashion Studies* (Oxford: Berg, 2005), p. 9; Wilson, *Adorned in Dreams*, p. 29.
10 Wilson, *Adorned in Dreams*, pp. 23–30.
11 Ulrich Lehmann, *Tigersprung: Fashion in Modernity* (Cambridge: MIT Press, 2000).
12 Mike Featherstone, Scott Lash and Roland Robertson (eds), *Global Modernities* (London: Sage, 1995).
13 Lynch and Strauss, *Changing Fashion*, pp. 165–169.
14 Roland Barthes, *The Fashion System* (Berkeley: University of California Press, 1990 [1967]).
15 Georg Simmel, "Fashion" (*International Quarterly*, vol. 10 no. 1, 1904), pp. 130–155.
16 Thorstein Veblen, *The Theory of the Leisure Class* (London: Allen and Unwin, 1957 [1899]).
17 Dana Thomas, *Deluxe: How Luxury Lost Its Luster* (New York: Penguin Books, 2007).
18 Pierre Bourdieu, *Distinction: A Social Critique of the Judgement of Taste* (Cambridge: Harvard University Press, 1984). Examples of studies in the footsteps of Bourdieu that also examine the role of cultural intermediaries are: Ben Crewe, *Representing Men: Cultural Production and Producers in the Men's Magazine Market* (Oxford: Berg, 2003); Anne Cronin, "Regimes of mediation: advertising practitioners as cultural intermediaries?" (*Consumption, Markets and Culture*, vol. 7 no. 4, 2004), pp. 349–369; Paul Du Gay and Sean Nixon, "Who needs cultural intermediaries?" (*Cultural Studies*, vol. 16 no. 4, 2002), pp. 495–500; Joanne Entwistle, *The Aesthetic Economy of Fashion: Markets and Values in Clothes and Modelling* (Oxford: Berg,

2009); Liz McFall, "Advertising, persuasion and the culture/economy dualism," in: Paul du Gay and Michael Pryke (eds), *Cultural Economy: Cultural Analysis and Commercial Life*, pp. 148–165 (London: Sage, 2002); Susanne Schulz, "Our lady hates viscose: the role of the customer image in high street fashion production" (*Cultural Sociology*, vol. 2 no. 3, 2008), pp. 385–405.

19 Erving Goffman, *Frame Analysis: An Essay on the Organization of Experience* (Boston: Northeastern University Press, 1974).

20 Entwistle, *The Aesthetic Economy of Fashion*. Entwistle uses the concept of "fashion market," but for the sake of simplicity I use that of "fashion field."

21 Ibid., pp. 13–15.

22 Lidewij Edelkoort, video clip <http://www.trendtablet.com>. Trendtablet.com is an online trend service that belongs to Lidewij Edelkoort's trend group.

23 A "baby boomer," according to the United States Census Bureau, is a person born during the demographic "baby boom" that followed the Second World War, between 1946 and 1964. Carrie Werner, *The Older Population: 2010*, report of the United States Census Bureau (Washington: United States Census Bureau, 2011).

24 See Weick, *Sensemaking in Organizations* and note 5 in Chapter 1.

25 The product life cycle model, often used in marketing, maps the lifespan of a commercial product over a set of five common stages: introduction, growth, maturity, stagnation and decline. See G. Day, "The product life cycle: analysis and applications issues" (*Journal of Marketing*, vol. 45, Autumn 1981), pp. 60–67.

Chapter 3

1 Pierre Bourdieu, "Le couturier et sa griffe: contribution à une théorie de la magie" (*Actes de la Recherche en Sciences Sociales*, vol. 1 no. 1, 1975), pp. 7–36; Pierre Bourdieu, *The Field of Cultural Production: Essays on Art and Literature* (New York: Columbia University Press, 1993); Pierre Bourdieu, *The Rules of Art: Genesis and Structure of the Literary Field* (Cambridge: Polity Press, 1996).

2 Agnès Rocamora argues, for example, that Bourdieu fails to account for the significance of popular fashion (i.e., mass-market fashion) and to explore how mass-market fashion and high fashion (i.e., designer fashion) continue to coexist successfully. Bourdieu's study was, Rocamora claims, limited to the subfield of high fashion without his recognizing it. Since Bourdieu's original study, many researchers have studied the blurring of boundaries between popular and high fashion. This transgression has been manifested in high-fashion brands' offering certain products, such as fragrances, eyewear, diffusion lines, capsule collections and collaborations, to a broader market. Today, a mix-and-match take on fashion is widespread, at least in the West, where high fashion is mixed with popular/mass-market fashion. Bourdieu is not concerned with legitimacy in terms of popular fashion but discusses legitimacy only in relation to high fashion. Furthermore, Rocamora maintains that Bourdieu fails to acknowledge consumers as active, creative agents who can relate to particular objects in numerous ways, both within and across class boundaries, for example, through mixing and matching. Bourdieu is criticized on similar grounds regarding the "trickle-down" model, as fashion often originates from the street, for example, from youth and ethnic groups, before being picked up by designers. The middle classes seldom represent the avant-garde that drives fashion change. Bourdieu's texts on fashion thus also lack analytical models beyond the idea of fashion as expressing class pretensions, distinction and necessity. As alternative reasons for consuming fashion, Rocamora mentions sensual pleasure, escapism, etc. Agnès Rocamora, "Fields of fashion: critical insights into Bourdieu's sociology of culture" (*Journal of Consumer Culture*, vol. 2 no. 3, 2002), pp. 341–362.

3 In *The Field of Cultural Production*, Bourdieu describes symbolic capital as "the degree of accumulated prestige, celebrity, consecration or honour." Such capital is based on a dialectic of knowledge and recognition. Cultural capital, on the other hand, refers to forms of cultural knowledge, competences or dispositions. In this book, I mostly use the term "symbolic capital" to stress the status that comes with this type of capital, but sometimes I refer to "cultural capital" to emphasize the knowledge dimension. Bourdieu has also described symbolic capital as "the form that one or another of these [other forms of capital] takes when it is grasped through categories of perception that recognize its specific logic or, if you prefer, misrecognize the arbitrariness of its possession and accumulation." Pierre Bourdieu and Loïc Wacquant, *An Invitation to Reflexive Sociology* (Chicago: University of Chicago Press, 1992), p. 119.
For an extended discussion of various forms of capital, see Bourdieu, *Outline of a Theory of Practice*, pp. 171–183; Pierre Bourdieu, *The Logic of Practice* (Stanford: Stanford University Press, 1990), pp. 112–121.

4 Entwistle, *The Aesthetic Economy of Fashion*.

Chapter 4

1 Fahrman is a Swedish fashion journalist who writes about fashion in the Swedish tabloid *Aftonbladet*.

2 Herbert Blumer, "Fashion: from class differentiation to collective selection" (*Sociological Quarterly*, vol. 10 no. 3, 1969), pp. 275–291.

3 Stanley Lieberson, *A Matter of Taste* (New Haven: Yale University Press, 2000).

4 Bourdieu, *Outline of a Theory of Practice*.

5 The magazine's and the designer's names were made fictitious in the interest of anonymity.

6 Ashley Mears, *Pricing Beauty: The Making of a Fashion Model* (Berkeley: University of California Press, 2011); Bourdieu, *The Field of Cultural Production*.

7 *Own-bought* implies that the department store buys the items and takes the entire risk for them. In a *concession*, the brand uses a particular space in the department store to sell its items and is solely responsible for the sales. The department store assumes no risk for the goods.

8 Harvey Nichols has department stores in the following cities: London, Bristol, Dublin, Manchester, Edinburgh, Birmingham, Leeds, Riyadh, Hong Kong, Kuwait, Dubai, Baku, Istanbul and Ankara.

9 Bourdieu, *Distinction*, p. 6.

10 Joanne Entwistle and Agnès Rocamora, "The field of fashion materialized: a study of the London Fashion Week" (*Sociology*, vol. 40 no. 4, 2006), pp. 735–751.

11 Robert Merton, "The Matthew effect in science" (*Science*, vol. 159 no. 3810, 1968), pp. 56–63; Daniel Rigney, *The Matthew Effect: How Advantage Begets Further Advantage* (New York: Columbia University Press, 2010).

12 Max Weber, *Economy and Society: An Outline of Interpretive Sociology* (Berkeley: University of California Press, 1978).

13 Morris Zelditch, "Processes of legitimation: recent developments and new directions" (*Social Psychology Quarterly*, vol. 64, 2001), pp. 4–17.

14 These are brand categories in the mid-segment between luxury and mass-market fashion. Selfridges regards brands such as Armani, Max Mara, Diane von Furstenberg and Elie Tahari as more commercial and categorizes them as "bridge."

15 The buyer's name was made fictitious in the interest of anonymity.

16 The stylist's name was made fictitious in the interest of anonymity.

17 The brand's and the designer's names were made fictitious in the interest of anonymity.

18 In addition, in February 2013, Net-A-Porter launched an online fashion magazine, *The Edit.*

19 Bourdieu, *The Field of Cultural Production*, pp. 71–81.

Chapter 5

1 The wording of the question brought about a focus on womenswear and menswear *in general*. Since the industry (e.g., media, department stores, blogs, brands and trend-forecasting agencies) organize their operations according to these categories, the question is indeed relevant. But obviously, there are variations within womenswear and menswear, respectively.

2 In brief, the concepts of *patriarchy* and the *gender order* refer, respectively, to a society dominated by men and to the power relationships between the genders at a structural level. For more in-depth discussions of these notions, see, for example, Valerie Bryson, *Feminist Political Theory* (New York: Random House, 1992) and Raewyn W. Connell, *Masculinities* (Cambridge: Polity Press, 1995).

3 Madeleine Heilman, "Description and prescription: how gender stereotypes prevent women's ascent up the organizational ladder" (*Journal of Social Issues*, vol. 57 no. 4, 2001), pp. 657–674.

4 See SOU 1998:6 Kvinnomaktutredningen (Stockholm: Fritze, 1998) and Susan Halford and Pauline Leonard, *Gender, Power and Organizations: An Introduction* (Basingstoke: Palgrave, 2001).

5 Weber, *Economy and Society*.

6 Jennifer Craik, *The Face of Fashion: Cultural Studies in Fashion* (London: Routledge, 1993), p. 176.

7 In the United States, only 13.2 percent of the thirty-eight most prominent fashion, retail and beauty companies had women CEOs; see Evan Clark, "Women at work: fashion's glass ceiling prevails" (*Women's Wear Daily*, October 29, 2012) <http://www.wwd.com/business-news/business-features/women-at-work-fashions-glass-ceiling-prevails-6459967?full=true> [accessed December 9, 2014]. Similar statistics apply to the UK and Sweden; see Catherine Neilan, "Fewer women are being given top fashion jobs" (*Drapers*, April 19, 2013) <http://www.drapersonline.com/news/exclusive-fewer-women-being-given-top-fashion-jobs/5048406.article> [accessed December 9, 2014]; Portnoff, *Modebranschen i Sverige.*

8 Jennifer Jones, "Coquettes and Grisettes: Women Buying and Selling in Ancien Régime Paris," in: Victoria de Grazia and Ellen Furlough (eds), *The Sex of*

Things: Gender and Consumption in Historical Perspective, pp. 22–48 (Berkeley: University of California Press, 1996).

9   Valerie Steele and Claudia Brush Kidwell (eds), *Men and Women: Dressing the Part* (Washington: Smithsonian Institute Press, 1989); Valerie Steele, *Fashion and Eroticism: Ideals of Feminine Beauty from the Victorian Era to the Jazz Age* (Oxford: Oxford University Press, 1985); Anna Wahl, Charlotte Holgersson and Pia Höök, *Ironi och sexualitet—om ledarskap och kön* (Stockholm: Carlssons, 2001), p. 116.

10 Fanny Ambjörnsson, *Rosa: den farliga färgen* (Stockholm: Ordfront Förlag, 2011), pp. 44–49.

11 Craik, *The Face of Fashion*, pp. 176–203.

12 *Metrosexual* describes men in large cities who, whatever their sexuality, dedicate substantial time and money to fashion, appearance and grooming.

13 *Retrosexual* describes men who spend as little time and money as possible on their appearance and embrace traditional masculinity in their self-presentation.

14 See, for example, Marie Nordberg's dissertation, in which she discusses reflexive masculinity: Marie Nordberg, *Jämställdhetens spjutspets? Manliga arbetstagare i kvinnoyrken, jämställdhet, maskulinitet, femininitet och heteronormativitet* (Stockholm: Arkipelag, 2005).

15 Lieberson, *A Matter of Taste*.

16 Ben Fine and Ellen Leopold, *The World of Consumption* (London: Routledge, 1993).

17 Efrat Tseëlon, *The Masque of Femininity* (London: Sage, 1997); Entwistle, *The Fashioned Body*; Sandra Lee Bartky, *Femininity and Domination: Studies in the Phenomenology of Oppression* (New York: Routledge, 1991).

18 Tseëlon, *The Masque of Femininity*; Jones, "Coquettes and grisettes"; Entwistle, *The Fashioned Body*.

19 Wilson, *Adorned in Dreams*, pp. 123–127. See for example Edith Head and Joe Hyams, *How to Dress for Success* (New York: Random House, 1967).

20 Michel Foucault, *Discipline and Punish* (Harmondsworth: Penguin, 1977).

21 See, for example, critiques by Entwistle, *The Fashioned Body*, pp. 23–26; Susan Hekman (ed.), *Feminist Interpretations of Michel Foucault* (University Park: Pennsylvania State University Press, 1996); Louis McNay, *Foucault and Feminism* (Cambridge: Polity Press, 1992); Tseëlon, *The Masque of Femininity*.

22 Magnus Mörck, "En reva i kostymen: Maskulinitet, mode och makt," in: Lizette Gradén and Magdalena Petersson McIntyre (eds), *Modets metamorfoser: Den klädda kroppens identiteter och förvandlingar*, pp. 286–307 (Stockholm: Carlssons, 2009); Ambjörnsson, *Rosa*.

23 Goffman, *Presentation of Self in Everyday Life*.

24 Rita Felski, *The Gender of Modernity* (Cambridge: Harvard University Press, 1995), p. 62.

25 Bourdieu, *Distinction*.

26 Entwistle, *The Fashioned Body*, p. 109.

27 Felski, *The Gender of Modernity*; Lawrence Birken, *Consuming Desire: Sexual Science and the Emergence of a Culture of Abundance, 1871–1914* (Ithaca: Cornell University Press, 1988).

28 Andrew Bolton and Harold Koda, *Schiaparelli & Prada: Impossible Conversations* (New York: Metropolitan Museum of Art, 2012).

29 See also Harrison White, *Markets from Networks: Socioeconomic Models of Production* (Princeton: Princeton University Press, 2002).

Chapter 6

1   Simmel, "Fashion."
2   Cline, *Overdressed*, p. 115.
3   Teri Agins, *The End of Fashion: How Marketing Changed the Clothing Business Forever* (New York: HarperCollins, 1999).
4   Cline, *Overdressed*.
5   Michèle Lamont, *Money, Morals & Manners: The Culture of the French and the American Upper-Middle Class* (Chicago: University of Chicago Press, 1992).
6   Cline, *Overdressed*, pp. 106–107; Craig Lambert, "Real fashion police: copyrighting clothing" (*Harvard Magazine*, July–August 2010), p. 9.
7   Douglas Holt, *How Brands Become Icons: The Principles of Cultural Branding* (Cambridge: Harvard Business School Press, 2004), pp. 13–35.
8   Ibid. Examples of marketing literature building on these principles include Philip Kotler and Gary Armstrong, *Principles of Marketing* (Upper Saddle River: Prentice Hall, 2009); Alina Wheeler, *Designing Brand Identity: An Essential Guide for the Whole Branding Team* (New York: Wiley, 2012); David Aaker, *Building Strong Brands* (London: Pocket Books, 2010).
9   Douglas Holt and Douglas Cameron, *Cultural Strategy: Using Innovative Ideologies to Build Breakthrough Brands* (Oxford: Oxford University Press, 2010).
10 Agins, *The End of Fashion*.
11 Lauren Cochrane, "Whistles conquers the 'middle market' of British womenswear" (*The Guardian*, August 24, 2012) <http://www.theguardian.com/fashion/2012/aug/24/whistles-middle-market-success> [accessed December 9, 2014].
12 Cf. Patrik Aspers, *Orderly Fashion: A Sociology of Markets* (Princeton: Princeton University Press, 2010), p. 41.
13 Karin Falk, *Det svenska modeundret* (Stockholm: Norstedts, 2011); "Acne växer snabbast" (*Svenska Dagbladet*, May 07, 2006) <http://www.svd.se/naringsliv/nyheter/sverige/acne-vaxer-snabbast_7148051.svd> [accessed December 9, 2014].
14 Bourdieu, *Field of Cultural Production*; Lantz, *Taste at Work*.
15 Agins, *The End of Fashion*.
16 The brand's and the designer's names were made fictitious in the interest of anonymity.
17 Bourdieu, *The Rules of Art*; Bourdieu and Wacquant, *An Invitation to Reflexive Sociology*.
18 Walter Powell and Paul DiMaggio (eds), *The New Institutionalism in Organizational Analysis* (Chicago: University of Chicago Press, 1991); Richard Scott, *Institutions and Organizations* (Thousand Oaks: Sage, 1995).
19 Agins, *The End of Fashion*.
20 Aspers, *Orderly Fashion*, p. 91.
21 Thomas, *Deluxe*.
22 The word "curate" comes from the art world, where a curator can be director of a museum or someone who assembles and organizes an exhibition. In current usage, it applies to marketing, online and social media in which criteria or personal sensibilities are used in filtering content.
23 Pierre Bourdieu, "But who created the 'creators'?" in: Pierre Bourdieu (ed.), *Sociology in Question* (London: Sage, 1993), pp. 139–148.
24 Rocamora, *Fields of Fashion*; Ted Polhemus, "In the supermarket of style," in: Steve Redhead (ed.), *The Clubcultures Reader: Readings in Popular Cultural Studies*, pp. 148–151 (Oxford: Blackwell, 1997). For more about the consumer as creator, see

Michel de Certeau, *The Practice of Everyday Life* (Berkeley: University of California Press, 1988); Paul Willis, *Common Culture: Symbolic Work at Play in the Everyday Cultures of the Young* (Boulder: Westview Press, 1990).

25   The brand's and the collection director's names were made fictitious in the interest of anonymity.

26   In connection with Hedi Slimane's appointment as creative director in the summer of 2012, the name was changed from Yves Saint Laurent (YSL) to Saint Laurent Paris (SLP).

27   Rocamora, *Fields of Fashion*, p. 348.

28   Agins, *The End of Fashion*, pp. 191–192.

29   Elizabeth Guffey, *Retro: The Culture of Revival* (London: Reaktion Books, 2006).

30   In the fashion field, in the relationship between manufacturers, marketers, distributors, tastemakers and consumers, clothes become *fashion*; cf. Kawamura, *Fashion-ology*.

31   In *Mode: En filosofisk essä* (Nora: Nya Doxa, 2006), Lars Svendsen argues that fashion has abandoned the previously characteristic *logic of replacement*, in which the new replaced the old. Instead, fashion is nowadays characterized by a *logic of supplementation*, in which all trends are old and the new fashion is not intended to replace the old but to supplement it. This evolution is apparent also in the art world, according to Svendsen; Svendsen, *Mode: En filosofisk essä*, pp. 32–33.

32   Alistair O'Neill, *London: After a Fashion* (London: Reaktion Books, 2007), p. 142.

33   Barthes, *The Fashion System*.

34   Simon Reynolds, *Retromania: Pop Culture's Addiction to Its Own Past* (London: Faber and Faber, 2011).

35   For more, see the Web site of FIT's exhibition, *Fashion & Politics* (New York: The Museum at FIT, 2009) <http://www.fitnyc.edu/5246.asp>

36   Western references are therefore more closely linked to fashion capital. On fashion as a self-referential system, see Ingrid Loschek, *When Clothes Become Fashion: Design and Innovation Systems* (Oxford: Berg, 2009), pp. 21–28. Studies of "ethnic fashion" demonstrate how it too is characterized by a Eurocentric idea of fashion that constructs it as "the other"; see, for example, Suzanne Baizerman, Joanne Eicher and Catherine Cerny, "Eurocentrism in the study of ethnic dress" (*Dress*, vol. 20, 1993), pp. 19–32; Joanne Eicher, "Ethnic dress," in: Valerie Steele (ed.), *The Berg Companion to Fashion*, pp. 260–263 (New York: Berg, 2010); Entwistle, *The Fashioned Body*.

37   Agins, *The End of Fashion*.

38   Aspers, *Orderly Fashion*.

Chapter 7

1   All financial analysts I interviewed were anonymized at their request; any names used in this connection are fictitious.

2   In 2011, Louis Vuitton was valued at USD 24.312 billion, twice as much as the second most valuable brand, Hermès; Cheryl Wischhover, "The world's ten most powerful luxury brands" (*Fashionista*, May 9, 2011) <http://fashionista.com/2011/05/the -worlds-ten-most-powerful-luxury-brands-2011/> [accessed December 9, 2014].

3   *Cyclicality* describes a company or a stock whose revenues, value or profits vary greatly according to the state of the market or season. *Volatility* is a measurement of

the price variations of a financial instrument, for example a stock, over time.

4   A company's *investor relations* department deals with communication and services primarily targeting financial markets and financial journalists.

5   Wilson, *Adorned in Dreams*, p. 13.

6   Norbert Elias, *The Civilizing Process, vol. 1: The History of Manners* (Oxford: Blackwell, 1994 [1939]).

7   Wilson, *Adorned in Dreams*, p. 14.

8   Gerald Epstein, "Introduction: financialization and the world economy," in: Gerald Epstein (ed.), *Financialization and the World Economy*, pp. 3–16 (Northampton: Edward Elgar, 2005), p. 3.

9   *Due diligence* is an inspection of a company, a method of gathering and analyzing information about a company's finances before an acquisition or any other strategic change for the purpose evaluating the company's soundness.

10   A *brand extension* is the application of a brand name to a new product category, for example, when a designer brand launches an interior design line.

11   *Market penetration* is a measure of the sales or use of a specific product or service relative to the total possible market for that product or service.

12   A *capsule collection* is a designer's mini-collection of a select few but important and representative pieces of clothing.

13   Goldman Sachs, *Europe: Branded Consumer Goods: Luxury Goods* (New York: Goldman Sachs, 2011).

14   These refer to an unofficial classification of Chinese cities according to local governance and, indirectly, population size: tier-two cities normally have over five million citizens (20–30 cities), while smaller tier-three cities are often provincial capitals (20–30 cities).

15   Cline, *Overdressed*, p. 20.

16   Bureau of Labor Statistics, *Consumer Expenditures—2011* (Washington, DC: United States Department of Labor, 2011).

17   Cline, *Overdressed*, p. 22.

18   Caroline Olsson, "Byxberg knäckte Lindex" (*Aftonbladet*, June 15, 2004) <http://www.aftonbladet.se/minekonomi/article10464285.ab> [accessed December 9, 2014].

19   EPS = earnings per share.

20   Aspers, *Orderly Fashion*, p. 146.

21   Day, "*The product life cycle*," see note 18 in Chapter 2.

22   Inditex, however, has a unique brand structure with separate stores for the brands Zara, Zara Home, Bershka, Massimo Dutti, Oysho, Stradivarius, Pull & Bear and Uterqüe.

23   Thomas, *Deluxe*.

24   Cline, *Overdressed*, p. 88.

Chapter 8

1   Credit Suisse Research Institute, *Global Wealth Report 2014* (Zurich: Credit Suisse 2014). This is, of course, a matter of definition. See "Burgeoning bourgeoisie—Special report: The new middle classes in emerging markets" (*The Economist*, February 14, 2009) <http://www.economist.com/node/13063298> [accessed December 9, 2014].

2   "Burgeoning bourgeoisie—Special report".

3 In a *monobrand store*, all products offered come from a single brand.

4 In January 2012, this regulation was lifted, allowing foreign direct investment of up to 100 percent in monobrand retailing. On the other hand, these retailers are required to use Indian suppliers to a large extent.

5 While fashion is considered a vital part of Western culture, Jennifer Craik points to the tendency in the West to construct the clothing of non-Western cultures as traditional, unchangeable reflections of social hierarchies, values and customs, that is, as distinct from fashion. To avoid such exoticization, she proposes that one instead examine techniques of dress and decoration using an ethnographic method. Only then, she claims, can one find parallels between Western and non-Western clothing systems. Even if the changes in fashion are fewer and not as marked in cultures with less emphasis on economic exchange, she maintains that changes do occur; Craik, *The Face of Fashion*, pp. 17–19.

6 The trend consultant's name was made fictitious in the interest of anonymity.

7 Wei Shi, *Intellectual Property in the Global Trading System: EU–China Perspective* (Berlin: Springer, 2008).

8 The content manager's name was made fictitious in the interest of anonymity.

9 The leaf fibers obtained from the raffia palm.

10 The project leader's name was made fictitious in the interest of anonymity.

11 The brand manager's name was made fictitious in the interest of anonymity.

12 *Franchise* is a business model in which an operator, a franchisee, for a fee is allowed to use a trademark and distribute a brand's goods.

13 *Mom-and-pop stores* are small independent businesses often run by families.

14 Characteristic blue-and-white porcelain from the Chenghua era, 1464–1487, during the Ming dynasty.

15 A classic body-hugging Chinese dress, *qipao* in Mandarin.

16 The trend consultant's name was made fictitious in the interest of anonymity.

17 Thomas, *Deluxe*.

18 The buyer's name was made fictitious in the interest of anonymity.

19 Andrew Downie, "In Brazil: for the love of shopping" (*The New York Times*, November 9, 2011) <http://www.nytimes.com/2011/11/10/fashion/in-brazil-for-the-love-of-shopping.html?_r=0> [accessed December 9, 2014].

20 In a class in the Fundação Getulio Vargas business school, Professor Evaldo Alves describes how, during high inflation, the lines to supermarket cashiers extended down the aisles at times of month when people were paid. One had to shop immediately for the whole month, because after just a few days, the value of one's money had eroded severely. Evaldo Alves, FGV. Lecture, February 23, 2011.

21 Ibid.

22 For more on ethnocentrism, see, for example, Edward Said, *Orientalism* (Stockholm: Ordfront, 2000). "The other" is a concept from Simone de Beauvoir's *The Second Sex* describing how men in Western culture and society have turned themselves into subjects by constructing the woman as the other; de Beauvoir, *The Second Sex* (New York: Vintage Books, 1973 [1949]).

Chapter 9

1 The trend forecaster's name was made fictitious in the interest of anonymity.

2 John Meyer and Brian Rowan, "Institutionalized organizations: formal structure as myth and ceremony" (*American Journal of Sociology*, vol. 83 no. 2, 1977), pp. 340–363.

3   Agins, *The End of Fashion*.
4   Simon Chilvers, "Hedi Slimane v Cathy Horyn: the story behind a fashion spat" (*The Guardian*, October 3, 2012) <http://www.guardian.co.uk/fashion/fashion -blog/2012/oct/03/hedi-slimane-cathy-horyn-fashion-spat> [accessed December 9, 2014]; Jacob Bernstein, "Fashion's most feared critic" (*The Daily Beast*, November 10, 2010) <http://www.thedailybeast.com/articles/2010/10/11/fashions-most-feared -critic.html> [accessed December 9, 2014].
5   Kellock, J. "J. Kellock on Current Trends," Conversation with Hope + Anchor, video clip from Vimeo <http://vimeo.com/43960633> [accessed December 9, 2014].
6   Michael Power, *Organized Uncertainty: Designing a World of Risk Management* (Oxford: Oxford University Press, 2007), pp. 5–6.
7   Peter Bernstein, *Against the Gods: The Remarkable Story of Risk* (London: John Wiley and Sons, 1996).
8   Max Weber, *The Protestant Ethic and the Spirit of Capitalism* (London: Routledge, 1992 [1930]); Lantz, *Taste at Work*.
9   See, for example, Derrick Chong, *Arts Management* (London: Routledge, 2002); Angela McRobbie, "Club to company" (*Cultural Studies*, vol. 16 no. 4, 2002), pp. 516–532; Lantz, *Taste at Work*; and David Hesmondhalgh, *The Cultural Industries* (London: Sage, 2007).
10   Nils Brunsson, *The Organization of Hypocrisy: Talk, Decisions and Actions in Organizations* (Chicester: John Wiley & Sons, 1989).
11   Ibid.
12   Jean Baudrillard, *The Consumer Society: Myths and Structures* (London: Sage, 1998 [1970]); Dick Hebdige, *Hiding in the Light: On Images and Things* (New York: Routledge, 1988); Douglas Holt, "Distinction in America? Recovering Bourdieu's theory of tastes from its critics" (*Poetics*, vol. 25, 1997), pp. 93–120; Patrik Aspers, *Markets in Fashion: A Phenomenological Approach* (Stockholm: City University Press, 2001); Virginia Postrel, *The Substance of Style: How the Rise of Aesthetic Value Is Remaking Commerce, Culture, and Consciousness* (New York: HarperCollins, 2003); Mike Featherstone, *Consumer Culture and Postmodernism* (London: Sage, 2007).
13   Manuel Castells, *Communication Power* (Oxford: Oxford University Press, 2009), pp. 54–71.
14   Bourdieu, *The Rules of Art*.
15   Veblen, *The Theory of the Leisure Class*.
16   Cf. Rocamora, *Fields of Fashion*.
17   Zygmunt Bauman, *The Individualized Society* (Cambridge: Polity Press, 2001).
18   Peter Berger and Thomas Luckmann, *The Social Construction of Reality: A Treatise in the Sociology of Knowledge* (New York: Doubleday, 1966).
19   Bourdieu, *Outline of a Theory of Practice*; Bourdieu, *The Logic of Practice*.
20   "Trend," *Collins English Dictionary* (Glasgow: HarperCollins, 2011).
21   Zygmunt Bauman, *Liquid Times: Living in an Age of Uncertainty* (Cambridge: Polity Press, 2007).

BIBLIOGRAPHY

Aaker, D. *Building Strong Brands*, London: Pocket Books, 2010.

"Acne växer snabbast." *Svenska Dagbladet*, May 7, 2006. <http://www.svd.se/naringsliv/ nyheter/sverige/acne-vaxer-snabbast_7148051.svd> [accessed February 21, 2013].

Agins, T. *The End of Fashion. How Marketing Changed the Clothing Business Forever*, New York: HarperCollins, 1999.

Ambjörnsson, F. Rosa. *Den farliga färgen*, Stockholm: Ordfront Förlag, 2011.

Aspers, P. *Markets in Fashion: A Phenomenological Approach*, Stockholm: City University Press, 2001.

Aspers, P. *Orderly Fashion: A Sociology of Markets*, Princeton: Princeton University Press, 2010.

Baizerman, S., J. Eicher and C. Cerny. "Eurocentrism in the Study of Ethnic Dress," *Dress* 20 (1993), pp. 19–32.

Barnett, E. "Trend-spotting is the new £36bn growth business," *Telegraph*, November 5, 2011.

Barthes, R. *The Fashion System*, Berkeley: University of California Press, 1990 (1967).

Baudrillard, J. *The Consumer Society: Myths and Structures*, London: Sage, 1998 (1970).

Bauman, Z. *The Individualized Society*, Cambridge: Polity Press, 2001.

Bauman, Z. *Liquid Times: Living in an Age of Uncertainty*, Cambridge: Polity Press, 2007.

Berger, P. and T. Luckmann. *The Social Construction of Reality: A Treatise in the Sociology of Knowledge*, New York: Doubleday, 1966.

Bernstein, J. "Fashion's Most Feared Critic." *Daily Beast*, October 11, 2011. <http://www .thedailybeast.com/articles/2010/10/11/fashions-most-feared-critic.html> [accessed October 22, 2012].

Bernstein, P. *Against the Gods: The Remarkable Story of Risk*, London: John Wiley & Sons, 1996.

Binkley, C. "What's out: the fashion trend," *The Wall Street Journal*, January 29, 2010. <http://online.wsj.com/article/SB10001424052748704320104575015141536429662 .html> [accessed October 1, 2012].

Birken, L. *Consuming Desire: Sexual Science and the Emergence of a Culture of Abundance, 1871–1914*, Ithaca: Cornell University Press, 1988.

Blumer, H. "Fashion: From Class Differentiation to Collective Selection," *Sociological Quarterly* 10 (1969), pp. 275–291.

Bolton, A. and Koda, H. *Schiaparelli & Prada: Impossible Conversations*, New York: Metropolitan Museum of Art, 2012.

Bourdieu, P. "Le Couturier et sa Griffe. Contribution à une Théorie de la Magie," *Actes de la Recherche en Sciences Sociales* 1 no. 1 (1975), pp. 7–36.

Bourdieu, P. *Outline of a Theory of Practice*, London: Cambridge University Press, 1977.

Bourdieu, P. *Distinction: A Social Critique of the Judgment of Taste*, Cambridge: Harvard University Press, 1984.

Bourdieu, P. *The Logic of Practice*, Stanford: Stanford University Press, 1990.

Bourdieu, P. "But Who Created the 'Creators'?" in P. Bourdieu (ed), *Sociology in Question*, London: Sage, 1993a.

Bourdieu, P. *The Field of Cultural Production: Essays on Art and Literature*, New York: Columbia University Press, 1993b.

Bourdieu, P. *The Rules of Art: Genesis and Structure of the Literary Field*, Cambridge: Polity Press, 1996.

Bourdieu, P. and L. Wacquant. *An Invitation to Reflexive Sociology*, Chicago: University of Chicago Press, 1992.

Brunsson, N. *The Organization of Hypocrisy: Talk, Decisions and Actions in Organizations*, Chicester: John Wiley & Sons, 1989.

Bryson, Valerie. *Feminist Political Theory*, New York: Random House, 1992.

Bureau of Labor Statistics, *Consumer Expenditures – 2011*, Washington, DC: United States Department of Labor, 2011.

"Burgeoning Bourgeoisie: A special report on the new middle classes in emerging markets." *The Economist*, February 14, 2009.

Castells, M. *Communication Power*, Oxford: Oxford University Press, 2009.

Chilvers, S. "Hedi Slimane v Cathy Horyn: the story behind a fashion spat." *The Guardian*, October 03, 2012. <http://www.guardian.co.uk/fashion/fashion-blog/2012/oct/03/hedi-slimane-cathy-horyn-fashion-spat> [accessed February 20, 2012].

Chong, D. *Arts Management*, London: Routledge, 2002.

Clark, E. "Women at Work: Fashion's Glass Ceiling Prevails." *Women's Wear Daily*, October 29, 2012. <http://www.wwd.com/business-news/business-features/women-at-work-fashions-glass-ceiling-prevails> [accessed June 26, 2014].

Cline, E. *Overdressed: The Shockingly High Cost of Cheap Fashion*, New York: Penguin Portfolio, 2012.

Cochrane, L. "Whistles conquers the middle market of British womenswear." *The Guardian*, August 24, 2012. <http://www.guardian.co.uk/fashion/2012/aug/24/whistles-middle-market-success> [accessed September 1, 2012].

Connell, R.W. *Masculinities*, Cambridge: Polity Press, 1995.

Craik, J. *The Face of Fashion: Cultural Studies in Fashion*, London: Routledge, 1993.

Credit Suisse Research Institute. Global Wealth Report 2014, report, Zurich: Credit Suisse, 2014.

Crewe, B. *Representing Men: Cultural Production and Producers in the Men's Magazine Market*, Oxford: Berg, 2003.

Cronin, A. "Regimes of Mediation: Advertising Practitioners as Cultural Intermediaries?" *Consumption, Markets and Culture* 7 no. 4 (2004), pp. 349–369.

Czarniawska, B. and Sevón, G. *Global Ideas: How Ideas, Objects and Practices Travel in the Global Economy*, Malmö: Liber, 2005.

Datamonitor. The United States: Clothing Industry Guide, report, Dublin: Research and Markets, 2011. <http://www.researchandmarkets.com/reports/1587109/united_states_clothing_industry_guide> [accessed January 18, 2013].

Day, G. "The Product Life Cycle: Analysis and Applications Issues," *Journal of Marketing*, 45 (Autumn 1981), pp. 60–67.

de Beauvoir, S. *The Second Sex*, New York: Vintage Books, 1973 (1949).

de Certeau, M. *The Practice of Everyday Life*, Berkeley: University of California Press, 1988.

Downie, A. "In Brazil: For the Love of Shopping." *The New York Times*, November 9, 2011. <http://www.nytimes.com/2011/11/10/fashion/in-brazil-for-the-love-of-shopping.html> [accessed October 22, 2012).

Du Gay, P. and S. Nixon. "Who Needs Cultural Intermediaries?" *Cultural Studies* 16 no. 4 (2002), pp. 495–500.

Eicher, J. "Ethnic Dress," in V. Steele (ed.), *The Berg Companion to Fashion*, New York: Berg, 2010.

Elias, N. *The Civilizing Process, vol. 1: The History of Manners*, Oxford: Blackwell, 1994 (1939).

Entwistle, J. *The Fashioned Body: Fashion, Dress and Modern Social Theory*, Cambridge: Polity Press, 2000.

Entwistle, J. *The Aesthetic Economy of Fashion: Markets and Values in Clothing and Modelling*, Oxford: Berg, 2009.

Entwistle, J. and A. Rocamora. "The Field of Fashion Materialized: A Study of London Fashion Week," *Sociology* 40 no. 4 (2006), pp. 735–751.

Epstein, G. "Introduction: Financialization and the World Economy," in G. Epstein (ed.), *Financialization and the World Economy*, Northampton: Edward Elgar, 2005.

Falk, K. *Det svenska modeundret*, Stockholm: Norstedts, 2011.

Featherstone, M. *Consumer Culture and Postmodernism*, London: Sage, 2007.

Featherstone, M., S. Lash and R. Robertson (eds), *Global Modernities*, London: Sage, 1995.

Felski, R. *The Gender of Modernity*, Cambridge: Harvard University Press, 1995.

Fine, B. and E. Leopold. *The World of Consumption*, London: Routledge, 1993.

Foucault, M. *Discipline and Punish*, Harmondsworth: Penguin, 1977.

Giddens, A. *New Rules of Sociological Method*, London: Hutchinson, 1976.

Goffman, E. *Presentation of Self in Everyday Life*, New York: Doubleday, 1959.

Goffman, E. *Frame Analysis. An Essay on the Organization of Experience*, Boston: Northeastern University Press, 1974.

Goldman Sachs. Europe: Branded Consumer Goods: Luxury Goods, report, New York, Goldman Sachs, 2011.

Guffey, E. *Retro: The Culture of Revival*, London: Reaktion Books, 2006.

Halford, S. and P. Leonard. *Gender, Power and Organisations: An Introduction*, Basingstoke: Palgrave, 2001.

Head, E. and J. Hyams. *How to Dress for Success*, New York: Random House, 1967.

Hebdige, D. *Hiding in the Light: On Images and Things*, New York: Routledge, 1988.

Heilman, M. "Description and Prescription: How Gender Stereotypes Prevent Women's Ascent Up the Organizational Ladder," *Journal of Social Issues* 57 no. 4 (2001), pp. 657–674.

Hekman, S. (ed.). *Feminist Interpretations of Michel Foucault*, University Park: Pennsylvania State University Press, 1996.

Hesmondhalgh, D. *The Cultural Industries*, London: Sage, 2007.

Holt, D. "Distinction in America? Recovering Bourdieu's Theory of Tastes from its Critics," *Poetics* 25 (1997), pp. 93–120.

Holt, D. *How Brands Become Icons: The Principles of Cultural Branding*, Cambridge: Harvard Business School Press, 2004.

Holt, D. and D. Cameron. *Cultural Strategy: Using Innovative Ideologies to Build Breakthrough Brands*, Oxford: Oxford University Press, 2010.

Jones, J. "Coquettes and Grisettes: Women Buying and Selling in Ancien Régime Paris," in V. de Grazia and E. Furlough (eds), *The Sex of Things: Gender and Consumption in Historical Perspective*, Berkeley: University of California Press, 1996.

Kawamura, Y. *Fashion-ology: An Introduction to Fashion Studies*, Oxford: Berg, 2005.

Kellock, J. "J. Kellock on Current Trends," Hope + Anchor, video clip from Vimeo. <http://vimeo.com/43960633> [accessed February 10, 2013].

Kim, E., A. M. Fiore and H. Kim. *Fashion Trends: Analysing and Forecasting*, London: Bloomsbury, 2013.

Kotler, P. and G. Armstrong. *Principles of Marketing: 13th edition*, Upper Saddle River: Prentice Hall, 2009.

Lambert, C. "Real Fashion Police: Copyrighting Clothing," Harvard Magazine, July–August 2010.

Lamont, M. *Money, Morals and Manners: The Culture of the French and the American Upper-Middle Class*, Chicago: University of Chicago Press, 1992.

Lantz, J. *Taste at Work: On Taste and Organization in the Field of Cultural Production*, Stockholm: Arvinius Förlag, 2005.

Lee Bartky, S. *Femininity and Domination: Studies in the Phenomenology of Oppression*, New York: Routledge, 1991.

Lehmann, U. *Tigersprung: Fashion in Modernity*, Cambridge: MIT Press, 2000.

Lieberson, S. *A Matter of Taste: How Names, Fashions, and Culture Change*, New Haven: Yale University Press, 2000.

Loschek, I. *When Clothes Become Fashion: Design and Innovation Systems*, Oxford: Berg, 2009.

Lynch, A. and M. Strauss. *Changing Fashion: A Critical Introduction to Trend Analysis and Meaning*, New York: Berg, 2007.

McFall, L. "Advertising, Persuasion and the Culture/Economy Dualism," in P. du Gay and M. Pryke (eds), *Cultural Economy: Cultural Analysis and Commercial Life*, London: Sage, 2002.

McKelvey, K. and J. Munslow. *Fashion Forecasting*, Oxford: Wiley Blackwell, 2008.

McNay, L. *Foucault and Feminism*, Cambridge: Polity Press, 1992.

McRobbie, A. "Club to Company," *Cultural Studies* 16 no. 4 (2002), pp. 516–532.

Mears, A. *Pricing Beauty: The Making of a Fashion Model*, Berkeley: University of California Press, 2011.

Merton, R. "The Matthew Effect in Science," *Science* 159 no. 3810 (1968), pp. 56–63.

Meyer, J. and B. Rowan. "Institutionalized Organizations: Formal Structure as Myth and Ceremony," *American Journal of Sociology* 83 no. 2 (1977), pp. 340–363.

Mörck, M. "En reva i kostymen: Maskulinitet, mode och makt," in L. Gradén and M. Petersson McIntyre (eds), *Modets metamorfoser. Den klädda kroppens identiteter och förvandlingar*, Stockholm: Carlssons, 2009.

Neilan, C. "Fewer Women Being Given Top Jobs in Fashion," *Drapers*, April 19, 2013. <http://www.drapersonline.com/news/exclusive-fewer-women-being-given-top-fashion-jobs/5048406.article> [accessed June 26, 2014].

Nordberg, M. *Jämställdhetens spjutspets? Manliga arbetstagare i kvinnoyrken, jämställdhet, maskulinitet, femininitet och heteronormativitet*, Stockholm: Arkipelag, 2005.

O'Neill, A. *London: After a Fashion*, London: Reaktion Books, 2007.

O'Neill, J. "Building Better Global Economic BRICs," Goldman Sachs, Global Economics Paper No: 66, November 30, 2001. <http://www.goldmansachs.com/korea/ideas/brics/building-better-pdf.pdf> [accessed February 9, 2013].

Olsson, K. 'Byxberg knäckte Lindex', *Aftonbladet*, June 15, 2004.

Panteva, N. *Trends Outfitting the Fashion Retail Sector*, Media Center, NY: IBIS World, 2012.

Polhemus, T. "In the Supermarket of Style," in S. Redhead (ed.), *The Clubcultures Reader: Readings in Popular Cultural Studies*, Oxford: Blackwell, 1997.

Portnoff, L. *Modebranschen i Sverige. Statistik och analys*, report by Volante for the Association of Swedish Fashion Brands and the Fashion Incubator in Borås, Stockholm: Volante, 2013.

Postrel, V. *The Substance of Style: How the Rise of Aesthetic Value Is Remaking Commerce, Culture and Consciousness*, New York: HarperCollins, 2003.

Powell, W. and P. DiMaggio. (eds) *The New Institutionalism in Organizational Analysis*, Chicago: University of Chicago Press, 1991.

Power, M. *Organized Uncertainty: Designing a World of Risk Management*, Oxford: Oxford University Press, 2007.

Prest, M. "Substance and style: The fashion courses that are a cut above," *The Independent*, April 14, 2011. <http://www.independent.co.uk/student/postgraduate/postgraduate -study/substance-and-style-the-fashion-courses-that-are-a-cut-above-2267507.html> [accessed November 8, 2012].

Reynolds, S. *Retromania: Popcultures Addiction to Its Own Past*, London: Faber and Faber, 2011.

Rigney, D. *The Matthew Effect: How Advantage Begets Further Advantage*, New York: Columbia University Press, 2010.

Rocamora, A. "Fields of Fashion: Critical Insights into Bourdieu's Sociology of Culture," *Journal of Consumer Culture* 2 no. 3 (2002), pp. 341–362.

Said, E. W. *Orientalism*, New York: Vintage Books, 1979.

Schulz, S. "Our Lady Hates Viscose: The Role of the Customer Image in High Street Fashion Production," *Cultural Sociology* 2 no. 3 (2008), pp. 385–405.

Scott, R. *Institutions and Organizations*, Thousand Oaks: Sage, 1995.

Shi, W. *Intellectual Property in the Global Trading System: EU-China Perspective*, Berlin: Springer, 2008.

Siegle, L. *Is Fashion Wearing Out the World?* London: Fourth Estate, 2011.

Silverman, D. *Interpreting Qualitative Data: Methods for Analyzing Talk, Text and Interaction*. London: Sage, 2001.

Simmel, G. "Fashion," *International Quarterly* 10 no. 1 (1904), pp. 130–155.

Skov, L. "The Role of Trade Fairs in the Global Fashion Business," *Current Sociology* 54 no. 5 (2006), pp. 764–783.

Slack, N. and M. Lewis. *Operations Strategy*, 2nd edition, Harlow: Financial Times Prentice Hall, 2008.

SOU *1998: 6. Kvinnomaktutredningen*, Stockholm: Fritze, 1998.

Steele, V. *Fashion and Eroticism: Ideals of Feminine Beauty from the Victorian Era to the Jazz Age*, Oxford: Oxford University Press, 1985.

Steele, V. and C. B. Kidwell. (eds), *Men and Women: Dressing the Part*, Washington, DC: Smithsonian Institute Press, 1989.

Svendsen, L. *Mode: En filosofisk essä*, Nora: Nya Doxa, 2006.

Taylor, M. "Culture Transition: Fashion's Cultural Dialogue between Commerce and Art," *Fashion Theory: The Journal of Dress, Body & Culture* 9 no. 4 (2005), pp. 445–460.

The British Fashion Council and Oxford Economics. The Value of the UK Fashion Industry, report, London and Oxford: The British Fashion Council and Oxford Economics, 2010.

Thomas, D. *Deluxe: How Luxury Lost Its Luster*, New York: Penguin Books, 2007.

Trend, Collins Dictionary, Glasgow: HarperCollins, 2011. <http://www.collinsdictionary .com/dictionary/english/trend> [accessed December 19, 2012].

Tseëlon, E. *The Masque of Femininity*, London: Sage, 1997.

Tungate, M. *Fashion Brands: Branding Style from Armani to Zara*, London: Kogan Page, 2008.

Veblen, T. *The Theory of the Leisure Class*, London: Allen and Unwin, 1957 (1899).

Vejlgaard, H. *Anatomy of a Trend*, New York: McGraw-Hill, 2007.

Wahl, A., C. Holgersson and P. Höök. *Ironi och sexualitet – om ledarskap och kön*, Stockholm: Carlssons, 2001.

Weber, M. *Economy and Society: An Outline of Interpretive Sociology*, Berkeley: University of California Press, 1978.

Weber, M. *The Protestant Ethic and the Spirit of Capitalism*, London: Routledge, 1992 (1930).

Weick, K. *The Social Psychology of Organizing*, Thousand Oaks: Sage, 1979.

Weick, K. *Sensemaking in Organizations*, Thousand Oaks: Sage, 1995.

Werner, C. The Older Population: 2010. 2010 Census Briefs, report, Washington: United States Census Bureau, 2011. <http://www.census.gov/prod/cen2010/briefs/c2010br-09.pdf> [accessed February 10, 2013].

Wheeler, A. *Designing Brand Identity: An Essential Guide for the Whole Branding Team*, New York: Wiley, 2012.

White, H. *Markets from Networks: Socioeconomic Models of Production*, Princeton: Princeton University Press, 2002.

Wilcox, C. (ed.) *The Golden Age of Couture: Paris and London 1947–57*, London: V&A Publications, 2007.

Willis, P. *Common Culture: Symbolic Work at Play in the Everyday Cultures of the Young*, Boulder: Westview Press, 1990.

Wilson, E. *Adorned in Dreams: Fashion and Modernity*, Revised and Updated Edition, New Brunswick: Rutgers University Press, 2003.

Wischhover, C. "The World's Ten Most Powerful Luxury Brands," *Fashionista*, May 09, 2011. <http://fashionista.com/2011/05/the-worlds-ten-most-powerful-luxury-brands-2011/2/> [accessed February 11, 2013].

Zelditch, M. "Processes of legitimation: recent developments and new directions," *Social Psychology Quarterly* 64 (2001), pp. 4–17.

INDEX